Researching Violently Divided

Researching Violently Divided Societies

Ethical and Methodological Issues

Edited by
Marie Smyth and Gillian Robinson

United Nations University Press

TOKYO • NEW YORK • PARIS

Pluto Press

LONDON

**First published 2001 in the United States of America and Canada by
the United Nations University Press**

United Nations University Press
The United Nations University, 53–70, Jingumae 5-chome,
Shibuya-ku, Tokyo, 150–8925, Japan
Tel: +81-3-3499-2811 Fax: +81-3-3406-7345
e-mail: sales@hq.unu.edu
http://www.unu.edu

United Nations University Office in North America
2 United Nations Plaza, Room DC2-1462-70, New York, NY 10017, USA
Tel: +1-212-963-6387 Fax: +1-212-371-9454
E-mail: unuona@igc.apc.org

United Nations University Press is the publishing division of
the United Nations University

**First published 2001 in Europe and the Commonwealth excluding Canada by
Pluto Press**

Pluto Press 345 Archway Road, London N6 5AA, United Kingdom
www.plutobooks.com

ISBN 92–808–1065–0 (UNUP edition)
ISBN 0–7453–1821–5 (Pluto hardback)
ISBN 0–7453–1820–7 (Pluto paperback)

British Library Cataloguing in Publication Data
A catalogue record for this book is available from the British Library

Library of Congress Cataloging in Publication Data
Researching violently divided societies : ethical and methodological
issues / edited by Marie Smyth and Gillian Robinson.
     p. cm.
Papers from an international workshop hosted by INCORE in March
1999—Cf. Foreword.
Includes bibliographical references and index.
   ISBN   — ISBN 0–7453–1821–5 (Pluto hardback) — ISBN 0–7453–1820–7
(Pluto paperback) — ISBN 92–808–1065–0 (UNUP paperback)
   1. Social sciences—Research—Moral and ethical aspects—Congresses.
2. Social sciences—Methodology—Congresses. 3.
Violence—Research—Congresses. 4. Social
conflict—Research—Congresses. I. Smyth, Marie, 1953– II. Robinson,
Gillian. III. INCORE.
   H62.A3 R47 2001
   303.6'07'2—dc21

                                                                                2001005083

10	09	08	07	06	05	04	03	02	01
10	9	8	7	6	5	4	3	2	1

Designed and produced for Pluto Press and UNUP by
Chase Publishing Services, Fortescue, Sidmouth EX10 9QG, England
Typeset from disk by Stanford DTP Services, Towcester
Printed in the European Union by TJ International, Padstow, England

Contents

Institutional Background

INCORE (the Initiative on Conflict Resolution and Ethnicity) is an initiative set up by the United Nations University and the University of Ulster with a remit to be a key global centre for research, policy and programme developments in the field of ethno-political conflict and conflict resolution. A major research theme identified in its current operational plan is 'Policy, Methodology and Evaluation'. Full details on the work of INCORE are available at its Website <http://www.incore.ulst.ac.uk>. Two services provided by INCORE are particularly important with respect to this work: the Conflict Data Service <http://www.incore.ulst.ac.uk/cds/> is an Internet-based service providing a host of information of relevance to researchers working in this subject area, and the *Ethnic Conflict Research Digest* <http://www.incore.ulst.ac.uk/ecrd/> launched in January 1998, provides an up-to-date review of all the recent publications and research reports in the area. INCORE also houses the Ethnic Studies Network (ESN) which now has almost 700 members from a broad disciplinary and geographic range. The main aim of the network is to encourage and facilitate comparative and collaborative research into conflict resolution and ethnicity. Gillian Robinson was Research Director of INCORE from 1997 to 2000. She continues as Senior Research Associate to work with INCORE to develop its work into methodology in divided societies.

The Cost of the Troubles Study was a three-year investigation, commencing in 1996, into the experiences and effects on the population of violent conflict in Northern Ireland. The study was initiated and directed by Marie Smyth, who was seconded full-time from the academic staff of the University of Ulster to conduct this work. The study aimed to provide reliable, non-sensationalist and ethically collected data on individual experiences of the so-called Troubles in Northern Ireland. The study adopted a participative action research paradigm, which involved members of the researched population in managing the study. The study explored, through a series of books, monographs, touring exhibitions and films, issues such as the longevity of impact, the geographical distribution of impact, and the relationship between Troubles-related difficulties and deprivation. This study has had implications for a range of policy areas.

Community Conflict Impact on Children, which commenced in 1999, was a two-year study of the impact of Northern Ireland's Troubles on children and young people. Like its predecessor, The Cost of the Troubles Study, it was initiated and directed by Marie Smyth and adopted a participative action research methodology. In June 2000, the study team organised the visit of Mr Olara Otunnu, Special Representative of the Secretary General of the United Nations on Children and Armed Conflict, and worked with Save the Children to ensure the participation of children and young people in the visit. The team also established a link between the Departments of Education in South Africa and Northern Ireland, focusing on the role of education in violently divided societies. CCIC also initiated a network of those working with children in violently divided societies in Northern Ireland and South Africa, and hope to extend this to other conflict zones. CCIC also provided evidence on Northern Ireland to the International Tribunal on War Affected Children. A range of publications was also produced. Following this study, Marie Smyth and other academics and practitioners founded the Institute for Conflict Research in Belfast, of which Marie Smyth is Chief Executive.

Introduction

Marie Smyth

With exceptions such as Britain's intervention under Margaret Thatcher in the Malvinas and the United States' Gulf War under George Bush – both strategic and brief strikes with a minimum of military casualties of the warring parties – the late nineteenth-century Rooseveltian perception of war as an ideal method of forging a nation's *manhood* has waned. The development of weapons of mass destruction, and the potential consequences of international disputes between combatants with nuclear weapons, together with increased documentation of the terrible consequences of war itself, have meant that overtly hawkish political approaches to disputes have, for the most part, fallen out of fashion.

Changes in the nature of war, with a majority – up to 90 per cent in some cases – of deaths in armed conflicts being of civilians, coming after the experience of two world wars, have altered attitudes to war itself. The United States' experience in Vietnam significantly contributed to subsequent shifts within the armed forces in the developed world. It is perhaps the world's most powerful armies that have least stomach for engagements likely to cause them significant military casualties. Bringing 'our boys' home in body bags is a political risk few contemporary First World politicians are anxious to take.

Furthermore, voters now, as never before, have access to information about some of the realities of war. With increased mass communication, the humanitarian consequences of such conflicts as Bosnia and Herzegovina have been – at least sporadically – presented to a wider audience, although some, such as Rwanda, are only brought to public attention after the worst has happened. Perhaps as a result of this combination – of increased communication, changes in the nature of war leading to massively increased civilian impact, and its destabilising effect – war and violent conflict has a worse press now than ever before as a means of resolving disputes. At the beginning of the twenty-first century, violent conflict and war is, for the present, fairly universally perceived to be a problem.

Global attention has increasingly focused on ethnic and intranational conflicts and their consequences. In the latter half of the twentieth century, one of the roles assumed by several major world leaders has been that of peace-broker in such conflicts, indicating that conflict is of concern to the most powerful political actors, even when their nations are seemingly not directly implicated. This concern may well be due to an increased capacity on the part of such leaders to embrace the humanitarian aspect of their role, the roles of their respective armies in international peacekeeping, or even their responsibilities as putative moral leaders. However, violent conflict – even when highly localised – may have a destabilising potential that can ultimately threaten and undermine the political status quo and may constrain economic penetration of global economic powers. Additionally, the significance of localised disputes in little-known and otherwise insignificant territories for global diaspora communities in the developed world may provide domestic political incentives for peacemaking initiatives on the part of First World political leaders. These factors cognately can provide sufficient incentive to interest and involve political leaders in dispute settlement.

Despite its apparent lack of mainstream political favour, however, armed conflict is as popular as ever as a method of resolving disputes over territory, sovereignty or other resources. Ongoing disputes in the Middle East, Eastern Europe, Central and Latin America and in several African countries provide many opportunities for peacemakers to practise their skills, and for researchers to enquire into the causes, effects and remedies for violent political conflict. A burgeoning literature on all three of these issues points to several conclusions. It is clear that the roots of ethnic conflict can often be traced to the legacy of colonialism, and to the specific form that colonialism took in a given location. In many instances, the nature of colonial relationships between the various ethnic groups and the colonial power in a given territory establish the grievances that ultimately may erupt under certain conditions into ethnic conflict, sometimes long after independence. A changed world order, with the end of the Cold War, has led to decentralisation and the political break-up of enormous political and ideological power blocs in the former Soviet Union. The shifts and associated realignment of loyalty that this entailed has contributed to a crisis of political identity which in turn partly explains the rise of nationalism and ethnic identification. The end of hegemonic power created conditions of uncertainty, rivalry for supremacy within the new order, and ambitions for autonomy. These factors, in the absence of centrist control, often created conditions in which violence could proliferate.

Yet it is difficult sometimes to draw a clear distinction between societies that are considered to be violently divided and those that are not. When we examine David Meddings' work on the use of epidemiological methods to examine small arms proliferation in this volume, it does not seem irrelevant to the issue of light weapons proliferation in the United States, and the increase in multiple killings there, some carried out by children. Indeed, work elsewhere would suggest other parallels between the United States and Northern Ireland (for example Morrissey and Smyth, 2001). The monitoring of so-called hate crime may well provide an early warning mechanism for predicting the escalation of ethnic, sectarian or racial violence. Comparisons between so-called peaceful societies and those considered to be violently divided can call into question the strict categorisation and demarcation between the two. For example the death rate due to political conflict in societies characterised as experiencing low-intensity conflict, such as Northern Ireland, the Middle East or South Africa, is surpassed by the death rate in several North American cities.

It may be true to say that all societies, such as the United States or Britain, are replete with conflict, divided by race, ethnicity, religion and class. However, in societies such as Britain and the US these tensions are contained and managed by social, economic and political mechanisms that function at some level, and about which there is a modicum of political consensus. Yet the societies studied by the researchers writing in this volume are distinguished from the US and Britain by one key feature. In the violently divided societies that provide the focus for the activities of researchers writing here, often there is no consensus about policing, law and order, the impartiality of the state apparatus to dealing with violence or indeed about the legitimacy of the state itself. This lack creates particular phenomena that are at one and the same time the subjects of inquiry, whilst simultaneously casting several obstacles in the path of such inquiry. Conflict researchers are often concerned with understanding the origins of the conflict, the conditions that sustain it, identifying the key forces within it and what drives it forward. Here, however, the focus is not on these questions – the content of conflict research – about which a great deal has been written, both about conflict in general and on specific regions. Here, our focus is on the conditions under which such inquiry is conducted, the obstacles in the path of the inquiry – obstacles, as stated earlier, that are inevitably linked to the conditions created by the violent conflict itself.

THE PURPOSE OF RESEARCHING CONFLICT

Whilst research for knowledge's sake is necessary, it is ethically difficult to justify the acquisition of knowledge for knowledge's sake in situations where lives are being lost. Perhaps for this reason, the ethical dimension of conducting research in violently divided societies was a recurring concern in our discussions in the international workshop. Improved knowledge about violent societies may not necessarily result in improved responses to the division and violence, yet the desire for such improvement is a motivator for much of the research that is carried out. The need to ensure that mediation and other forms of intervention are informed by robust information on divided societies in general and by specific knowledge about the specifics of each situation often requires research to be carried out. A sound understanding of the way conflict is caused and maintained is the key to successful intervention, and, indeed, to the work of recreating a social fabric in the wake of violent conflict.

Sound research carried out in violently divided societies may, if effectively communicated to the appropriate actors, eventually lead to an improved response to the management of conflicts. There is no blueprint or set of established procedures by which violent conflicts in and between societies can be resolved. However, any emergent principles can be enhanced in their effectiveness by being contextualised in a thorough knowledge of local circumstances and causes of violence therein.

THE GEOGRAPHICAL DISTRIBUTION OF RESEARCH

Research in and on divided societies differs greatly between the Northern and the Southern hemispheres. This is partly determined by the level of resources available to fund such research. Research interest in Northern Ireland, for example, continues to rise whilst research on divided societies in the developing world is difficult to fund. Furthermore, the availability of funding is also determined by various governments' perception of how particular potential and actual conflicts have a direct impact on their own countries' security. Thus, which conflicts are studied, and how well or thoroughly, is often beyond the control of researchers. Rather, such work is at the mercy of donors' or funders' depth of understanding of and commitment to its importance from a humanitarian and world-citizenship perspective.

Much work has been done, for instance, on Bosnia, while very little research was done until recently on Somalia or on Rwanda. Some governments in divided societies perceive research on division and conflict as undesirable activity and oppose it. Furthermore, publicly supported research on violent conflict has mostly been reactive, conducted after the conflict, rather than proactively antici-pating violence and feeding into early warning systems. In the context of extremely limited resources, particularly in the Southern hemisphere, there has been little interest in funding research on the roots of conflicts prior to their eruption.

ETHICAL CONCERNS

Ethical concerns assume a more urgent and stark form in this field of research than elsewhere. The geographical distribution of attention discussed above can have a significant ethical dimension. Conflicts in former Yugoslavia, for example, have attracted a range of humanitarian aid programmes and research projects. These programmes and projects have concentrated on those who have survived ethnic cleansing and the dislocation, displacement, death, maiming, rape, torture, loss of family and loss of identity that this has entailed. Much of the research has been done without due regard for the contextualisation of the data in the Yugoslav context. Nor in many instances have there been efforts to ensure that these projects lead to beneficial effects for those participants who have undergone the traumatic experience of ethnic war. Conducting research in a manner that uses people as objects without due regard to their sub-jectivity, needs and the impact of the research on their situation is ethically questionable. This becomes particularly apparent in psy-chological terms, since respondents may be at a stage of denial in relation to the horrors that have happened to them. The timing of research, and subsequent intervention should take account of the subjective experience of those studied. Inappropriate timing, in the case of early shock and denial reactions, can result in the under-reporting of impact and thus compromise or reduce subsequent humanitarian assistance. Timing is also significant in terms of the assessment of the longer-term impact of conflict. Substantial commitment is needed on the part of researchers and aid agencies alike to establish and address the longer-term consequences of violent conflict, yet support for such work is often short term, and focused on the current situation and the immediate future. The principle that research in violent societies must at least do no harm to participants and at most have a beneficial effect for those partici-pating is an aspiration that is complex to realise. None the less, ethically, the researcher owes that much to research participants.

Other ethical challenges face the researcher whose focus is not on the victims of conflict, but rather on combatants or perpetrators of violence. Researching guerrilla movements, for instance, and establishing and maintaining the trust and confidence of respondents creates a whole range of practical ethical and legal dilemmas for researchers. In such circumstances, researchers must solve problems and make agreements with those studied about their role and its limits. Studying a guerrilla movement, for example, may entail observing acts of violence, or being party to prior knowledge of such acts. These are complicated and difficult areas that are not often openly discussed, nor is there good guidance available to those embarking for the first time into such a potentially dangerous field. Yet such research is an important contribution to an overall understanding of violent conflict. Similarly, the purpose of such research and the application of any findings create ethical and practical dilemmas. If such research is used for the purpose of out-manoeuvring, militarily defeating or negotiating with such groups, what is the responsibility of the researcher in relation to informed consent of participants? Some researchers – such as those in the military – may be more personally comfortable (or trained) than others with an *undercover* role. In scientific terms however, such a role is clearly ethically dubious and is likely to jeopardise the researcher's safety.

DOES RESEARCHING DIVIDED SOCIETIES MAKE ANY DIFFERENCE?

Does it have a positive effect? Is research done to satisfy researchers' quest for knowledge, or need to enhance their publication record, rather than to have a positive impact on the conflict studied? These, too, are ethical questions. Researchers have a responsibility to balance the contribution that their work makes to the situation, with careerist or academic goals. Conflict research in particular faces grave responsibilities in this matter. If research is to inform international organisations, policy makers and the public both outside and within divided societies, then the researcher must be able to communicate with integrity in several *languages*: as a specialist, as a generalist, as an academic, as a populist, as a public speaker, and as a journalist.

Researchers from divided communities have the potential to fulfil an educational function within their own society, providing reflexive observations and analyses on what divides or integrates the society. Violently divided societies are notoriously caught in a reactive and bifurcated social and political dynamic, in which public discourse on contemporary issues is narrowed and constricted by the very divisions within the society itself. Researchers, by offering inputs on externally and internally conducted research on aspects of the society, may aim to assist in broadening this discourse and thereby inhibit the deepening of division and escalation of conflict. The skills involved in successfully fulfilling this role, and the lessons learned by those who have attempted to do so could, however, fill another volume.

ISSUES AND DIFFICULTIES IN RESEARCHING VIOLENTLY DIVIDED SOCIETIES

Contextualisation is a crucial issue in the design, collection of data and analysis of research in violently divided societies. The embedding of conceptualisations of conflict or its consequences in their local contexts is essential to the robustness of analysis. For example, an analysis of the contemporary street conflict in Northern Ireland that ignores the historical significance of political marching to the pro-Unionist community and the history of violent sectarianism between the two communities will conclude that current disputes are easily resolved, whereas the contextual information alone explains why this is not the case.

An allied difficulty to that of contextualisation is the difficulty in the transfer of concepts between languages and cultures in comparative or international work. At the micro-level, conceptual frameworks may not translate easily between one context and another, and other methods may need be found to overcome this difficulty. Lack of attention to conceptual differences between cultures or contexts can run the risk of confusing rather than illuminating issues.

IDENTITY

Finlay, in his contribution, raises the issue of identity of the researcher and its impact on analysis, a theme elaborated on by Hermann. The issue of who conducts the research has implications for the way the research is conceptualised, carried out, analysed and subsequently used. To take Africa, for example, most of the research on African conflicts is done by non-Africans. The limited or non-existent involvement of African researchers in such research severely restricts its local relevance or applicability and as a result, much of the research conducted has little policy impact. The intervention of aid and humanitarian assistance agencies has forced some governments to support educational institutions and as a result there are now increased opportunities in local universities to research violent conflict. However, these opportunities are concentrated in South Africa, and only very gradually has there been an improvement in other parts of the continent. Furthermore, since European and North American scholarship in this field has predominated, more emphasis on local approaches to conflict and dispute management is urgently required.

Both Hermann and Finlay, however, address the difficulties inherent in the 'insider' versus 'outsider' researcher role. There are numerous methodological and ethical issues raised by the position of the insider or outsider researcher, researching the conflict in one's own society or conflict elsewhere, or in researching one's own group or the other side of a conflict. The extent to which the researchers' identity impacts on the research, how inside researchers might study the conflict in their own society without taking sides, the dangers that an insider researcher is exposed to, the degree to which an insider gains access to information that is often off limits to outside researchers are all issues addressed by Hermann, Finlay and others.

Another effect of conducting research in situations of violent societal division is that the researchers may become identified either in their own mind or that of influential others, with those researched. This identification may lead to a range of effects. A perceived loss of *impartiality* or *neutrality*, can produce a kind of con-tamination effect in the eyes of others. On the other hand, the researcher may feel the need to either produce a research antidote to this effect, by researching the *equal and opposite* topic, or the researcher may regard the identification as unproblematic and limit future work to one faction or field.

The fraught issue of neutrality raises further difficulties. Much discussion amongst contributors to this volume revealed a majority view that neutrality in researching violently divided societies was not achievable. At best, researchers can identify their position, to whom they are accountable, and then proceed to conduct the research in as comprehensive, rounded and detached or objective a manner as possible. Emotional involvement with the humanitarian plight of those studied, or strong feelings about the behaviour of some of the armed parties to the conflict are all issues likely to influence the researcher's judgement and the type of information gathered. Whilst researchers are scientists, in pursuit of knowledge, they are simultaneously human, and responsive to what they observe. In the face of human suffering, for example, it may be ethically impossible to remain rigidly within a research role, and not cross the line into intervention. Indeed, some research paradigms, such as action-research, call into question rigid demarcation between research and intervention in the first place. Some researchers would argue that such research paradigms are therefore more appropriate to research in violent or challenging fields, for this reason.

Several other challenges are routinely faced by researchers operating in violent or volatile societies. A lack of good baseline statistics, particularly those collected by governments can impede research. Difficulty in accessing such data, inconsistencies in the way statistics are collated or difficulties in using such data for internal analysis or international comparisons due to inconsistent categorisation are not infrequently encountered. Real or perceived difficulties in access to certain populations may also be a feature of research in divided societies. Often the identity of the researcher is a factor in such access difficulties, and access may well be much easier with one side than with the other, leading to obvious difficulties in conducting comprehensive research.

Gaining access may require the researcher to overcome difficulties due to populations' previous experience of being researched – or over-researched in some instances. Research has been a disempowering and objectifying experience for some respondents. Access may be denied because of fears of outsiders within divided societies. These fears may be compounded in situations where they have no control over the research, where the researcher has no accountability to community or where respondents have previous bad experiences of the media. In some situations, the violent conflict has led to a suspicion of all intervention, and an expectation that everything, including the research, will be used against them. Such fear must be overcome and relationships of at least minimal trust and accountability established between researcher and the researched if successful in-depth research is to be conducted.

Perhaps the most obvious difficulty faced by researchers in violently divided societies is that of physical danger and personal safety. Researchers must not only manage physical danger and their own personal safety, but also their own fears and those of their family and colleagues. Fear is not always experienced in proportion to the actual amount of risk. In situations of armed conflict, there are often quite marked gender differences between men and women, not only in the level and nature of material risk they face but also in their respective abilities to assess such risk, and to be seen to withdraw from situations without losing face. Risks of physical violence, injury and death are often higher for men, whereas risks of rape and sexual attack are higher for women. In some cases, the gender of the researcher facilitates or inhibits access to particular situations.

Consideration also to the impact of the research process and outcomes on those researched takes on a dimension in violently divided societies that it may not have in less sensitive environments. The very act of conducting research can exacerbate conflict or can perpetuate uneven distribution of research attention. The reported findings of research in polarised settings may be used by one faction or other to reinforce certain political factions' views of the situation.

Nor is the impact of conducting the research felt exclusively by those researched. The impact on the researchers is not often acknowledged, which perpetuates the myth that research is a neutral and technical matter. Yet researchers working in situations of violence and division may experience marked psychological and emotional impacts from, for example, conducting interviews with those affected by violent societal division. It is clear that adequate prophylactic measures to protect researchers must be part of the research design.

Finally, much of what has already been discussed hinges on the accountability of the researcher within the research process. The researcher is accountable to a considerable number of parties, and often for different reasons – to the academic community, government agencies, private foundations, NGO and humanitarian communities, respondent populations, or various political causes. All these shape the research agenda, design and, possibly, the research results. The academic community (or one's academic employer) offers and withholds approval of the research plan, approves or disapproves of one's work, promotes or discontinues *unproductive* or *productive* researchers. The legitimacy, quality and scientific value of one's work is assessed in peer reviews before its utility is deemed worthy for publication in journals or books.

Governments and private foundations often provide the financial resource for research – or deny the same. Research needs to be valuable for adaptation in policy processes – however, this often only happens if there is an ideological congruence with the funders' own principles.

Often, those researched are those with the least influence over how the research is conducted, analysed or used. This lack of accountability to the researched population can create and reproduce many of the other problems discussed above – lack of access, contextualisation and problems with safety of the researchers. Many of these problems can be alleviated by democratising the process of the research itself: by involving those researched in the design, collection of data, analysis and dissemination of the research.

Respondent populations can inform the direction and methodology of the research. They can assist in negotiating ethical dilemmas and guide the researcher's agenda. The researcher's political and ideological stance, and that of the donor or funder – whether implicit or explicit – inevitably influence the research agenda and process, and they shape the collection and interpretation of information, and the selection of respondents. Democratisation of the management and process of research is a means of achieving greater accountability and improving the quality of the work itself. In actualising such accountability, some limits must be maintained in the interests of practicality. The researcher must retain responsibility for the implementation of scientific method and analysis. However, many other areas can be managed in partnership with the population researched. Democracy in research, as in society, may be more time-consuming than totalitarian or autocratic approaches, but in the long run it may offer a more complete and diverse result. At the very least, in studying violently divided societies, which are often the result of totalitarian, autocratic or anti-democratic circumstances, as researchers, we could be assured that we were not replicating in our work the worst features of that which we study.

The contributors to this volume, and the editors continue to explore these and other issues raised in these pages with each other. Through the accounts in the chapters that follow, the reader can acquire a flavour of the state of these explorations. Research on violently divided societies, and on violence itself, can offer the potential to learn from past bitter and difficult experience. Researchers working in the field bear the responsibility of conducting research in the most effective and ethical way possible, in order that such learning can be maximised, and perhaps some future violence avoided. There can be very little work that is more crucial.

REFERENCE

Morrissey, M. and Smyth, M. (2001) *Northern Ireland After the Good Friday Agreement* (London: Pluto).

1 The Role and Function of Research in Divided Societies: The Case of Africa

Eghosa E. Osaghae

This chapter examines the role and function of research in Africa's problematic multi-ethnic states, referred to here as 'divided societies'. Briefly, the role and function consist of interrogations of the nature of conflicts which characterise these states, as well as the strategies for managing and resolving them. This requires not only knowledge of the diverse groups, the nature of diversity including particularly the intricate recursive linkages between ethnic and other co-extant cleavages – religious, racial, regional, class and gender. It also requires knowledge of the historical, political, economic and sociological frameworks within which the conflicts are embedded.

Despite the pervasiveness of violent ethnic and other conflicts, and the commonplace presumption that political conflicts in Africa are generally ethnic-laden, conflict studies remains an underdeveloped field of study. Research in the area faces a number of serious problems. As discussed below, these range from the hostile terrain of research to the paucity of funds and local expertise. As a result, and also because of the scant regard for a policy-science approach to solving problems, the role and function of research remains largely a potential to be actualised. This demonstrably has a direct implication for the protracted character of conflicts, and the inability to deal with them. The challenge posed, especially in the 1980s and 1990s, by the intensification of virulent conflicts that threatened to destroy the fragile foundations of the postcolonial state all over the African continent however forced greater attention to be paid to conflict research.

What followed was the rise of governmental and non-governmental research organisations, study groups, research networks, and a massive expansion of scholars and policy makers involved in the study and management of conflicts. Although this has not eliminated the problems and pitfalls of research, serious efforts have been made to overcome them, and the need for research into conflict is now widely acknowledged. This acknowledgement is most marked on the part of governments that had a tendency in the past to deal with conflicts by suppressing or simply ignoring them.

This chapter examines the opportunities for retrospection, fresh beginnings and new paradigms offered by the new frontiers of research and the ways in which these opportunities can be further enhanced. The chapter is divided into four sections. The first maps the contours of conflict studies in Africa in a panoramic way, as a background to the rest of the chapter.

The second section examines the nature of Africa's divided societies. The third section presents a critical appraisal of the state of research on conflicts and their management in these societies, the dominant paradigms and methodologies as well as their problems and pitfalls, and the search for new paradigms in view of the intensified conflict situations examined by most researchers in the 1980s and 1990s. The final section presents the conclusions.

A PANORAMIC OVERVIEW OF CONFLICT STUDIES IN AFRICA

Although Africa provides one of the most potentially fruitful laboratories for the production of knowledge on conflict situations in general, and ethnic conflicts in particular, it remains a rather difficult terrain for research and researchers in these areas of study. For a long time, when forces of nationalism and state-led developmentalism held sway, research on ethnic and other forms of conflict was considered epithetic, and researchers who studied them were labelled 'unprogressive', 'subversive', and 'agents of opposition and imperialism' (Magubane and Magubawe, 1969; Mafeje, 1971; Arrighi and Saul, 1973). Governments also tended to be intolerant of research on conflicts, which many of them viewed as subversive. The hostile terrain stultified the development of local research expertise, but even foreign scholars who consequently dominated the scene were equally castigated for giving intellectual muscle to a supposedly neo-colonial project to keep the fragile African states weak and divided.

This conspiratorial thesis was subscribed to by the radical (dependency-underdevelopment) scholars who dominated African social science from the 1960s up until the 1980s. This thesis led to the dubbing of the discipline of anthropology as a colonial discipline (Mafeje, 1976), since it was popularised as a familiarisation course for colonial officers, and its initial focus was on groups that *combine but do not mix*, and the divisions and conflicts among them. A similar fate befell the modernisation paradigm that dominated what was perceived to be 'Western social science' and therefore an instrument of imperialism (Ake, 1979).

There were three main consequences of the disabling environment for research into ethnic and other forms of conflict. First was the underdevelopment of research expertise in the areas of conflicts and violence. Very few tertiary institutions offered conflict studies, much less strategies of resolution, management and mediation in their social science curricula. This was especially true of francophone countries where the existence of ethnicity and other divisions and conflicts was denied for a long time by scholars, policy makers and state officials.

Second was the underdevelopment (or absence in many countries) of research institutions devoted to the study and monitoring of conflict, war or violence, and their management and resolution. The research network on ethnic conflicts in Africa initiated by the Council for the Development of Social Science Research in Africa (CODESRIA) in 1990 was the first major attempt to overcome this deficit on a continent-wide scale. Up until the late 1990s, there was no major centre for the study and management of ethnic and other forms of conflict on the continent.

Third was the poor state of knowledge of the nature of groups and conflicts. The initial leads provided by the disciplines of history and anthropology were not followed up, and little contemporary knowledge was being generated. In Liberia, to take one example, the exact number (or even the names in some cases) of ethnic groups, and the nature of their historical and contemporary relations were and still are not known. This had partly to do with the overwhelming attention given to American-Liberian versus tribal-Liberian division, but it was also because very few Liberians were encouraged to undertake such studies (Osaghae, 1996). For reasons already stated, the state of knowledge on conflicts in francophone Africa was similar to, if not worse than, that of Liberia. The situation in Nigeria, which typifies other conflicts in Africa was surprisingly not very different. Social scientists in that country hold that the escalation of complex ethnic conflicts since the 1980s was partly due to the paucity of knowledge.

The later half of the 1980s, and 1990s, however, witnessed something of a reinvigoration in the overall state of research on conflicts in Africa's divided societies. To some extent, this was part of the monumental search by scholars for new openings, paradigms and directions in the study of Africa's development. The crises and trajectories of Africa's development seemed to have defied all conventional wisdoms, and this quest for new approaches was set in the context of the global search that followed the evolution of new post-Cold War realities and the global forces of democratisation and market reforms (Himmelstrand et al., 1994; Osaghae, 1994).

The new lease of life owed more to the ethnic revival, violent conflicts and the protracted civil wars that ravaged virtually every country on the continent, rendering asunder the fragile postcolonial states and their peoples. The need to manage and resolve conflicts and salvage the collapsing states became more urgent (Hansen, 1987; Zartman, 1995; Olukoshi and Laasko, 1996), but this could not take place without a massive upgrading of knowledge of conflict situations.

A number of emerging factors suggest remarkable responses to the challenges posed by the devastating face of (the mostly newly-formed) conflicts in Africa: the phenomenal rise in the number of governmental and non-governmental organisations (NGOs) involved in the study and management of conflicts;[1] the importance now attached to conflict studies in the curricula of tertiary institutions; the growing recognition of ethnic and regional mobilisation as legitimate means of interest and grievance articulation, and the increased research output on the subject, especially by left-wing radical scholars who have not only become convinced of the reality of ethnic conflicts but are in the forefront of championing ethnic interests in the resurgent clash of nationalisms.

Underneath this apparent improvement in the state of research on division and conflict, however, remains a number of causes for concern. One is the great disparity in the regional and national locations of centres of research production. The more notable institutions dealing with conflicts are concentrated in South Africa and Southern Africa which account for roughly 60 per cent and 70 per cent respectively of all such institutions in Sub-Saharan Africa. With the exception of a few flashpoints of protracted conflicts such as Burundi and Senegal, conflict studies institutions continue to be absent in francophone countries.

Another factor is that the research arena continues to be dominated by foreign scholars who mostly import and employ Western unilinear paradigms encapsulated in neo-modernisation frameworks (Apter and Rosberg, 1994). Although there has been an increase in the number of African researchers this has not led to the emergence of an indigenous paradigm or framework. Often indigenous scholars, especially those of the radical mien, have become so intimately involved as champions of ethnic interests that the validity of their work is constantly questioned. It would seem that, for the converted radicals, the passion for waging a class war which now seems more unlikely, has simply been transferred to the ethnic battlefield. Finally, despite these new openings and emergent frameworks, and the expansion in the volume of research output, knowledge on the subject remains at an early stage of development. This serves as a point of departure for our review of the nature of Africa's divided societies.

AFRICA'S DIVIDED SOCIETIES

What is the extent of division in Africa's divided societies? How much of the complexity of the divisions do we perceive? In particular, how much of the violent conflict that constantly threatens the stability and survival of the states in Africa is, as conventional wisdom on Africa suggests, ethnic? And what are the implications of the adequacy or inadequacy of our knowledge of Africa's conflict situations for the management of these conflicts? Does the intractability of these conflicts and the seeming failure of standard strategies of resolution, management and peacemaking suggest that we need to do more? These are the key questions to be addressed in this section.

The term 'divided society' is often used to refer to a polity in which ethnic, religious, racial, regional and allied cleavages are so fundamental that most political relations, especially involving competition for power and scarce resources, hinge on these differences. In Sub-Saharan Africa, ethnic cleavages are the most significant for politics, though, due to the overlap with religious, regional, racial and class cleavages, they rarely exist in pure forms (Nnoli, 1978). This explains why conflicts that are not strictly ethnic, such as those between Northerners and Southerners and people from different states in Nigeria, and between Northerners and Southerners, Muslims and Christians in Sudan, are described as ethnic. It is precisely because of the recursive nature of the cleavages that they are salient and pervasive in political relations.

However, the extent to which ethnic and other cleavages are fundamental and pervasive differs from country to country. Using the operational measure of the degree of *corporate ethnic distance* and the degree of conflict, multi-ethnic, multicultural and multi-religious polities can be classified into *less divided*, *divided* and *more divided* or *deeply divided* societies. Many francophone African states and a few others like Tanzania which have experienced less virulent conflicts may be regarded as *less divided*, while most anglophone states, notably Ghana, Sierra Leone and Kenya, belong to the category of *divided* societies. At the extreme of *deeply divided* societies are countries like South Africa, Rwanda, Nigeria and Sudan. In these countries, the fundamentality of ethnic, racial and regional cleavages underlie various separatist agitations and perennial violent conflicts which in turn render issues of nationality deeply divisive, and threaten the very survival of the state.

The definition and elaboration of *divided societies* should not be interpreted as suggesting that the mere existence of diversity renders ethnicity (or racism or religion) an inevitable or given basis of political relations and mobilisation. Neither should it be assumed that people in such societies are obdurately fixed to ethnicity as an organising principle for society. Some have even fallen into the racist error of believing that ethnic division and conflict are natural to African peoples. The fluidity and pragmatic location of ethnic boundaries and identities in Africa is related to the process of recreating and consolidating ethnic groups within the postcolonial states, which is ongoing. The overlapping multiple identities assumed by individuals, and the historical location of ethnic relations, and contemporary theorising about such processes is sufficient to invalidate such suggestion (Bhabha, 1994; Yeros, 1999).

If ethnicity does not naturally arise from diversity, how can the salience of ethnicity and ethnic conflicts be explained? The experience of African states and other states in the world, suggests that the answers should be sought in the history of inter- and intra-group relations within the particular polity, and the history of the management of difference-based conflicts. In relation to Africa where, to borrow Geertz's perceptive description, we have 'old societies and new states', this raises the question how far back in history is it necessary to go? Arguments could be advanced for a retrospective analysis to the pre-colonial era, the colonial or, in view of the radical changes that accompanied independence in a country like South Africa, the postcolonial era. This question will be revisited in the next section where methodological questions are raised. At this point, it suffices to establish that division and conflicts are historically located and can only be understood as such. The key goal in the review of that history is to evaluate how conflicts are managed or mismanaged. In postcolonial African states certainly, the proliferation of conflicts can be attributed, without danger of reduction-ism, to the violent and non-democratic strategies employed by postcolonial governments.

Given the arbitrary ways in which the boundaries of the present-day African states were drawn by colonisers, and the forcible incorporation of the diverse groups that compose them, the states were always going to be difficult to govern and sustain. To begin with, many of the ethnic groups incorporated into such states were strange bedfellows with long histories of unequal relations and antagonism. But the effects of these antagonisms could have been ameliorated if the colonial authorities had not been driven by the motives of colonial enterprise that subordinated the interests of the colonised peoples to those of the colonisers. This led to the pursuance of policies of forced and migrant labour, ethnic and racial discrimination, and the elaboration and consolidation of pre-colonial inequalities.

In effect, the inept, explicitly violent strategies and policies pursued by the colonial authorities to (mis)manage diversity made the proliferation of conflicts somewhat inevitable. These strategies included policies such as ethnic ranking and stratification which seemed to engender rigid hierarchical divisions (as in the so-called 'warrior tribe' policy of recruitment into the military and police, and the entrenchment of domination by favoured groups like the Fulani in Nigeria and the Baganda in Uganda). Elsewhere, ethnic differences were created or invented through administrative restructuring, as was the case in several British colonies where the indirect rule system concretised nascent ethnic identities and boundaries (Mamdani, 1996). The development of standard languages and language families, and division of labour along ethnic lines also reinforced ethnic affinities and consciousness. The pursuit of these policies accentuated uneven development among regions and ethnic, racial and regional groups, together with the violent repression of ethnic demands and grievances, led in short, to ethnic countermobilisation.

There were no fundamental changes in strategies and policies when erstwhile colonies became politically independent. As scholars like Ake (1994) have argued, independence did not mean the dis-mantling of the imperial state which had been established to serve the interests of Western colonialists; the significant change was only in the change of guards. To achieve a real change of strategy, the state would have needed to be democratised, to be appropriated by its citizens, and to be reorientated towards serving the interests of those citizens rather than the interests of its erstwhile colonial bene-factors. This would have required a new social contract or an outright revolution (Olukoshi and Laasko, 1996).

That none of this happened had partly to do with the peripheral location of African states in the global capitalist system and partly with the fact that the old order of ethnic stratification and inequal-ities was preserved, despite the nationalist fervour that attended independence movements. The last thing Western powers wanted in the context of the Cold War was the coming into power of unpre-dictable and unreliable ruling coalitions. The preservation of erstwhile power relations resulted in the transfer of power to favoured or dominant ethnic interests and coalitions which patron mother colonies such as France were prepared to defend at all costs.

Thus began the march towards *ethnocracy* or exclusionary rule by and in the interest of a few elite ethnic groups. Public services, police, armed forces and universities were dominated by members of these groups, and development efforts were concentrated in their areas, at the expense of the development of other areas. The ascendancy of single-party and military governments was conducive to this march (Horowitz, 1985). Ostensibly in the name of holding the fragile state together and building a unified nation out of multiplicity and division, contesting cultures and identities were to be excluded and assimilated, in a version of the melting pot approach, into a new hegemonic structure or simply marginalised and repressed out of existence (Kasfir, 1976). This tendency was in the opposite direction of the *multi-ethnic democracy* which, according to Horowitz (1994) and Osaghae (1999), is necessary for the survival of divided societies. The hallmarks and goals of multi-ethnic democracy are inclusive-ness, accommodation and conflict reduction.[2]

The tendency of the state to dominate the public sphere and effect unalloyed control over public life ensured its centrality to the mode of material and non-material reproduction. As the main determinant and allocator of development (the private sector barely existed in many countries for a long time and even when it did, operated under state control), the centrality of the state ensured ethnocracy and allied forms of exclusionary hegemonic rule became the cradle of the mostly zero-sum political conflicts in the postcolonial era. The resulting diminution of any remaining legitimacy of the postcolo-nial era engendered further contest over citizenship, group rights, equity, social justice and the sanctity of the extant state.

The contests took various forms. The most widespread were separatist agitations and movements to assert the right of nationalities to self-determination (for example, Biafra in Nigeria, Katanga in Congo, right-wing Afrikaners in post-apartheid South Africa, and Oromo in Ethiopia). Added to these struggles were demands for local political autonomy to reduce the effects of centrist domination by one ethnic group (for example, the Ogoni and other minority nationalities in Nigeria's Niger Delta region). The contests also took the form of vigorous and sometimes violent challenges to the ruling status quo and its eventual overthrow through military *coups d'état*, opposition politics, electoral defeats and underground activities. Responses by the ruling status quo were mixed, but mostly involved violent suppression of ethnic (opposition) parties and movements, and attempts to outlaw and delegitimise ethnicity. In a few extreme cases, suppression was pursued by means of genocide and ethnic cleansing.

Only in a few cases (Nigeria, South Africa and, more recently, Uganda and Ethiopia) were contesting forces recognised and serious attempts made to respond peacefully to conflicting demands through one form of multi-ethnic democracy or the other. Even in these cases, the absence or fragility of democracy together with the scant regard for the values of tolerance and reciprocity soon foreclosed the potential benefits inherent in federalism, devolution and consociational principles. As military rule in Nigeria became an instrument of ethno-regional hegemony, it desecrated what would otherwise have been a model federal system for governance of divided societies.

In the case of Ethiopia, which went as far as granting the right of secession to nationalities in its ethnic federation, Amharic dominance and hegemony has continued to stoke the fire of Oromo and Tigrean separatism. South Africa with its federal and consociational instrumentalities, emergent culture of constitutionalism, and the counterbalance to state power provided by a highly developed capitalist sector and civil society, has one of the better capacities and frameworks for peaceful management of conflicts. Yet these have not prevented Afrikaner and Zulu separatist agitation, nor have they removed the increasingly loud allegations of marginalisation and domination by the Coloureds and most black-African minority groups (the latter allege Xhosa domination of the ruling African National Congress and the post-apartheid government).

Whilst ethnic and other sectional conflicts were poorly managed in the period after independence, this mismanagement served to consolidate and accentuate state-directed and intergroup conflicts which have deep roots in precolonial and colonial histories. Other global and local forces from the late 1970s onward were to exacerbate further these conflicts. Economic depression, declining resources and the implementation of poverty-aggravating structural adjustment programmes which were the defining features of the late 1970s, lasting to the end of the 1990s, demonstrably heightened the conflicts (see Adekanye, 2000; Osaghae, 1995; Olukoshi and Laasko, 1996). Exiles who became particularly active and made use of information technology available in the developed world (e-mail, the Internet, radio networks and so on) to draw attention to and oppose unpopular governments at home, further accentuated the conflicts themselves.

Bringing multiparty government and opposition politics back in served to legitimise previously suppressed demands by minorities and other dominated and marginalised groups. This brought the full weight of the international community to bear on these states, ensuring that they conformed to the growing global human rights culture and liberalisation. The simultaneous process of democratisation created the conditions for more desperate and uncompromising demands to be voiced. These demands were for income redistribution, local political autonomy, and equity – the latter came to be euphemistically known as 'ethnic justice'.

This was the context within which the movement for *majimboism* or regionalism revived in Uganda and Kenya. Aggrieved groups in Nigeria also demanded a restructuring of the federation along confederal lines, and ethnic agitations intensified all over the continent. Given their authoritarian character, most states were unable to respond adequately to the challenges of the ethnic implosions that, in a literal sense, demanded the dissolution of the state itself. It was this inability and in some cases, the intensification of violent state strategies, that led to the escalation of state-threatening conflicts in the 1980s and 1990s. By the close of the 1990s, virtually all African states were embroiled in one form of internal war or the other, with Liberia, Sierra Leone, Ethiopia, Sudan, Equatorial Guinea, Senegal, Rwanda, Burundi, Democratic Republic of the Congo, Angola, Uganda, Niger, Chad and Nigeria being some of the most troubled.

This is a familiar, if simplistic, summary of Africa's divided societies and major conflict situations. Such summarising creates the false impression that ethnicity in Africa is easily understood, simply because the virulent conflicts are mostly ethnic. But can they really be seen as ethnic, given that, as several studies have shown, ethnicity is often mobilised by and dependent on other crucial divisions such as class? This aspect of the complexity of Africa's divided societies is well articulated in the literature (Nnoli, 1978, 1998) and is beyond the remit of this chapter.

Here the immediate concern is with ethnic complexity which is fundamental to conflicts in Africa. How much of these complex ethnic situations is really known or understood? If conflict therapies or 'medicine' (Zartman, 2000) can be meaningful only when there is adequate knowledge of the conflict, does the seeming intractability of these conflicts not suggest that what is known is far from adequate? The tendency to proffer catch-all and supposedly universalist solutions to conflict situations suggests that this is the case, as is argued elsewhere with regard to the multiple ethnic minority problems in Nigeria (Osaghae, 1998). Calls for more discerning management strategies, based on concrete analyses of concrete situations by several international NGOs involved in peacemaking in Africa (see International Alert, 1994; Smock, 1996) would confirm this suggestion.

More evidence can be adduced to show that, indeed, our knowledge of Africa's divided societies and the conflicts emanating from them is far from adequate or satisfactory. This is however at the empirical rather than theoretical level where much of the sometimes diversionary and unproductive debates and controversies that dominate ethnic studies in Africa have taken place (Osaghae, 1990). At the empirical level, not much advance has been made on the ethnographic profiles and analyses of intergroup relations and conflicts in the context of social change. Work by anthropologists, historians and sociologists in the period before the 1970s was produced in a context where mapping the contours of the African terrain was for colonial and neo-colonial use.

As a result, there is a problem of incomplete baseline data. These ethnographic profiles were largely exploratory and tentative, since at that time there was no agreement on the criteria for identifying ethnic groups. Thus the field continues to rely on old data and racial stereotypes. In the earlier section, the poor state of knowledge of ethnicity in Liberia was referred to. There, such basic things as the names of ethnic groups are still contested (see Dunn and Holsoe, 1985). Many scholars will be surprised to learn that the situation in Nigeria, which is perhaps the most popularly cited divided society in Africa, is not very different.

For example, the number of (distinct) ethnic groups in the country is still not known. If the mixed criteria of objective definition (language, culture, locality, name) and subjective definition (in-group/out-group differentiation, myth of common origin, self-definition) are used, is it 248 (Coleman, 1958), 62 (Murdock, 1975), 161 (Gandonu, 1978), 143 (Odetola, 1978), or 374 (Otite, 1990)? Or following the linguistic criterion, is it 394 (Hoffman, 1974), or 619 (Wente-Lukas, 1985)? The discrepancies could be attributed to the fluid character of ethnic identities. However, field studies conducted by this author and several others suggest that the problem is even more fundamental and has to do with the paucity of comprehensive and systematic attempts (with the exception of Otite's study) to map the ethnic profile of Nigeria.

It is the absence of such a map that explains the rather simplistic and reductionist explanations of ethnic conflicts and problems in the country as those between the north and south or between the majority and minority groups, and among the three major ethnic groups (Hausa/Fulani, Igbo and Yoruba). This approach erroneously assumes a high degree of homogeneity within the ethnic and tends to gloss over the enormous intra-group and intra-category differ-ences and conflicts. In many cases these conflicts are more severe than those between the categories. The recent redefinitions and reconstructions by relevance-seeking elites of ethnic identities, which have created scores of new minorities within the major ethnic groups, is partly a response to the inadequacies of extant concep-tions and articulations of the ethnic configuration in the country.

What is true of Nigeria is also generally true of other Sub-Saharan African countries (Nnoli, 1998). For example, Sithole (1980, 1995) has made similar observations about the situation in Zimbabwe, as have Muigai (1995) about Kenya, and Azevedo (1995) about Cameroon and Gabon. In the earlier section, the special case of fran-cophone countries, where the illusion of ethnic homogeneity discouraged and stultified the study of ethnic configurations and conflicts for a long time, was made.

The case of South Africa today is a mish-mash reproduction of several of the anomalies of ethnic studies and conflict research in the rest of Africa. First, most of the analyses remain fixated on racial and regional categories which gloss over other equally – if not more – troubling ethnic problems, especially amongst black Africans. An even more serious error results from the popular Marxist analytical framework that denies ethnic consciousness or regards it as false consciousness. Then there are the nationalist scholars who argue that ethnic divisions were mobilised within the apartheid discourse (Posel, 1987), and insist on a successful melting-pot of black African ethnicities in urban centres like Soweto and other townships (Maphai, 1995). For a more comprehensive discussion of the state of ethnic studies in South Africa, see Bekker (1993).

This perception of homogeneity and harmony is in marked contrast to the insistence of some non-white scholars that blacks are ethnically divided (Adam and Giliomee, 1979). The perception survives in spite of contrary evidence of strong ethnic attachments and increasing opposition to what is perceived as Xhosa domination of the African National Congress and the post-apartheid government. All this, especially the highly partisan approaches to the ethnic problem, has prevented ethnicity from being taken seriously. The increased occurrence of deadly black-on-black violence is partly attributable to this.

The overall implication of the foregoing is that a lot more work is needed on the nature of Africa's divided societies and the conflicts that ensue therefrom. We not only need to return to the drawing-board of ethnic mapping, but also need to update knowledge of ethnic configurations. This can be achieved by studying the ways in which domestic and global social, economic and political forces have affected and (re)shaped ethnic configurations. Unless this is done, no serious and enduring solutions can be found to the conflicts in Africa.

Let us next turn to examine the state of research on these subjects in Africa. This will hopefully throw light on the shortcomings of ethnic studies, and how they can be improved.

THE STATE OF RESEARCH

This section begins with some observations on the state of the public policy process in Africa, and the role of research in that process. Long ago, Hirschman (1963) described the policy-process role of developing countries as 'failure-prone'. A number of factors account for this assessment: unrealistic goals, reactive and emergency rather than proactive and comprehensive approaches to policy making, a dearth of relevant data, reliance on foreign expertise, and poor implementation, feedback and evaluative strategies (also see Clark, 1978). This assessment could also be applied to the flaws in the policy process of most African states. Here the aspect of the problem in focus is the *ad hoc* and emergency rather than comprehensive approaches to problem solving.

Central to understanding this problem is the disconnection between research output and policy-making structures. In the formulation and implementation of policy, very little consideration is given to (independent) research, other than that undertaken directly by foreign donors or at their behest. Once again, Nigeria typifies this policy malady in Africa. This is in spite of the existence of numerous tertiary institutions and research institutes in that country, including the elite National Institute for Policy and Strategic Studies, together with highly trained staff, official think-tanks and study groups. Social scientists in Nigeria 'have been confronted with the problem of the relevance of their vocation to public policy' (Ajakaiye and Roberts, 1997: 190; also Sanda, 1980; for comparative African experiences, see Rukobo, 1990; Goncalves, 1992; Rasheed, 1993; Ndongko, 1993).

This disconnection is particularly found in policy making with regard to political conflicts, and their management, which require continuous research and monitoring. It must count as one of the shortfalls of conflict management in Africa that, even in those countries which have experienced the most devastating conflicts, there are no specialised research institutions dealing with conflicts, including ethnic conflicts. One additional reason for this is the fear by state managers that researching ethnic conflicts may confer some form of legitimacy on ethnicity and thereby encourage ethnic agitations against the state.

It may be an exaggeration to hold the absence of research bodies or networks responsible for the prevalence of conflict. However, the basic state of conflict management which leaves violent repression and confrontation as the current centrepiece of conflict management practice can be attributed to that absence. This seems likely to change, due to the incorporation of conflict management into the agenda of the donor community to which many governments are beholden. One of the positive results of this has been the influx of international NGOs whose humanitarian activities of necessity include conflict resolution and peacemaking. This has been accompanied by the emergence of local independent research and activist NGOs funded by foreign donors.[3]

With so much going on, African governments, especially those embroiled in severe crises and protracted wars, can no longer afford to ignore research findings and the recommendations based on them. The case of Sierra Leone illustrates this. There, International Alert, an international NGO, became highly involved in the resolution of the protracted war and actually helped to broker peace between the government and Foday Sankoh, the rebel leader. This intervention illustrates the potential direction and practical benefits of increased collaboration between government and non-governmental agencies, and the research community. Indeed, the involvement of non-state actors in conflict issues makes such collaboration very unlikely, although governments usually remain highly suspicious of independent research and other initiatives on conflict. Notwithstanding, I think there is a strong argument for researchers to finally assert their relevance to the conflict situation in Africa, and the critical appraisal that follows is predicated on this position.

It bears repeating that the state of conflict research in African divided societies leaves much to be desired. For example, more scientifically oriented scholars could lament the fact that the prevalent methodology is more often qualitative rather than quantitative. The central problem is partly conceptual and partly methodological. Conceptually, two theoretical paradigms dominated and shaped social science research in Africa from its inception: first, modernisation, and second, dependency/underdevelopment, or the 'radical school', for short. Both were dismissive of ethnicity.

Both saw it as part of the residue of the pre-modern past, which was bound to wither away as African societies became more industrialised, and more peasants and others in the pre-capitalist economy were drawn into the modern way of life. In addition, the inherent nationalist ideology of the two schools, especially the radical school, theorised ethnicity as a (dangerous) obstacle to nationhood that had to be eradicated. In the period between independence and the late 1970s, these were the predominant views in the literature, and they also seemed to inform and justify the nation-building strategies pursued by African governments.

The nation-state project was a monumental failure because a uni-nation model is incompatible with a divided multi-nation situation. This failure finally forced a re-examination of conventional wisdom on ethnic conflicts and the tools of research. Violent conflicts and civil wars became the order of the day in most countries, including those like Côte d'Ivoire and Senegal where it was said the ethnic problem did not exist. This situation led not only to the acknowledgement of the reality of ethnicity, ethnic consciousness and associated concepts, but also to the development of new concepts for handling conflict situations.

New approaches and concerns appeared: liberalisation; democratisation; pluralism; the national question, including power sharing, federalism, decentralisation and local political autonomy; human and group rights, including the right to self-determination; conflict management and prevention; peacemaking, and globalism. These replaced the earlier approaches of nation-building, charismatic authority, one-party democracy, economic regulation, peacekeeping and separatism. Today, the literature of the new radical school and neo-modernisation alike have adopted a revised attitude towards ethnicity. Ethnicity is accepted as a problem to be managed rather than repressed, since repression only exacerbates conflicts.

Indeed, the radical school now sees ethnicity as a weapon of struggle from below, and not simply as a mask for class privilege or false consciousness as was previously thought. The enthusiasm generated by the new-found approach and instrumentality of ethnicity, has seen the unprecedented influx of local African researchers into the field of study. This has, however, created a new problem: that of maintaining objectivity in conflict research. As many of the new researchers are involved because of their own ethnicity, in the same way that class analysts were involved in trying to bring about a class revolution, their analysis carries great passion and emotion. In an emotionally charged field like ethnicity, the need for discipline cannot be over-emphasised, otherwise research risks becoming counterproductive, and exacerbating the very problem it is meant to elucidate and solve.

This conceptual shift in ethnic analysis has led to much methodological soul-searching and redirections that now characterise conflict studies in Africa. First, ethnic analysis now goes beyond investigations of the association of ethnicity with class, to include its linkages also with regionalism, religion, gender and so on. As a corollary of this, the old argument that ethnicity was wholly a dependent variable to be explained only in terms of elite manipulation and competition for scarce resources is now being re-examined. The independent variables of language and culture that are key components of ethnicity are now accorded greater attention. These developments seem to be finally getting closer to the roots of the ethnic complex.

Second, ethnicity is increasingly analysed as an historical and problematic phenomenon. The argument in the past was that ethnic groups developed their contemporary characters and patterns of political involvement within the context of the new states. Since most of these states were colonial creations, the farthest most analysts were prepared to go was the colonial period which, according to Nnoli (1978) is the cradle of ethnicity in Africa. Many scholars subsequently tended to see the pre-colonial – and even colonial – historical context(s) of inter-group relations as separate from the contemporary situation.

In the aftermath of persistent violent conflicts, the deeper pre-colonial and colonial roots of inter-group conflicts are now being emphasised and investigated. Thus, recent analysis of ethnic minority politics and problems in Nigeria focus extensively on how pre-colonial relations and changes occurring under colonialism have shaped present-day political attitudes and conflicts (Ekeh, 1996; Osaghae, 1998). This has helped to shed light on the complexity of minority problems which previously were incorrectly analysed. They were seen as a problem that emerged with the regionalisation of the country and ended with the demise of the regions. Admittedly, there are serious difficulties in reconstructing Africa's pre-colonial history. However, there is enough at present, by way of oral traditions, documentary sources, art forms, rituals and religious practices, to enable meaningful analysis. Nor have all resources been explored, for example, not much use has been made of the chronicles of the famous Islamic scholars.

There are other dimensions of the historicity of ethnic conflicts that are now recognised as requiring re-examination. One of these is the global context of Africa's integration into and location within the world (capitalist) system. There are huge gaps in how the history of globalism has affected contemporary ethnic conflicts. The consequences of the slave trade, for example, have yet to be more thoroughly investigated. Likewise the effects of the powerful Islamic intrusions into Africa have tended to be ignored or undermined in ethnic analysis, with the focus strictly maintained on so-called forces of Western imperialism.

The manner in which the arms trade has contributed to the escalation of violent conflicts in Africa over time also requires further examination. Were Africans really as violent as they were portrayed before the influx of arms from the outside world? In what way do the economic interests behind the arms trade depend on ethnic and other conflicts remaining unresolved, and is this a factor in the failure to resolve them?

Finally, more careful examination is required of the continuities and changes that have characterised the external forces at play in Africa's conflict situation. In particular, against the background of the continuities and changes, there is a need to examine thoroughly the contradictory forces of the post-Cold War period that have seen the escalation rather than the expected de-escalation of conflicts. In this regard, the emergence and the role of diaspora communities made up of former members of the opposition, 'brain drain' scholars, and professional and economic exiles requires further scrutiny. These diaspora communities who often find succour and support from foreign governments in their pursuit of political intervention back home need to be thoroughly investigated.

The deterioration of conflict situations has, however, led to positive responses in conflict prevention, management and resolution. Most African conflicts, notably those of Somalia and Sudan, have defied conventional wisdom and this provided an incentive to examine more creative and innovative strategies for intervention (International Alert, 1994). Accordingly, there has been a movement away from advocating universal, catch-all solutions to more discerning approaches and strategies informed by the historical, as well as economic, social and political circumstances at play in the particular situation.

One of the resulting advances is the greater attention now paid to indigenous knowledge of conflicts, and to traditional or indigenous systems, strategies and practices of conflict prevention, management and resolution (Osaghae, 2000). This development has great promise for the integration of the rich anthropological and historical literature into mainstream conflict studies in Africa. Paradoxically, it must be pointed out that African researchers have been rather slow in accepting responsibility for this form of research.

CONCLUSION

Research into African conflict situations has finally been launched. It could be argued – erroneously – that the pervasive violence of the 1980s and 1990s would have been reduced if research in this area had been better developed or if mechanisms had existed, as they now do, for anticipating, monitoring and managing conflicts. Although there is certainly some merit in this line of reasoning, it underplays the role of forces from outside Africa that have historically propelled and shaped conflicts in Africa (Osaghae, 1995).

Therefore, investigations of internal sources of conflicts must be balanced with those of powerful external sources beyond the control of local actors. In particular, in view of the increased participation of outside actors in the conflict arena, there is a need to pay greater attention to the roles they play. Finally, research on Africa's divided societies should not be reactive, focusing only on conflicts that have already erupted. There is need to devote greater energy to conflict prevention and the management of ordinary day-to-day conflicts. There has been the realisation that every competition or conflict even at the inter-personal level has the potential of escalating into violent and still more violent conflict if not managed at the appropriate stage. But the management of such situations is dependent on a thorough understanding of the exact nature of Africa's divided societies.

NOTES

1. At the continental and sub-continental levels, the Organisation of African Unity (OAU) and various subregional organisations have created departments for conflict management and resolution.

2. As elaborated by Horowitz (1994: 52–3), multi-ethnic democracy requires a coherent or even redundant package of conflict-reducing techniques which include 'electoral systems to create ongoing incentives for interethnic cooperation ... federalism or regional autonomy ... [and] devolution', although he admits that 'All such innovations are difficult to introduce with coherence to have their intended effect.'

3. As was pointed out earlier, South Africa has a large concentration of research and activist NGOs which produce volumes of interesting and insightful material. One of the more notable organisations is the Helen Suzman Foundation which produces, amongst others, the *KwaZulu-Natal Briefing and Focus* every month. Another, with an Africa-wide focus which spans the study, mediation, management and resolution of conflicts is the African Centre for the Constructive Resolution of Disputes (ACCORD), which is based at the University of Durban–Westville. The Institute for Strategic Studies, whose focus is more on the military dimensions of security, is also active in this field.

   Some semi-governmental agencies have been established in a number of countries, such as the Centre for Peace Research and Conflict Resolution which is an arm of the National War College in Nigeria. Progress has also been made at the continental and sub-continental levels where international organisations such as the Organisation for African Unity, the Economic Community of West African States (ECOWAS) and the South African Development Community (SADC) have set up conflict-resolution initiatives which also receive funds from the donor community. These are in addition to the African Commission on Human and Peoples' Rights and the African Human Rights Charter which serve as rallying points for groups struggling to assert their rights to self-determination.

REFERENCES

Adam, H. and Giliomee, H. (1979) *Ethnic Power Mobilised: Can South Africa Change?* (New Haven: Yale University Press).

Adekanye, J.B. (1995) 'Structural Adjustment Democratisation and Rising Ethnic Tensions in Africa', *Development and Change*, vol. 26, no. 2.

Adekanye, J.B. (2000) *Comparative Military Ethnic Relations in Post Cold War Africa* (London: Ashgate).

Ajakaiye, D.O. and Roberts, F.O.N. (1997) 'Social Science Research in Nigeria: The Problems of Policy Relevance', *Journal of Humanities and Social Sciences*, vol. 8, no. 2.

Ake, C. (1979) *Social Science as Imperialism: The Theory of Political Development* (Ibadan: Ibadan University Press).

Ake, C. (1994) *Democratization and Disempowerment in Africa* (Lagos and Oxford: Malthouse).

Apter, D.E. and Rosberg, C.G. (eds) (1994) *Political Development and the New Realism in Sub-Saharan Africa* (Charlottesville & London: University Press of Virginia).

Arrighi, G. and Saul, J. (1973) *Essays on the Political Economy of Africa* (New York: Monthly Review Press).

Azevedo, M. (1995) 'Ethnicity and Democratisation: Cameroon and Gabon', in H. Glickman (ed.), *Ethnic Conflict and Democratisation in Africa* (Atlanta: African Studies Association Press).

Bekker, S. (1993) *Ethnicity in Focus: The South African Case* (Durban: Indicator South Africa).

Bhaba, H. (1994) *The Location of Culture* (London: Routledge).

Clark, R.P. (1978) *Power and Policy in the Third World* (New York: John Wiley).

Coleman, J.S. (1958) *Nigeria: Background to Nationalism* (Berkeley: University of California Press).

Dunn, D.E. and Holsoe, S.E. (1985) *Historical Dictionary of Liberia* (Metuchen & London: Scarecrow Press).

Ekeh, P.P. (1996) 'Political Minorities and Historically Dominant Minorities in Nigerian History and Politics', in O. Oyediran (ed.), *Governance and Development in Nigeria: Essays in Honour of Professor Billy J. Dudley* (Ibadan: Oyediran Consult).

Gandonu, A. (1978) 'Nigeria's 250 Ethnic Groups. Realities and Assumptions', in R.E. Holloman and S.A. Arutiunov (eds), *Perspectives on Ethnicity* (The Hague: Mouton).

Geertz, C. (1963) *Old Societies and New States: The Quest for Modernity in Asia and Africa* (New York: The Free Press).

Goncalves, J. (1992) *The Social Sciences in Angola, Cape Verde, Guinea-Bissau, Mozambique and Sao Tome and Principe* (Dakar: CODESRIA Monograph series).

Hansen, E. (1987) 'Development', in E. Hansen, (ed.) *Africa: Perspectives on Peace and Development* (London & New Jersey, United Nations University and Zed Press).

Himmelstrand, U., Kinyanjui, K. and Mburugu, E. (eds) (1994) *African Perspectives on Development: Controversies, Dilemmas and Openings* (London: James Currey).

Hirschman, A.O. (1963) *Journeys Toward Progress: Studies of Economic Policy Making in Latin America* (New York: Twentieth Century Fund).

Hoffman, C. (1974) 'The Languages of Nigeria by Language Families' (Mimeograph, Department of Linguistics, University of Ibadan).

Horowitz, D.L. (1985) *Ethnic Groups in Conflict* (Berkeley, University of California Press).

Horowitz, D.L. (1994) 'Democracy in Divided Societies', in L. Diamond and M.F. Plattner (eds) *Nationalism, Ethnic Conflict, and Democracy* (Baltimore and London: Johns Hopkins University Press).

International Alert (1994) *The Challenge of Peacemaking in Africa: Conflict Prevention and Conflict Resolution – Report of the Conference held in Addis Ababa, Ethiopia, 12–15 September 1994* (London: International Alert).

Kasfir, N. (1976) *The Shrinking Political Arena: Participation and Ethnicity in African Politics, with a Case Study of Uganda* (Berkeley: University of California Press).

Mafeje, A. (1971) 'The Ideology of Tribalism', *African Studies Journal of Modern Africa Studies*, vol. 9, no. 2.

Mafeje, A. (1976) 'The Problem of Anthropology in Historical Perspective: An Enquiry into the Growth of the Social Sciences', *Canadian Journal of African Studies*, vol. 10, no. 2.

Magubane, B. and Magubawe, A. (1969) 'Pluralism and Conflict Situations in Africa. A New Look', *African Social Research*, vol. 7, no. 2.

Mamdani, M. (1996) *Citizen and Subject: Contemporary Africa and the Legacy of Late Colonialism* (Princeton: Princeton University Press).

Maphai, V.T. (1995) 'Liberal Democracy and Ethnic Conflict in South Africa', in H. Glickman (ed.), *Ethnic Conflict and Democratisation in Africa* (Atlanta: African Studies Association Press).

Muigai, G. (1995) 'Ethnicity and the Renewal of Competitive Politics in Kenya', in H. Glickman (ed.), *Ethnic Conflict and Democratisation in Africa* (Atlanta: African Studies Association Press).

Murdock, G.P. (1975) *Outline of World Cultures* (New Haven: Human Relations Area Files).

Ndongko, W.A. (1993) 'Social Science Research and Policy-Making in Africa: Status, Issues and Prospects', paper presented at Conference on Social Sciences in Post-Independence Africa: Past, Present and Future, Dakar, Senegal.

Nnoli, O. (1978) *Ethnic Politics in Nigeria* (Enugu: Fourth Dimension).

Nnoli, O. (ed.) (1998) *Ethnic Conflicts in Africa* (Dakar: CODESRIA).

Odetola, T.O. (1978) *Military Politics in Nigeria, Economic Development and Political Stability* (New Brunswick: Transaction Books).

Olukoshi, A.O. and Laasko, L. (eds) (1996) *Challenges to the Nation-State in Africa* (Uppsala: Nordiska Afrikainstitutet).

Osaghae, E.E. (1990) 'Redeeming the Utility of the Ethnic Perspective in African Studies: Towards a new Agenda', *Journal of Ethnic Studies*, vol. 18, no. 2.

Osaghae, E.E. (ed.) (1994) *Between State and Civil Society in Africa: Perspectives on Development* (Dakar: CODESRIA).

Osaghae, E.E. (1995) 'The Fire Behind the Smoke: External Sources of Ethnic Conflicts in Africa', *Forum for Development Studies*, no. 1.

Osaghae, E.E. (1996) *Ethnicity, Class and the Struggle for State Power in Liberia Ethnicity, Class and the Struggle for State Power in Liberia* (Dakar: CODESRIA Monograph Series).

Osaghae, E.E. (1998) 'Managing Multiple Minority Problems in a Divided Society: The Nigerian Experience', *Journal of Modern African Studies*, vol. 36, no. 1.

Osaghae, E.E. (1999) 'Democracy and National Cohesion in Multiethnic African States: Nigeria and South Africa Compared', *Nations and Nationalism*, vol. 5, no. 2.

Osaghae, E.E. (2000) 'Applying Traditional Strategies of Conflict Management to Modern Conflicts in Africa: Possibilities and Limits', in I.W. Zartman (ed.), *Traditional Cures for Modern Conflicts*: *African Conflict Medicine* (Boulder: Lynne Rienner).

Otite, O. (1990) *Ethnic Pluralism and Ethnicity in Nigeria* (Ibadan: Shaneson).

Posel, D. (1987) 'The Language of Domination, 1978–1983', in S. Marks and S. Trapido (eds), *The Politics of Race, Class and Nationalism in Twentieth Century South Africa* (London: Longman).

Rasheed, S. (1993) 'Social Sciences and Policy-Making in Africa: A Critical Review', paper presented at the conference on Social Sciences in Post-Independence Africa: Past, Present and Future, Dakar, Senegal.

Rukobo, A.M. (1990) *The Social Sciences, Policy Research and Development in Zimbabwe*, Research Paper Series no. 4 (Harare: Zimbabwe Institute of Development Studies).

Sanda, A.O. (1980) 'Social Science and Policy: The Nigerian Experience', *Africa Development*, vol. 4, no. 4.

Sithole, M. (1980) 'Ethnicity and Factionalism in Zimbabwean Nationalist Politics 1957–1979', *Ethnic and Racial Studies*, vol. 3, no. 1.

Sithole, M. (1995) 'Ethnicity and Democratisation in Zimbabwe – From Confrontation to Accommodation', in H. Glickman (ed.), *Ethnic Conflict and Democratisation in Africa* (Atlanta: African Studies Association Press).

Smock, D.R. (1996) *Humanitarian Assistance and Conflict in Africa* (Washington: United States Institute of Peace).

Wente-Lukas, A. (1985) *Handbook of Ethnic Groups in Nigeria*, Studien zur Kulturkunde 74 (Stuttgart: Franz Steiner Verlag Weisbaden).

Yeros, P. (ed.) (1999) *Ethnicity and Nationalism in Africa: Constructive Reflections and Contemporary Politics* (Houndmills: Macmillan).

Zartman, I.W. (ed.) (1995) *Collapsed States: The Disintegration and Restoration of Legitimate Authority* (Boulder: Lynne Rienner).

Zartman, I.W. (2000) *Traditional Cures for Modern Conflicts*: *African Conflict Medicine* (Boulder: Lynne Rienner).

2 Does Research Make Any Difference? The Case of Northern Ireland

Marie Smyth and John Darby

In 1999, whilst conducting a review of the Good Friday Agreement in Northern Ireland, former US Senator George Mitchell proposed a media black-out – not for the first time – to the political parties participating. Information on the progress of the talks was withheld from the media for almost a week during the most delicate phase of the negotiations. Mitchell was attempting to preclude the negative impact of these activities in his suggestion of a media silence. And if anyone in the local or international media understood the implied judgement of their role in the earlier peace process, they gave no indication of such understanding, nor did they indicate that they were reflecting on their role or responsibility.

The media play an enormously powerful role in the shaping of political life, and one that is especially sensitive at times of political crises. Over the thirty years since 1969, Northern Ireland has had recurring experiences of political crises. In this chapter, the less prominent but none the less potentially significant role of researchers in the understanding and resolution of the conflict provides the focus of attention. Would George Mitchell have admitted researchers to information about the talks? Are researchers to be trusted or are they likely to behave in any more or less trustworthy ways than other observers? Does the activity of researchers make a difference? And if it does, what kind of impact can it be expected to make? What lessons can be learned for those researchers who would maximise the societal impact of their work?

Researchers tend to overestimate the impact of their research on policy. Policy makers tend to underestimate it. It is hardly novel for academics to regard their fields of study as central, and their own work within the field as important. In reality, policy decisions emerge from a much broader range of influences: the particular interest of ministers, their advisers and civil servants, parliament, political exigency, lobbying groups. It is not easy to separate and grade the

failure to be explicit' (Horowitz, forthcoming, Chapter 12). Collier and Mahoney (1996) suggest that it is important to be open about the research's distinctive 'frame of reference' so that readers can judge for themselves the boundaries within which the research is located. So, to be explicit, the case studies that follow do not attempt to cover all aspects of social policy research in Northern Ireland. They were selected to illuminate research which was undertaken to affect social policy in Northern Ireland; all relate to Northern Ireland's central sectarian division; they are intended to cover both *successes* and *failures*; they reflect the research experiences of the authors, both of whom have spent most of their academic careers working – separately – on such issues. These are the paper's frame of reference. It is, of course, possible and even likely that a different selection would have produced different conclusions.

CASE STUDIES IN RESEARCH

Local Government Discrimination – Research Conducted by the Fermanagh Civil Rights Association

A strong body of evidence now available demonstrates that successive Unionist administrations from 1921 to the mid-1960s openly discriminated politically, economically and socially against the Nationalist minority in Northern Ireland (see Whyte, 1991). Despite this, apart from periodic noises from the British Labour Party (for a recent review, see Rose, 2000, especially the first two chapters), there was little organised opposition and even fewer research investigations into the abuses until the formation of the Campaign for Social Justice in 1964 and the Northern Ireland Civil Rights Association (NICRA) three years later.[1] The campaigns carried out by these organisations during the late 1960s were modelled on the American civil rights campaigns – sit-ins, marches (a familiar form of protest in Northern Ireland), rallies and publications. Alongside these emerged the first explicit attempts to adopt research techniques as a means of both informing public opinion of abuses and lobbying for their reform. In 1969 the Fermanagh Civil Rights Association, a branch of NICRA, produced a report, *Fermanagh Facts*, investigating discrimination against Catholics in the allocation of public housing and jobs by the Unionist local council. This publication stood out from the more polemical ephemera by its thoroughness. The claims of gerrymandering and bias in employment by Unionist-controlled Fermanagh County Council were supported by detailed data. For example, they tracked down the religious affiliation of all the full-time council employees in April 1969, excluding those working in schools. The results needed no additional rhetoric. Out of a total of 370, and in a county that was approximately equally divided between the two religious communities, only 32 employees were Catholic.

The significance of the research was its comprehensive nature. It was not uncommon for critical social research in the early years of Northern Ireland's violence to be systematically attacked as incompetent or politically biased. *Fermanagh Facts* was able to withstand the closest scrutiny because the sample studied was the total population. It and other evidence was accepted completely and incorporated into the Cameron Report (1969), the first official investigation of Northern Ireland's peculiar practices. Indeed it had a major effect on Cameron's main finding, that 'much of the evidence of grievance and complaint which we heard, when analysed, was found, as might be expected, to be concentrated on two major issues – housing and employment. Jobs and houses are things that matter and touch the life of the ordinary man more than issues of "one man, one vote" and the gerrymandering of ward boundaries' (Cameron Report (1969), Paragraph 129).

Research on the Population Shifts and Increasing Segregation in Derry Londonderry[2] – Templegrove Action Research

In 1994, a group of people from both sides of the sectarian divide in Derry Londonderry became concerned about the deepening sectarian divide in the city and the movement of Protestants out of the city. A group of people from both sides of the sectarian divide (later known as the Guildhall Group) began to meet secretly to discuss sectarian divisions in the city. Some of these people were prominent in their own community and had views which would lead some on their own side to suspect them of treachery were it known that they were meeting with 'the enemy'. One of the authors was invited to participate. A set of common concerns emerged from those meetings, related to sectarian division. A central concern related to the exodus of Protestants from the city, and what this exodus meant for the city's future. No accurate statistics on the scale of the population shift were available, opening the way to rumour, speculation and scaremongering. Furthermore, there seemed to be a dearth of public policy on the issue. In consultation with the Guildhall Group, which was composed of those from both sides of the sectarian divide, a two-year research project to document the scale of the movement of population, and investigate aspects of sectarian division in the city was undertaken. One of the authors acted as the researcher.

The gathering of robust data on the scale of population movement in the City of Derry area over the period since the Troubles began was one of the goals of the research. The establishment of reliable figures was aimed at undermining the rumours and the talk of 'ethnic cleansing' that in turn exacerbated sectarian tensions. A review of estimates that were in use by, for example, local political parties, revealed widely divergent methods of estimation, with most methods presenting significant problems for the reliability and validity of the estimates produced. The production of robust figures however was not straightforward for two reasons. The most obvious source of population data was the Census of Population. Censuses had been conducted in 1971, 1981 and 1991, allowing a longitudinal analysis that revealed shifts in population. But there were problems. First, the ward boundaries had changed between the three censuses, so no longitudinal analysis could be conducted using wards as the basis for measurement; second, the 1981 census was regarded as unreliable because of a census boycott in certain areas. However, census data for the three census periods was used at grid square level to produce figures on population movement. Analysis of these data showed the following trends: an overall decrease in the Protestant population of the cityside (–7,052); an increase in the Protestant population in the Waterside (+1,903); a small increase in the Catholic population in the Waterside (+324); a decrease in the number of Protestants in the city as a whole (–5,149). Analysis of population figures for a Catholic enclave in the city showed an increase in the percentage of Catholics and a marked decrease in the percentage of Protestants, whereas analysis of the population of a Protestant enclave showed marked decreases in all denominations, associated with dramatic decline in the total Protestant population. Overall, there was a trend towards deepening segregation.

The results were published in monograph form (Smyth, 1995), and presented at local public meetings, including those attended by politicians. The scale of the exodus of Protestants from the city was established and the data was generally accepted as authoritative, thereby ending most of the speculation and rumour. The research subsequently examined other aspects of sectarian division in the city, and public policy on segregation and sectarian division, making recommendations on policy and generating public discussion on the position of minorities within the city.

Research into Educational Provision – Standing Advisory Commission on Human Rights (SACHR) (a Government-Appointed Body) and the Nuffield Foundation

Barritt and Carter's first survey of Northern Ireland's community relations problem (1962) placed a heavy responsibility for Northern Ireland's divisions and intransigence on its highly segregated school system (see Gallagher, 1989 for an overview). They have not been alone. By the late 1970s, segregated schooling had become one of the most popular subjects for academics working on the Northern Ireland conflict and it still absorbs a large amount of research energy. In 1993, the year of the most recent comprehensive register of research on Northern Ireland subjects, 88 projects were devoted to education (Ó'Maoláin, 1993). As the research interest developed, it developed a number of different foci. One stream explored the relationship between educational segregation and socio-religious divisions. Another highlighted funding issues, both for schools attended by Catholic and Protestant pupils, and on the financial problems facing the new integrated schools. Two interventions, one a research study relating to differential funding, the other an innovative intervention by a charitable trust to support integrated schools, together throw light on how educational policy changes were made in Northern Ireland.

In 1990, the Standing Advisory Commission on Human Rights (SACHR), an independent body advising government on human rights issues, commissioned a research study of how schools were funded in Northern Ireland. SACHR's motivation for initiating the research was its growing conviction that lower academic performance from Catholic schools were caused in part by their inferior funding, and that lower performance helped to explain Catholic disadvantage in employment. Since the formation of the Northern Ireland state, Catholic schools, in return for retaining greater independence, had been provided with less public funding support than state schools, leaving the resulting state schools as *de facto* Protestant establishments. The SACHR research examined the *per capita* spending in schools, and confirmed that spending per pupil was substantially lower for Catholic children. The publication of the research was followed in 1992 by an increase in state financial support to Catholic (maintained) schools to the level enjoyed by state schools.

At first sight, this episode appears to demonstrate an outstanding example of how an alliance between strategic research and a public organisation can effectively lobby for change. This view, while true, needs to be tempered by regarding the matter from a broader perspective. In fact, the effective lobbying had been carried out before the research had been commissioned. To decrease the differential employment of Catholics, and to respond to changing political attitudes both within government and the Catholic Church, there was already a strong predisposition towards altering the funding arrangements for schools, and no effective lobby against it. It was not the first time, nor the last, that research had been commissioned to justify a decision already reached in political terms.

If Catholic schools suffered *vis-à-vis* funding, the new category of integrated schools were in an even more difficult situation during the 1980s. These schools, which welcomed both Catholic and Protestant pupils, were permitted to open from the early 1980s, but were deprived of public funding support until each school had demonstrated its ability to attract and sustain a satisfactory school population. To many advocates it seemed a classic Catch-22 problem. The condition required for success seemed unattainable. At this point the Nuffield Foundation, a United Kingdom-based charitable trust, entered the lists. In an outstanding example of strategic intervention, Nuffield established a fund from which prospective integrated schools could borrow interest-free to purchase or build accommodation and cover essential costs until the schools qualified for government funding. The money was then repaid and recycled to support further integrated initiatives. The experiment helps to locate the relative importance of research as a factor in policy making. There was a growing body of research into the new integrated schools during the Nuffield initiative, and it certainly helped to raise the profile of the integrated issue and to inform policy developments, but the real breakthrough came from an imaginative financial intervention rather than from research.

Fair Employment – Various Researchers, and the Standing Advisory Commission on Human Rights (SACHR)

It is certainly true that some researchers in Northern Ireland have been associated either overtly and sometimes unwillingly with particular political parties or lobbies. Indeed, it is perhaps surprising that research investigations are not more partisan. Perhaps the most controversial and bitter dispute on public policy is research into the distribution of employment and unemployment between Catholics and Protestants. Curiously enough there is little disagreement on the basic facts. Catholic unemployment rates have always been higher than those for Protestants, operating at a differential of around 2.5:1 for males, around 2:1 for females, although both differentials have been diminishing. The dispute is about the reasons for the differential. The dispute has taken on a strong political flavour, with politicians from the Democratic Unionist Party and Sinn Fein, entering the contest. The spectrum of explanations ranges between those who argue that sectarian discrimination sets the pattern and still maintains it, those who believe it is caused by demographic and geographical patterns which disadvantage Catholics, and those who suggested that the principal cause was related to higher Catholic birth rates.

The third charge is probably the most controversial, as it overlaps the emotional issue of political demographics. A number of research studies and surveys have suggested that a continuation of past demographic trends could lead to a Catholic majority in Northern Ireland within a quarter-century (see Gallagher, 1991 for an excellent review of the arguments). This trend has been given added political significance by the increased residential segregation resulting from violence. In 1994, 37 per cent of electoral wards in Northern Ireland were highly – more than 90 per cent – religiously exclusive (Clark, 1994). Religious demographics is a hot political issue.

The controversy about fair employment research has cooled but not disappeared during the 1990s. The production of three reports on fair employment by the Standing Advisory Commission on Human Rights (1996), dealing respectively with the law, policy aspects and public views and experiences, has added a much-needed dimension of impartiality. But the bitterness of the dispute, the exchange of implications that the research has been influenced by sectarian bias, and the willingness of some political parties to exploit the debate for sectarian purposes, are all reminders that research is never neutral. Researchers working on controversial subjects within divided societies often find it difficult to avoid charges that they are partisan.

Religious Imbalances in Northern Ireland's Civil Service – David Donnison, Centre for Environmental Studies

In 1973, Professor David Donnison, at the time director of the Centre for Environmental Studies, published an article on employment in Northern Ireland in *New Society*. He cited a study of 477 senior

Northern Ireland civil servants, from the grade of deputy to assistant principal upwards, which revealed that 95 per cent of these officials were Protestants. These figures had not been previously published, and the article was widely copied by mainstream newspapers. Shortly afterwards, a press notice from the Northern Ireland Civil Service (NICS) alleged that Donnison's figures were incorrect and claimed that 15 per cent of the senior grades mentioned were Catholics, adding 'moreover, not all the remaining 85% were Protestants' (NICS, 1973). The lower official figure, provided for the first time solid confirmation of a serious imbalance and remained the basis for debate on public services employment until the Fair Employment Agency began producing religious breakdowns of employment practices some years later. Donnison's original figures were guesstimates, and had the desired effect of drawing more reliable data from official sources by way of challenge to his figures.

Research on the Impact of the Troubles on the Population of Northern Ireland – The Cost of the Troubles Study (COTTS)

In the period following the paramilitary cease-fires of 1994 in Northern Ireland, a new atmosphere of hope prevailed. In the atmosphere of new optimism, the position of those who had been bereaved and injured was in danger of being ignored. In the early peace process after 1994, whilst it was clear that prisoners played an essential part in the establishment and maintenance of cease-fires thus affording them a powerful and central role, those who had been bereaved or injured in the conflict had no such role or access to power. The constituency of those bereaved and injured was a fragmented one, divided by politics and geography, and isolated within a culture of silence and a lack of support services. The initiative to bring a group of bereaved and injured people from across the political spectrum together in order to collaborate on research and documentation of the effects of the Troubles came from one of the authors. The Cost of the Troubles Study (COTTS), the organisation that was formed, had two concerns: first, there was a lack of robust evidence of need on which any new services could be based; and second, that the interests of those bereaved and injured in the Troubles would be overlooked in the broader maelstrom of political change. As such, COTTS was part of the process of social construction of *victim* identity, and played a part in the subsequent development of *victim* politics, documented elsewhere (Smyth 2000a, 2000b).

The significant feature of the project was that those bereaved and injured in the Troubles held executive positions within the project, and participated not merely as informants but also as decision makers in the project as a whole.

The main goals of the project were:

- to provide robust and comprehensive evidence of the level of exposure to, and the effects of, the Troubles on the population of Northern Ireland; and
- to raise the level of public and official awareness of the situation of those bereaved and injured through the use of research and documentation and dissemination of that documentation.

In order to establish a sampling frame for a survey of Northern Ireland that was designed to examine experience and effects of the Troubles, the study compiled a database of all deaths due to the conflict since 1969. This database was then analysed to show which geographical areas had the highest death rates, and the survey was conducted accordingly. The database was then further analysed to show comparative death rates for gender, age, religion, affiliation, year and location. The results were published commercially in 1999 (Fay et al., 1999). The study also conducted a survey of Northern Ireland investigating exposure to Troubles-related events and the effects of the Troubles, and conducted in-depth interviews that were used to produce a touring exhibition, a book of personal accounts of the Troubles and a video to be used for training human service professionals.

CONCLUSIONS: RESEARCH AND POLICY

Patterns of research, as well as patterns of conflict itself, change constantly. Since the early 1970s, there has been an extensive, if fluctuating, interest in the Northern Ireland conflict from outside Ireland – educationalists studying its segregated school system, churchmen examining the apparently denominational basis of the conflict, students of violence and its effects, and medical researchers examining the emergency procedures and surgical techniques in its hospitals. More recently there has been a shift towards comparative analysis of ethnic conflicts and approaches to conflict resolution. INCORE, for example, is currently researching peace processes in societies recently engaged in ethnic violence (Darby and MacGinty,

2000). The move towards comparative analysis is likely to continue, as those involved in peace processes across the world are looking abroad for practical guidance. This development, already well established, will certainly create new opportunities and problems for policy researchers, but it is likely that it will elaborate existing problems. Six of these problems are presented as propositions below.

Policy Research Without a Dissemination Strategy is a Contradiction in Terms

If policy research is to be effective, it must start with a dissemination strategy which takes account of the kind of research undertaken and how it can impact on the social and political situation. Reports, books or articles may be effective methods of dissemination, but only if the publication ends up on the desk of those the researcher wishes to influence. Ensuring this kind of policy impact requires the abandoning of purist notions of 'appropriate' roles for researchers. Personal contact through formal presentation of results is often essential, and both INCORE and COTTS have organised seminars for Northern Ireland politicians for this purpose. Research seminars for civil servants may achieve the same goal. Diversity of outputs, such as exhibitions that tour town halls, videos that can be used for training, and that are produced in language that is easily accessible to a wider audience, can also improve dissemination. This diversification takes time and energy and, in the case of COTTS, the expenditure of money to employ professional help with publicity.

In order to render research meaningful to an audience wider than the research team, it is necessary to devise a strategy for ensuring that the findings impact on policy targets. This strategy starts at the inception of the research and continues until the publication of results and beyond. The fact that research is being carried out in the first place may be publicised in order to draw attention to a set of issues. When conducting large field surveys on issues of political sensitivity, it may be wise to provide information to participating communities and constituencies about the researcher's intentions and credentials. This publicity can allow a process of drawing out any questions or doubts before embarking on the collection of data, and a means of publicising the later research findings.

Often research that is expensive to undertake and time-consuming to document attracts little attention because it is written up in technical language or published in outlets with restricted circulation. University libraries in Northern Ireland, as elsewhere, are replete with research reports that have been read by few and had little influence. A dissemination strategy is required if this is to be avoided. In the case of the Fermanagh Civil Rights Association study, the research was undertaken not by a research organisation, but by a body which wished to use research to document their concerns about discrimination, and to contribute to a wider civil rights campaign. A pre-existing network of civil rights campaigners was able to use the research to further its campaign. In the case of COTTS, a network of victims' organisations, many of whom participated in the study, were provided with copies of the work, and a touring public exhibition brought the results of the work within the reach of the general public. A public relations officer was also employed by COTTS for a three-month period in order to maximise the media coverage and dissemination of the findings.

Both of these examples are uncommissioned research, where the onus to disseminate – and the ownership of data – lies clearly with the researcher or researching organisation. Where research has been commissioned, the commissioning agent may own the data, and the prerogative to publish and disseminate results. In such cases, the researcher is in a much less powerful position, and will, more often than not, have to negotiate dissemination with the commissioner of the research, who may well decide that it is not in their interests to disseminate the work, or be willing to provide the extra funding necessary to ensure this happens.

Here, it is important to mention the role of the media in publicising research. Whilst censorship in the media at certain points in Northern Ireland's history would have precluded certain issues being effectively highlighted, in both the examples cited, the media were important (if not entirely accurate) agents of research dissemination. News media are often more interested in 'controversial' stories, in certain conditions where censorship is not severe. Critical research is likely to be more controversial and therefore more likely to be considered newsworthy – a mixed blessing, of course.

Finally, dissemination of research results does not, of itself, ensure that the research will make an impact. The ability to anticipate and plan for resistance to the influence of the research information is an important part of planning a research strategy. In violently divided societies, perhaps a disproportionate share of the population tend towards conspiracy views of social and political processes. Research critical of the status quo is often subject to criticism and attack from predictable quarters, often taking the form of attacks on the methodological soundness of the study, or on the credibility of the researcher. A 1972 report into housing by four academics at the University of Ulster produced a counter-blast by the Northern Ireland Housing Trust (then responsible, with the local councils, for housing) substantially longer that the report it attacked, detailing spelling and grammatical infelicities and typing errors as well as substantive criticisms (Birrell et al., 1972). The COTTS researchers also became aware that a government department assigned a statistician to 'vet' the study after the designated person concerned wrote to the researchers with a list of minor concerns. It is therefore important to iron out any methodological worries early in the project, and to give consideration to the way the research is presented – and the credentials of those who do the presentation. There are few enough examples of research that policy makers would have liked to ignore but couldn't, such as Fermanagh Civil Rights Association's unanswerable documentation of housing inequality. There are many more examples of research that officialdom wished to ignore, and could and did manage to do so.

The Researcher's Credibility is Essential in Determining the Research's Impact

The orientation of the researcher is a factor in the way the research is disseminated and presented. The researcher's faith in the ability of the system to change will influence the success of the dissemination strategy. In many cases where research is addressing concerns of injustice, inequality and violence, those undertaking the work are caught in a dilemma between aiming to achieve change through their work and wishing to discredit the system responsible for the abuses they have uncovered. In both the Fermanagh Civil Rights Association and the COTTS example, this dilemma was marked.

Is it an advantage to come from outside the society one is researching? Outsider status in a researcher will usually raise concerns about trustworthiness in certain local communities within violently divided societies. Nationality and previous work are factors in this, and it is not unknown in violently divided societies for researchers to be suspected and accused of espionage. Questions about a researcher's credentials in such circumstances can be critical and potentially fatal for the researcher and colleagues, and will usually neutralise any potential impact that the research might have.

On the other hand, David Donnison's exploration of the composition of the Northern Ireland Civil Service was enhanced by his academic reputation and lent authority to the figures for the religious composition of the NICS that he published in *New Society* (Donnison, 1973). Furthermore, Donnison was an outsider, assumed to be 'neutral' with no axe to grind in the Northern Ireland conflict. His Englishness symbolised and compounded his trustworthiness. Had he been from Northern Ireland, his data, and the motivation for publishing it, would have been suspect.

Other studies, such as Templegrove Action Research or COTTS, were conducted by local researchers, and the issue of their identity was explicitly addressed in the presentation of the findings. Measures, such as co-working with colleagues from the other side of the divide, or the use of advisory group members with such perspectives, were included as part of the research's strategic attempt to produce inclusive analysis and reduce researcher bias (Smyth, 1996d). These strategies were described in the write-up of the research, so that the reader could assess the methods used to achieve this end as well as the success or failure of the results of its use.

In COTTS, where a comprehensive survey of a divided population was conducted, it was necessary for the researcher to establish credentials in a wide range of fields within a divided society. With former members of the security forces, for example, who have no history of working with civilians, this presented a challenge, in more ways than one. Gaining credentials within one constituency in a divided society may entail losing credentials in another.

Timing is Everything

On reviewing the impact of the selected pieces of research in Northern Ireland, the issue of the timeliness of the project is central. Arguably, had Fermanagh Civil Rights Association produced their research earlier, in the absence of a growing demand for civil rights, and without the increased articulation of concern about discrimination against Catholics, the work may not have had the impact it did. The timing of a research initiative may be a function of the foresight or good judgement of the researcher or the commissioner of the research, or it may be a fortuitous accident. Timing may be a function of the need on the part of a public body to draw attention to a particular issue at a particular point in time, as when SACHR commissioned its research on educational funding. Other public bodies may also use research as a form of procrastination, to avoid being launched into what they consider precipitate action. Action can then be postponed until the research is completed, and then the results may be seen as inconclusive and more research called for, in the time-honoured fashion.

The timing of COTTS research into the human costs of the Troubles was fortuitous, in that the study had collected data not available elsewhere at a time when government was beginning to address the issues with which the study was concerned. As a result, the researchers were in a key position to influence the government's own commission into the impact of the Troubles, and the data collected was used as baseline data in preference to the official statistics available from government. Had the study been conducted earlier, the data might have been considered to be dated by government, and had it been conducted later it would have been too late to affect policy. The approach adopted by the researchers, in terms of inclusive definitions of 'victims' – which went against the earlier government positions adopted by, for example, the Compensation Agency – was readily adopted by the Bloomfield Commission, in part due to the influence of the work of COTTS. Later, the inclusive definition of victims was to come under attack from certain quarters of Unionist and Loyalist opinion, but by then, inclusion had been adopted as policy.

The Indirect Influence of Research is Greater than Direct Influence: There is a Non-linear Relationship between Results and Impact

The indirect, or unintended, impact of research may, on occasion, be greater than the intended impact. An example of this is research on the labour market in Northern Ireland that showed the extent of employment and unemployment inequality between Catholics and Protestants (see Gallagher, 1991). This fuelled a furious and ongoing debate (the so-called Catholic disadvantage debate) about the causes of employment inequality in Northern Ireland. This, in turn, contributed to a campaign in North America for disinvestment in firms in Northern Ireland whose employment practices were not manifestly egalitarian. However, the findings of the original research by Cormack and Osborne also led to the reworking of employment statistics by academics such as Gudgin and Breen (1996) and politicians like Gregory Campbell of the Democratic Unionist Party who contest either the extent and causes for Catholic disadvantage. During a debate on the progress of measures guaranteeing equality in government in June 2000, Mr Gregory Campbell said it was 'a nonsense and a fallacy to keep saying people are discriminated against in Northern Ireland because they are Roman Catholic ... The reality is it's our [Protestant] community that's being discriminated against, day in, day out' (*Irish Times*, 2000). Thus, although a piece of research may have intended consequences, such as the raising of a debate in the first place, it may have unintended consequences such as stimulating others to rework data, in this case statistics, in increasingly *creative* and unorthodox ways.

He Who Pays the Piper May Have Another Tune in Mind Than That Assumed by the Researcher

The research commissioned by SACHR on how schools in Northern Ireland were financed revealed the inequity in the *per capita* funding for each school, which in turn was used to recommend and implement 100 per cent funding of Catholic schools. This would suggest that the government, through SACHR, sought and found evidence for reforms or changes that they wished to implement in any case, with the research providing the justification for doing so. A similar approach may apply to research commissioned in 1998 by government into educational selection in Northern Ireland.

In such cases the commissioning body was reasonably confident that the research findings would support the proposed policy initiative. When research findings produce unexpected findings, especially if they are controversial, the outcome may be very different. Research into intimidation, carried out in 1972 by staff members of the Northern Ireland Community Relations Commission (Darby and Morris, 1972) found evidence of collusion between some police members and Loyalist paramilitaries in north Belfast. The Commission established a sub-committee of its members to consider the matter of publication, which attempted to persuade the researchers to remove the controversial section and effectively delayed publications for more than a year. The report was leaked to the media by another Commission member and, after an unsuccessful enquiry into the source of the leak, the report was published in its original form (Darby and Morris, 1974). The incident underscores the importance of researchers clarifying the terms of publication with the commissioning agency before research is started. When the research is directly commissioned by government, or is conducted in-house as the intimidation research was, the researchers' hands are often tied. When there is an intermediate or private funding source, flexibility is usually possible. It is probable that the intimidation report, which had a considerable effect on government policy and practices, would not have been published had it not been leaked to the media.

Expect your Research to be 'Spinned'

Once a piece of research is placed in the public domain, through publication of some kind, then the researcher or author loses control of how it is used. Findings and even statistical results will be presented in ways that do not accurately reflect the original findings, results will be selectively read and represented in ways that suit a particular agenda. 'Spinning' – the process of manipulating the research results to fit in with pre-existing agendas – often ignores the overall meaning of a set of findings, ignores complexity, and goes for a simple and inevitably partial version of the findings. Donnison's publication of unconfirmed figures about the proportion of Catholics in the senior ranks of the Civil Service demonstrates the point. After the publication, and the rebuttal, the issue became one of considering whether Donnison's estimate of 5 per cent or the Northern Ireland Office's claim of 15 per cent was correct; but one could be reasonably certain that the true figure fell somewhere between the two estimates. The debate can then start. The key lesson is that researchers need to be aware of the process and to present their findings in a form that diminishes the potential for misrepresentation and accentuates the most significant findings.

In the case of COTTS, the media used the data on responsibility for deaths in the Troubles to highlight the predominant role of the IRA in Troubles-related killing. However, the media misquoted the research and attributed to the IRA all deaths caused by Republican paramilitaries in general. Furthermore, they chose to ignore other equally newsworthy aspects of the research, such as the consistently greater death rate amongst Catholics than Protestants. The spinning of research by the media in this case led to researchers being confronted (or congratulated) by politicians. Journalists who report the research may have a limited grasp of, for example, statistics and may misinterpret or overgeneralise the results in the interests of a 'good story'. The careful preparation of press releases, the provision of press briefings, and the cultivation of key relationships with journalists can help reduce these tendencies, although the press is unlikely to become a reliable outlet for accurate and detailed research dissemination. The Templegrove project is an example of how research can be designed to provide an antidote to a press spin – in this case about so-called 'ethnic cleansing' in Derry Londonderry. In that project, the response of the Protestant community to the research was crucial, as was the involvement of politicians in research, so that dialogue and agreement about methods and results would generate an authoritative set of figures about population movement. In a sense, the Templegrove research was designed to be the antidote to a media spin on so-called ethnic cleansing.

DOES RESEARCH MAKE ANY DIFFERENCE?

The famous Hawthorne experiments showed that conducting research in itself alters that which is studied (Homans, 1965). The act of researching conveys to those who are the subject of inquiry a number of messages about the nature of their situation and the level of outside interest in it. In violently divided societies, where world attention may well be a factor in the conflict itself, it is clear that doing research is unlikely to be without effects of some kind. It seems that research may well make a difference, although the nature of that difference may not always be the difference that was intended. Violently divided societies are complicated and often unpredictable research environments and when the nature of division is the subject of research, the lack of predictability and complication are further enhanced.

NOTES

1. An admirable exception was a book compiled by Denis Barritt and Charles Carter (1962). This attempted to lay out a template for Northern Ireland's political and social institutions, by means of informal surveys. It was an essential reference until the publications boom began in the early 1970s.
2. The name of the city is a matter of contention, Nationalists referring to it as Derry, whilst Unionists refer to it as Londonderry. Templegrove Action Research conducted research on the topic and concluded that the city should be called 'Derry Londonderry', hence the nomenclature in the text.

REFERENCES

Barritt, D. and Carter, C. (1962) *The Northern Ireland Problem* (Oxford: Oxford University Press).

Birrell, D. et al. (1972) 'Housing Policy in Northern Ireland', Belfast, *Community Forum*, 2 February.

The Cameron Report (1969) *Disturbances in Northern Ireland* (Belfast: HMSO).

Clark, L. (1994) 'Apartheid takes root after 25 years of segregation', *Sunday Times*, 14 August.

Collier, D and Mahoney, J. (1996) 'Insights and Pitfalls: Selection bias in Qualitative research', *World Politics*, vol. 49, no. 1.

Darby, J. and MacGinty, R. (2000) *The Management of Peace* (London: Macmillan).

Darby, J. and Morris, G. (1972, 1974) *Intimidation in Housing* (Belfast: Northern Ireland Community Relations Commission).

Donnison, D. (1973) 'The Northern Ireland Civil Service', *New Society*, 5 July.

Fay, M.T., Morrissey, M. and Smyth, M. (1999) *Northern Ireland's Troubles: The Human Costs* (London: Pluto).

Flackes, W.D. and Elliott, S. (1994) *Northern Ireland: A Political Directory 1968–1988*, 4th edn (Belfast: Blackstaff).

Flackes, W.D. and Elliott, S. (1999) *Northern Ireland: A Political Directory 1968–1999*, 5th edn (Belfast: Blackstaff).

Gallagher, A.M. (1989) *The Majority-minority Review, no. 1, Education and Religion in Northern Ireland* (Coleraine: Centre for the Study of Conflict).

Gallagher, A.M. (1991), *The Majority-minority Review, no. 2, Employment, Unemployment and Religion In Northern Ireland* (Coleraine: Centre for the Study of Conflict).

Gudgin, G. and Breen, R. (1996) *Evaluation of the Ratio of Unemployment Rates as an Indicator of Fair Employment* (Belfast: Central Community Relations Unit).

Homans, G.C. (1965) 'Group Factors in Worker Productivity', in H. Proshansky and L. Seidenberg (eds), *Basic Studies in Social Psychology* (New York: Holt).

Horowitz, Donald (forthcoming) *The Deadly Ethnic Riot* (California: University of California Press).

Irish Times (2000) 'Anti-Catholic bias: a fallacy', 7 June.

NICS (1973) Northern Ireland Office press release, 6 July.

Ó'Maoláin, Ciaran (1993) *Register of research on Northern Ireland* (Coleraine: Centre for the Study of Conflict).

Rose, P. (2000) *How the Troubles came to Northern Ireland* (London: Macmillan).

Smyth, M. (1995) *Sectarian Division and Area Planning: a commentary on the Derry Area Plan 2011*, April (Derry Londonderry: Templegrove Action Research).

Smyth, M. (1996a) *Life in Two Enclave Areas in Northern Ireland. A Field Survey in Derry Londonderry after the Cease-fires*, June (Derry Londonderry: Templegrove Action Research).

Smyth, M. (1996b) *A Report of a Public Hearing on the Experiences of Minorities in Derry Londonderry*, April 1996 (Derry Londonderry: Templegrove Action Research).

Smyth, M. (1996c) *A Report of a series of Public Discussion on Aspects of Sectarian Division in Derry Londonderry, held in the period December 1994 – June 1995*, March 1996 (Derry Londonderry: Templegrove Action Research).

Smyth, M. (1996d) 'Researching Sectarianism', in *Three Conference Papers on Aspects of Sectarian Division*, May (Derry Londonderry: Templegrove Action Research).

Smyth, M. (1996e) *Two Policy Papers: Policing and Sectarian Division (with Ruth Moore) and Urban Regeneration and Sectarian Division*, April 1996 (Derry Londonderry: Templegrove Action Research).

Smyth, M. (2000a) 'Burying the past? Victims and community relations in Northern Ireland since the cease-fires', in N. Biggar (ed.) *Burying the Past: Making Peace and Doing Justice after Civil Conflict* (Washington DC: Georgetown University Press).

Smyth, M. (2000b) 'The role of victims in the Northern Ireland Peace Process', in A. Guelke and M. Cox (eds), *A Farewell to Arms: From War to Peace in Northern Ireland* (Manchester: Manchester University Press).

Smyth, M. and Moore, R. (1996) *Three Conference Papers on Aspects of Sectarian Division: Researching Sectarianism; Borders within borders: material and ideological aspects of sectarian division; and Limitations on the capacity for citizenship in Post-Cease-fires Northern Ireland*, May (Derry Londonderry: Templegrove Action Research).

Standing Advisory Commission on Human Rights (1996) *Employment Equality in Northern Ireland* (Authors: Magill and Rose; McLaughlin and Quirk; McVey and Hutson), (Belfast: SACHR).

Whyte, John (1991) *Interpreting Northern Ireland* (Oxford: Blackwell).

3 Reflexivity and the Dilemmas of Identification: An Ethnographic Encounter in Northern Ireland

Andrew Finlay

I'll tell you this much now, and I don't care if you are recording it or not. I'm not a bit ashamed. Now I don't want to hurt your feelings, [but] if you were a Protestant and no matter what mistake you made it was overlooked. Now I'm being honest and truthful ... anything ... anywhere in the factory, if you made a mistake, no matter how big it was, that was overlooked. But if you were a Catholic you were put out on your mouth and nose in the street if you made a mistake. And they had Protestants in high up jobs and [they] hadn't a brain in their head. And I'll tell you that much, making more mistakes than enough that people on the ground then ... rectified when it came to our Department ... They [that is, Protestant workers] hadn't a call for a trade union you see. The firm was their trade union, they were their stand-by.

THE ENCOUNTER

The above quote is from an interview that I conducted 15 years ago when I was a postgraduate student of social anthropology. I was researching trade unionism and sectarianism in the Derry shirt industry (Finlay, 1989). My respondent was a retired trade union activist; Ms Cosgrave was the pseudonym I gave her at the time. The focus of my research was a series of conflicts between Protestant and Catholic workers that took place in the 1950s. The proximate origin of the conflicts was in the secession of the local branch of the (British) National Union of Tailor and Garment Workers. The secessionists initially constituted themselves as an independent union, but soon transferred to the Irish Transport and General Workers Union. At this point, trade unionists in the shirt industry divided according to their sectarian identities: the local branch of the Irish union became exclusively Catholic in its composition, and the British union became mostly Protestant. The subsequent rivalry between the two unions gave rise to strikes, walkouts and physical confrontations between groups of Catholic and Protestant workers, most of them women. Ms Cosgrave had been an activist in the Irish-based union. Her generalisation about Protestant workers did not come out of the blue: it was prompted by a question that I had asked about why so few Protestants had been unionised prior to the breakaway.

Ms Cosgrave's response troubled me. At the time, I can remember recoiling inwardly from the bitterness of her feelings towards Protestant workers. But it was not primarily the bitterness that I found troubling; on the contrary, her frankness flattered my pretensions as an interviewer. I was more troubled by the way she prefaced her comment about Protestant workers: 'I'll tell you this much now, and I don't care if you are recording it or not. I'm not a bit ashamed. Now I don't want to hurt your feelings, [but] if you were a Protestant and no matter what mistake you made it was overlooked. Now I'm being honest and truthful ... .' This was a tortuous challenge to the neutral role that I had cast for myself in the course of my research. Her prefatory remarks made me uncomfortably aware that my identity as someone from a Belfast Protestant background might have influenced what she and other respondents had said in previous interviews or, more importantly, not said.

Having grown up in Northern Ireland, I was instinctively aware of the cultural protocols governing communication between strangers. I was also familiar with Rosemary Harris's (1986) and Frank Burton's (1978) influential analyses of these protocols. First published in 1972, Harris's book is based on fieldwork conducted in rural Northern Ireland before the onset of the recent Troubles. She notes that Protestants and Catholics 'have close relationships whilst remaining essentially separate' (1986: ix) and discusses the various mechanisms through which distance is maintained even in close relationships. She argues that 'all social relationships are pervaded by a consciousness of the religious dichotomy' (1986: xi) and that

so important is it ... to be able to determine the allegiances of strangers that many Ulster people seem to have developed an extreme sensitivity to signs other than explicit badges that denote the affiliations of those that they meet. Each looks automatically for slight indications from another's name, physical appearance, expression and manner, style of dress and speech idiom to provide the clues that will enable the correct categorisation to be made. [1986: 148]

The indicators described by Harris are used to 'tell' whether the strangers we encounter are Catholic or Protestant, and Burton later defined the process as 'telling' (1978: 37). Both Harris and Burton agree that the divide between Catholics and Protestants, maintained through 'telling' and other mechanisms, is such that inter-cultural communication is problematic. According to Burton, the sectarian consciousness 'seems to lead to a form of social relations which have almost a congenital inability to communicate across religious boundaries as each side inures itself to dialogue, making only "pseudo communication", or what Habermas ... has called "systematically distorted communication", possible' (1978: 67).

My argument about 'telling' and its pervasive influence on inter-cultural relations and communication contradicts the image that many Northern Irish have of themselves as straight-talking: we are not, at least not in my experience. Against this self-congratulatory stereotype, I would set the vernacular injunction: 'whatever you say, say nothing.' Seamus Heaney uses this injunction as the title of a poem that encapsulates the phenomenon that I am describing:

> Northern reticence, the tight gag of the place [...]
> Smoke signals are loud-mouthed compared to us:
> Manoeuvrings to find out name and school,
> Subtle discrimination by addresses. [1990: 79]

Although Ms Cosgrave confronted me with the possible implications of 'telling' for interview-based research, I did not reflect long on the issues that she raised. My response was to pay more careful attention to the discrepancies between the accounts that different respondents gave me of the same events and to compare the oral record of those events with the contemporary documentary record in trade union minutes and local newspapers. I placed my confidence in the capacity of textbookish triangulation to yield something close to the truth of the matters that I was investigating. I was also mindful of the then hotly contested debate about the extent to which Protestant workers constituted a labour aristocracy. I argued that, while it might be true that the attitude of some Protestant workers to trade unionism was coloured by their position in the workforce and their relationship with managers, most of whom were also Protestant, the poor representation of Protestants in the Garment Workers Union prior to the breakaway could not be explained in terms of some generalised hostility to trade unionism inherent in the Protestant condition. Rather the poor representation could only be understood as a historical process constructed through the practices of actual individuals operating in a particular social milieu (see Finlay, 1989: 183–9).

Ms Cosgrave was not to be dismissed so easily. My experience of researching sectarianism and trade unionism had been an extended process of disillusionment – the encounter with Ms Cosgrave was somehow bound up with that process. I left Northern Ireland as soon as my PhD was finished, and embarked on a new and entirely different programme of research that was driven more by the exigencies of career considerations and the priorities of the policy maker than of personal interest. Nevertheless, the memory of my encounter with Ms Cosgrave, and doubts about the adequacy of my response to it, continued to trouble me. Having recently regained an appetite for Irish cultural and political affairs, I feel compelled to return to my encounter with Ms Cosgrave as unfinished business and a necessary (see Stanley, 1996) prelude to further work. My initial purpose is to discover why this particular encounter affected me in the way that it did, but I hope that by analysing my encounter with Ms Cosgrave, I might also illuminate issues of more general interest to do with the importance, and difficulties, of reflexivity in the study of ethnic and national conflicts.

My lack of reflexivity at the time is, I think, understandable if not excusable. If my memory is correct, concern within social anthropology about the researcher's identity was then focused on the political and moral implications of white metropolitans doing fieldwork in former colonies (for example, Asad, 1973). I thought that by studying my own society I had avoided this dilemma.[1]

Certainly, my lack of reflexivity was not unusual in the prevailing conditions of Northern Ireland. Liam O'Dowd (1990) and Bill Rolston (1998a) have written about the pressures on social researchers, exerted from within sociology and the Northern Ireland academy more generally, to maintain a distance from, and certainly not to take sides in, the Troubles. Marie Smyth and Ruth Moore go further to argue that researchers in Northern Ireland have hidden 'behind the veil of academic language and method ... laying claim to scientific objectivity claiming scholarly or scientific detachment', and that the corresponding lack of reflexivity has been detrimental in two ways. First, they argue that the 'academic community largely unreflexively mirrors and re-enacts the divisions occurring in the society it is observing and writing about' (1996: 17).[2] Second, they note a 'resistance to the exploration of personal experiences and emotions in relation to sectarian division' (1996: 12). The lack of reflexivity on the part of researchers has meant that the subjective and emotional aspect of conflict has been neglected: 'The possibilities or implications of incorporating subjectivity into traditional methodological approaches in research and writing on sectarianism would entail the writer declarating [*sic*] his or her position, and/or ... providing data on his or her socialisation in relation to the sectarian divide' (1996: 18).

Smyth and Moore's claim that social researchers in Northern Ireland have failed to be reflexive is overstated. An early example of self-criticism is provided by Hastings Donnan and Graham McFarlane's review of qualitative research on sectarianism. They note the 'coexistence of different views on [Northern Irish] society' (1983: 134) or two sets of assumptions among researchers interested in the micro-sociology of Catholic–Protestant relations:

> One set, usually held by sociologists, is that Northern Ireland has a core problem which hides beneath a veneer of superficial good relations. This core problem erupts at certain times and in certain places, and subsides beneath the veneer at others. The other set of assumptions, seemingly shared by most social anthropologists, is that Northern Irish society has a reasonable balance at its core, which is only temporarily disrupted by dramatic events. [1983: 135]

They offer two potential explanations for the coexistence of these different views. First, they suggest that 'the small community or network of people whose affairs are investigated are not representative of Northern Irish society' (1983: 134). Second, they suggest that the discrepancy

> ... might derive from inappropriate methods. We pointed out in our introduction that we were not going to discuss research which used questionnaire surveys because they are too unreliable. However, even in the research carried out by more personalised methods, there are certain to be differences in emphasis. It is perfectly reasonable to conjecture that the tolerance and harmony to be found in many reports is simply a product of using

interviews more than any research tool. Everyone in Northern Ireland knows that few people are willing to be frank and open about their strong opposition to the other side, especially seemingly educated researchers. The solution here is probably to carry out more research using the more informal methods and to be more explicit about the methods which are used. [1983: 134–5]

I would suggest that what matters most is not the researcher's educational status, but that interviewers and interviewees both engage in 'telling' and, depending on the outcome of the process, may never, or only rarely, get beyond the bland, superficial, coded communication described by Heaney, Harris and Burton.

'Telling' is confronted more directly in two recent monographs, but still there is a tendency to dismiss or minimise the problems it poses for researchers. Madeline Leonard mentions that her interviews with respondents in a Nationalist area of Belfast 'were often preceded by attempts by respondents to pry into my background'. However, she grew up close to the locale she was researching, and 'Once it was established that I was "one of them", trust and confidence was easily secured' (1994: 41).

John Brewer and Kathleen Magee are admirably frank about the potential problems posed by the latter's identity as a Catholic conducting ethnographic fieldwork among the mainly Protestant Royal Ulster Constabulary (RUC), but conclude that 'on the whole we feel knowledge of the fieldworker's religion was not detrimental to the research' (1991: 26). They justify this conclusion by pointing out that the fieldworker's identity 'did not prevent some respondents expressing disparaging remarks about Catholics, nor dissuade them from giving opinions on controversial political issues' (1991: 25). They also argue that members of the RUC distinguish between 'good' and 'bad' Catholics, and,

> Once the fieldworker was categorized as conforming to the typification of a 'good' Catholic ... then her religion was no longer as important as it appears at first sight, although the extent to which it had a residual effect is impossible to estimate. But it only remained of crucial importance to that small minority of bigoted constables who classify all Catholics as equally evil and nefarious. [1991: 25]

And yet, as Burton points out, 'In calling the process of telling part of the sectarian consciousness I do not mean to suggest that thinking in such terms is an exclusive domain of the bigot' (1978: 63). Brewer and Magee's conclusion that 'the RUC's sectarianism tends to be localised' has been disputed by several critics who 'questioned the capacity of the ethnographic method to support such claims' (Brewer, 1994: 237).

My point is that 'telling' and its effects are more insidious than Brewer and Magee allow. Burton, like Brewer and Magee, conceives 'telling' as a cognitive, ethnic identification device, but Burton recognises that there is more to 'telling' than classifying the social world. Let me develop my point with reference to Moerman's discussion of ethnic identification among the Lue of North Thailand (1974). Moerman notes the apparent triviality of the traits used by the Lue to identify themselves as a discrete ethnic group and argues that, too often, ethnographers take such folk identifications for granted or, even, recycle them as analytic categories and explanations when what is required is that ethnographers ask themselves why the people they are studying are preoccupied with ethnic identity rather than with the other possible identifications available to them.[3]

Burton explains the salience of 'telling' among Northern Irish people by demonstrating its role in the routine, everyday management of sectarian alienation. 'Telling' operates at many levels: 'At the order of face-to-face interaction it is a necessary social skill if the embarrassment endemic in a sectarian milieu is to be avoided' (Burton, 1978: 64). Similarly, Harris describes how Catholics and Protestants use 'telling' to avoid offending one another. But 'telling' also has a more sinister significance. The example Burton gives is of it being used 'when the identity of an individual is being determined for intended military, political and criminal activity'. He continues:

This threat of danger which is endemic in Belfast underlines a second feature of telling: the way it can be used to create areas of trust. As Suttles poignantly illustrates, territorial segregation amongst ethnic groups has the seeming advantage of creating personal and local pools of predictability ... Within one's own physical area there is a built in moral arena, a normative order, which helps to structure the possible types of interaction. The potential conflict in cross-ethnic interaction is limited by territory.

I would suggest that telling, in a like manner, creates order in the anomic climate of a sectarian society. In one sense Protestants and Catholics do not know how to interact. Their restricted knowledge of each other prevents communication. Telling contributes to shutting out this anomie before it starts. (1978: 65–6)

In a more recent discussion which emphasises the sinister aspect of the process, Feldman (1991) has described 'telling' as the embodiment of sectarianism.

Burton's notion of 'telling' as a method of managing sectarianism and his allusion to its role in mitigating the anomie created by sectarianism might usefully be supplemented by recent work in the sociology of emotion. Thomas Scheff (1994) has argued that at the heart of any protracted conflict there are deep-seated and unacknowledged emotional issues to do with the quality of relations between the contending parties and that it is these, as much as the ostensible *topics of conflict*, that make it protracted. Arlie Russel Hochschild, in her analysis of the work done by flight attendants, develops the notion of emotional labour:

This labor requires one to induce or suppress feeling in order to sustain the outward countenance that produces the proper state of mind in others ... I use the term emotional labor to mean the management of feeling ... emotional labor is sold for a wage and therefore has exchange value ... these same acts done in a private context ... have a use value. [1983: 7]

Although Hochschild is concerned with flight attendants, she makes it clear that the management of feeling is involved in routine social encounters of various kinds.

Let me illustrate the relevance of Scheff's and Hochschild's work by returning to my interview with Ms Cosgrave. I had not told Ms Cosgrave that I was from a Protestant background – given my knowledge of 'telling' I did not think that I needed to be explicit about this. In the tortuous preface to her generalisation about Protestants and trade unionism she was not only indicating that she had got the message, she was also engaging in what Hochschild would call feeling management. Before transgressing the norms of Catholic–Protestant interaction, she had to clear the way. In saying that she 'was not a bit ashamed' and that she was 'being honest and truthful', she was addressing the possibility that I might dismiss what she was about to tell me as bigotry. In saying 'I don't want to hurt your feelings', she was acknowledging the possibility that I might be upset by her condemnation of what she took to be my co-religionists and was seeking to diminish its immediate impact.

I am tempted to take this further, even though it is not yet resolved in my mind. In the light of Scheff's work, it is perhaps interesting that Ms Cosgrave alludes to shame, for, of all the emotions, Scheff assigns a special significance to shame and shamelessness in protracted conflict. He also elaborates the connection between shame and morality: 'For most people shame provides unmistakable signals of where they stand in the moral universe at any particular moment' (1994: 53). In her condemnation of Protestant workers, Ms Cosgrave was self-consciously entering the moral universe. She was apportioning blame. As Heaney notes in his poem, 'Whatever You Say Say Nothing', blame is usually avoided in social encounters between Catholics and Protestants by circumlocutions such as 'One side's as bad as the other', – 'never worse' (1990: 79). Certainly, 'telling' as a way of managing sectarianism is more than a cognitive device, it has an emotional and moral valency (see Feldman, 1991: 59).

My response to Ms Cosgrave's generalisation about Protestant shirt workers was to make reassuring noises to the effect that she should feel free to say to me whatever she wanted. I had interviewed her before, and we had already established a relationship that had a warmth that went beyond what the textbooks call rapport. The point is that the interview was not fraught; nor are most routine encounters between Catholics and Protestants. Nevertheless, I would agree with Harris that 'all social relationships are pervaded by a consciousness of the religious dichotomy' (1986: xi). I would go further to suggest that deep-seated emotional and moral issues that I have alluded to are immanent even in routine encounters between Catholics and Protestants and I suspect that it is this that makes 'telling' necessary and so difficult to escape, even for the social researcher. The fact that these issues do not surface on most occasions attests to the insidious efficacy of 'telling' as a mechanism for managing sectarianism. To the extent that the foregoing is true, I would agree with Smyth and Moore (1996) when they imply a connection between a lack of reflexivity on the part of researchers and their failure to deal with the subjective and emotional aspects of sectarianism and their lack of reflexivity.[4]

The point of my brief excursion into the sociology of emotion was to suggest that 'telling' and its effects are more insidious than Brewer and Magee allow and that the issues it raises for ethnographic and interview-based research cannot be reduced to the familiar problem of 'reactive effects' (1991: 25). In developing this point I have also come closer to understanding what it was about my encounter with Ms Cosgrave that troubled me. To get closer still, I need to refer to Game's (1991) discussion of reflexivity and the manner in which radical sociologists authorise their research and writing. She notes that Marxist and feminist sociologists acknowledge their partisanship, but they make a particular connection between

> ... a political position and truth. In Marxist and feminist sociology the determining dynamics are characterised by conflict ... Marxism ... is not just a theory of the class struggle and conflict, it is a class theory – the theory of the subject of history. Thus Marxist sociologists authorise themselves by putting themselves in the movement of history, in the class narrative; and they are the voice of the narrative. Feminist sociologists have been critical of 'male' sociologists who speak on behalf of the working class, but their authorisation is based on similar assumptions. While it is problematic for sociologists to speak for the working class, feminist sociologists, as women, can speak on behalf of women ... this assumes a unity, women, and fails to acknowledge questions of difference and the production of the other to the subject of feminist knowledge. [1991: 24]

Game argues that in making these assumptions radical sociologists evade difference, they evade otherness, and they do this 'precisely through a process of identification with "objects" of research ... accounts of the other are about an "affirmation of identity" [by the researcher], a sense of self ... through an identification with the objects of research, the autobiographical is not fully acknowledged' (1991: 29).

Earlier, I mentioned that in the course of my fieldwork I cast for myself a neutral role. It would be more precise to say that I cast for myself a role that I imagined might transcend sectarian divisions and evade the usual strictures on communication between strangers in Northern Ireland. My role was not that of the disinterested academic, but that of a socialist who was steeped in an established – though much reduced – indigenous labourist tradition that was critical of both Unionism and Nationalism and sought to unite the Catholic and Protestant workers on a class basis. This role was not an artifice, it was organic. It was part of my family history and my own adult experience. My interest in researching sectarian divisions within the Derry shirt industry was not purely academic. The research was conceived during the early 1980s when socialism seemed more viable than it does now, and it was initially motivated by the hope that a micro-sociology of Catholic–Protestant relations in the Derry shirt industry might contribute to a larger political project of working-class unity in Northern Ireland.

Until I met Ms Cosgrave, it had seemed reasonable – though, with hindsight, naive – to assume that the women I was interviewing would, irrespective of the practical problems that they had encountered in their time as trade union activists, identify to some extent with ideals similar to my own and that, on the basis of this mutual identification, we could establish a trust and rapport that was sufficient to ensure valid communication. As I have already indicated, Ms Cosgrave's forthrightness *was not reassuring* for, in transgressing the norms of communication between Catholic and Protestant, she implicitly refused my identification with her and, by implication, with other Nationalist trade unionists I had interviewed. I had constructed myself as a non-sectarian, secular socialist and her moral equal; she constructed me as a Protestant.[5]

Ms Cosgrave confronted me with difference, with the dangers of a self-serving, over-identification with the people we research and with the need for researchers to reflect honestly and critically on their own identities and the influence of these on what they research, what they find and how they analyse it. Ultimately, she did me a service, but, at the time, my encounter with her crystallised an already growing disillusionment with the intellectual and political adequacy of socialism and Marxist theory in the face of ethnic and national conflict. Having had the rug pulled out from under my socialism, I could find no other tenable and personally satisfying position from which to prolong my intellectual and political engagement in Irish cultural affairs.

Now it seems that reflexive sociology might, itself, provide a stable position from which to re-engage, but the foregoing discussion of 'telling' also illuminates the difficulty of adopting a fully reflexive position in situations of ethnic and national conflict. It is not so much that there is a physical risk involved in identifying oneself or in being identified (see Lee, 1995 and Rolston, 1998a); even before the recent paramilitary cease-fires, such a risk was sometimes overstated. A more insidious and ongoing difficulty is the cultural reticence – summed up here in the concept of 'telling' – that has evolved as a means of managing conflict and tension, but which acts as a barrier not only to inter-cultural communication, but also to reflexive expression. This cultural reticence is internalised such that it is only now, 15 years after the event, that I have been able to write this reflexive piece, and still with some anxiety.

There is another problem with reflexivity in small, intimate, ethnically divided societies such as Northern Ireland, where identities have an ineluctable quality.[6] As with me and Ms Cosgrave, so with the people who read research reports: they know or think that they know where the author is coming from and interpret or dismiss what is written accordingly (see Brewer 1994 and Rolston 1998a). Smyth and Moore's (1996) injunction that the researcher should declare 'his or her position, and/or ... provid[e] data on his or her socialisation in relation to the sectarian divide' is simultaneously asking a lot and yet scarcely sufficient. I am reminded of the following quote attributed to Foucault: 'I am ... not the only one who writes in order to have no face. Do not ask who I am and do not ask me to remain the same: leave it to our bureaucrats and our police to see that our papers are in order' (quoted in Poster 1997: 152).

In the context of Northern Ireland, effacing oneself remains an enduring temptation, and yet, the possibilities afforded by reflexivity are such that one should struggle with this temptation. The potential of reflexivity is not only that, as Smith and Moore argue, it might help us to better understand animosity and the other emotions implicated in communal conflict and division, but that, as Peter Shirlow and Mark McGovern have recently suggested, 'a project in which each community or tradition begins its own introspection' might contribute to the 'deconstruction of cultural animosity and division' (1997: xii). Shirlow and McGovern are symptomatic of what seems to be a more general introspective mood among intellectuals from Northern Protestant backgrounds (for example, Foster, 1991; Hall, 1994; Hyndman, 1996). All of these introspective, reflexive efforts are laudable and important, but the methodologies upon which they are based may ultimately be inadequate to the promise held out by Shirlow and McGovern. A review of different forms of reflexivity would seem to be in order.

FORMS OF REFLEXIVITY

Steve Woolgar makes a useful distinction between what he calls 'benign introspection' and 'constitutive reflexivity'. Woolgar is a sociologist of scientific and technical knowledge, and he elaborates the distinction between different forms of reflexivity in the context of an argument against those of his colleagues who treat scientific knowledge as having been socially constructed, but persist in seeing their own research in realist terms. Against the latter, Woolgar advocates a constitutive reflexivity in which 'the fact that the author constitutes and forms part of the "reality" she creates is axiomatic to the analytical style' (1988: 22). He contrasts his preferred constitutive reflexivity with 'benign introspection', which is compatible with a realist view that there is some pre-existing reality that is independent of our efforts to describe it. Benign introspection 'entails loose injunctions to "think about what we are doing", it is usually concerned with improving the adequacy of the connections between the analyst's statements and the objects of those statements' (1988: 22).

A parallel can be drawn between benign introspection and Smyth and Moore's minimalist reflexive requirement for the researcher to declare his or her position and Shirlow and McGovern's introspective project. Woolgar is not completely dismissive of benign introspection. He suggests that it can generate '"fieldwork confessions", which provide the "inside story" on how the research was done' (Woolgar, 1988: 22), and that it might lead the researcher to constitutive reflexivity. More often, the researcher is content to preface his/her report with descriptive biographical details which remain unconnected with the substance of their report. Thus, Shirlow and McGovern (1997) advocate introspection as a means of deconstructing cultural antagonism in Northern Ireland, but in their edited collection they seem to do little more than state that they themselves, and most of their contributors, are from Protestant backgrounds, but hold diverse political views.

The benign, descriptive reflexivity advocated by Smyth and Moore and practised by Shirlow and McGovern is not adequate to the task that these authors set themselves. Woolgar's constitutive reflexivity has more potential, but first we must confront the fact that it is inherently relativistic. Social constructionists and postmodernists would not see relativism as a problem. And it is true that in the conditions of Northern Ireland the postmodern premise that there is no possibility of fixed, final authoritative meaning has a compelling quality. As Henry Patterson has implied, there is always at least two meanings or truths in Northern Ireland:

There is no 'civil society' in Northern Ireland. 'Civil society' has collapsed into competing religio-political blocs. There are two 'civil societies' which display many of the characteristics of what … Hannah Arendt called 'communities of meaning'. Such communities exist where each group shows a strong tendency to degenerate into mutually opposed self-absorbed worlds. [1999]

I broadly agree with Patterson, but wish to note the role of 'telling' in sustaining these two self-absorbed 'communities of meaning' and suggest that they have existed for longer than Patterson allows. Patterson attributes the emergence of the two 'communities of meaning', in significant measure, 'to three decades of violence'. The self-absorption and cultural reticence that I have discussed have been characteristic of Northern Irish society for longer than the last three decades. After all, Harris's (1972) discussion of 'telling' was based on fieldwork conducted well before the onset of the recent Troubles, and John Jackson (1983) was immediately struck by the difficulty in sustaining authoritative social scientific explanations in Northern Ireland when he arrived there in the early 1970s.

In Northern Ireland, as elsewhere, a scepticism about claims to truth is healthy, but the relativist denial of the possibility of faithful accounts of reality is potentially disabling. Thus poised, uneasily between social constructionism and realism, I turn to the work of feminist standpoint theorists who have attempted to reconcile these tensions.

Donna Haraway (1988) defines the problem:

So, I think my problem, and 'our' problem is how to have *simultaneously* an account of radical historical contingency for all knowledge claims and knowing subjects, a critical practice for recognizing our own 'semiotic technologies' for making meanings *and* a no-nonsense commitment to faithful accounts of a 'real' world … . [1988: 579, Haraway's emphasis]

The solution that she develops revolves around notions of situated knowledge and embodied objectivity: what Marcus (1994: 571 and 572) has called 'reflexivity as a politics of location' and 'as a practice of positioning':

Not so perversely, objectivity turns out to be about particular and specific embodiment and definitely not about the false vision promising transcendence of all limits and responsibilities. The moral is simple: only partial perspective promises objective vision. All western cultural narratives about objectivity are allegories of the ideologies governing the relations of what we call mind and body, distance and responsibility. Feminist objectivity is about limited location and situated knowledge, not about transcendence and splitting of subject and object. It allows us to become answerable for what we learn how to see. [1988: 583]

Haraway emphasises that: 'situated knowledges are about communities, not about isolated individuals':

The only way to find a larger vision is to be somewhere in particular ... [feminist objectivity] is about ... the joining of partial views and halting voices into a collective subject position that promises a vision of the means of ongoing finite embodiment, of living within limits and contradictions – of views from somewhere. [1988: 590]

She notes the currents within feminism that privilege or prefer the vantage point of the subjugated, and agrees that 'there is good reason to believe vision is better from below' (1988: 584). She further argues:

Such preferred positioning is as hostile to various forms of relativism as to the most explicitly totalizing versions of claims to scientific authority. But the alternative to relativism is not totalization whose power depends on systematic narrowing and obscuring. The alternative to relativism is partial, locatable, critical knowledges sustaining the possibility of webs of connections called solidarity in politics and shared conversations in epistemology. Relativism is a way of being nowhere while claiming to be everywhere equally. The 'equality' of positioning is a denial of responsibility and critical inquiry. Relativism is the perfect mirror twin of totalization in the ideologies of objectivity; both deny the stakes in location, embodiment, and partial perspective; both make it impossible to see well. Relativism and totalisation are both 'god tricks' promising vision from everywhere and nowhere equally and fully ... . [1988: 584]

In short, Haraway resolves the tension between social construction-ism/relativism and realism/objectivism by privileging the vantage point of the subjugated.

As a man[7] who was born, and grew up, in a community that in various degrees sustained and benefited from an oppressive regime, I cannot claim 'the vantage point of the subjugated'. Nor would I wish to; rather, I want to take issue with Haraway's claim that 'vision is better from below'. The notion that there are privileged subjects of history who, by virtue of their social position, can see more clearly than others is a persistent one: for Marx, drawing on Hegel (see Hammersley and Gomm, 1997: para 3.5), it was the working class, for some feminists it is women, for Homi Bhaba it seems to be the hybrid and diasporic subjects created by colonialism: 'the truest eye may now belong to the migrant's double vision' (1994: 5). Given their origins as a colonial settler community, their uneasy relation-ship with their British 'motherland' and with Irish Catholics – historically subordinate to one and superordinate to the other – one might be tempted to stretch Bhaba's notion of hybridity to include Northern Protestants. However, the experience of dislocation or oppression is as likely to produce confusion and fundamentalism as insight (see Friedman, 1997); certainly, the notion that Northern Protestants suffer from an identity crisis has recently gained much currency in the academic literature (see Cochrane, 1997, for a review). I remain sceptical about the notion that there are privileged subjects of history.

For me, the virtues of reflexivity as a politics of location and a practice of positioning do not reside in its association with oppressed strata; more important is the emphasis on what Haraway calls 'critical positioning' and what Liz Stanley (1996) refers to as 'analytical accountability'. Haraway speaks of the danger 'of roman-ticising and/or appropriating the vision of the less powerful while claiming to see from their positions', argues that 'the positionings of the subjugated are not exempt from critical examination', and warns that 'Identity, including self-identity, does not produce science; critical positioning does, that is, objectivity'. For Haraway the 'split and contradictory self is the one who can interrogate posi-tionings and be accountable' (1988: 584, 586 and 587).

Stanley develops the notion of analytical accountability in relation to her observation that feminist research is often motivated by, amongst other things, 'felt *necessity*' in the sense that the topic of the research, or the approach to it, resonates with the 'personal context of the researcher' (1996: 48, Stanley's emphasis). The 'personal context' of feminist researchers was characterised in an earlier publication, Stanley and Wise (1983), in terms of the experience of oppression in a sexist society. Rejecting the unsustainable notion of the detached researcher, Stanley and Wise proposed 'making the researcher and her consciousness the central focus of research'. Such an approach demands that the researcher comes to grips 'analytically (not just descriptively)... with the everyday experiences of the processes of finding out' and renders this analytical engagement in 'research accounts which display their argumentative processes in detailed ways which can be critically engaged with by readers'. They advocate a form of intellectual autobiography which explicates 'the processes by which understanding and conclusions are reached' and which 'positions an experiencing and comprehending subject at the heart of intellectual and research life, a subject whose ontologically-based reasoning processes provide the grounds for knowledge claims and thus for all epistemological endeavour' (1996: 46–7).

CONCLUSION

The critical and analytically accountable forms of reflexivity advocated by Haraway and Stanley offer a 'more secure methodological basis' for the kinds of introspective project advocated by Smyth and Moore, and Shirlow and McGovern. In developing her notion of research as 'necessity', Stanley speaks of 'the resonance between the intellectual or ideational, and the experiential, emotional and political aspects of our lives' (1996: 48). Following Alvin Gouldner (1970), I would suggest that social research often arises from dissonance. Such dissonance is not merely personal, it is often the introjection of, and a clue to, larger social, political and moral contradictions; nor is it the preserve of researchers born into subordinate or oppressed strata (see Sartre's discussion of Memmi, 1990). Ms Cosgrave made visible to me the dissonance which permeated the whole of the research project in which I was engaged. Rather than suppress such dissonance for fear of transgressing a spurious notion of objectivity or of appearing self-indulgent, would I have been better served, and served better, by analysing the broader social, political and moral contradictions that created the feeling of dissonance, and the limitations of my self-identification as a socialist as a means of dealing with or, perhaps, evading them?

ACKNOWLEDGEMENTS

I have incurred many debts in the development of this paper. The research upon which it is based was funded by a Research Studentship from the Department of Education for Northern Ireland. The research was supervised by John Gledhill and Rosemary Harris; any shortcomings discussed here were of my own making, and occurred despite their best efforts and careful supervision. Earlier versions of the paper were read at two conferences: World Congress on Violence and Human Coexistence, University College Dublin, 17–21 August 1997, and INCORE International Workshop on Researching Violent Societies, Derry/Londonderry and Belfast, 28–31 March 1999. A subsequent version of the paper was published in *Sociological Research Online*, vol. 4, no. 3, September 1999. I am grateful to all those who have commented on the paper. My biggest debt, however, is obviously to Ms Cosgrave.

NOTES

1. *Writing Culture* (Clifford and Marcus, 1986) was published around the time of the events I describe. Here, Clifford mentions the virtues of 'narrating interpersonal confrontation' in ethnography; however, I did not read *Writing Culture* until later, and it is only recently that I have come across examples that resonate with my experience (for example, Bowes, 1996, and Song and Parker, 1995).
2. Two recent publications (Miller, 1998 and McVeigh, 1995b) have discussed the social composition of academics in Northern Ireland's universities and questioned their neutrality; however, they are less concerned with the specific implications of this for social research, than with advancing an argument about the continuing relevance of British colonialism to explanations of the Northern Ireland conflict as against the prevalence in academic debate of the *internal conflict model*.
3. There is more that could be said about the conflation of folk models and analytic models in the discourse of academics and policy makers. Arguably such a conflation has contributed to a tendency for the cultural categories, Protestant and Catholic, to be taken as givens – objectified and frozen – rather than being understood as actively constructed and contested. Such reification seems to have had a pernicious effect on cultural policies initiated by the British state in the wake of the Anglo-Irish Agreement, 1985 (see Bell, 1998 and Rolston, 1998b). However, my present concern is with the implications of 'telling' for social research.
4. The failure on the part of social researchers to address the passions aroused by ethnic conflict in Northern Ireland has been commented upon by other writers, notably Whyte (1983). I would not pretend that this failure can be reduced to the lack of reflexivity on the part of researchers; one would also need to consider, for example, the influence on social researchers of the tension in Enlightenment thought between reason and

romanticism and the subsequent tendency to privilege rationality over emotion.

5. It is difficult to explore the shifting power relations between myself and Ms Cosgrave at this remove. Moreover, we should be wary, as Rhodes has pointed out in relation to debates about white researchers interviewing black people, of the danger 'of confusing cultural misunderstanding with the unequal power relationships constructed around racial differentiation' (1994: 55). However, there were clearly issues of power at stake, and the interview should be seen in light of the fact that Protestants in Ireland have, historically, held power at the expense of Catholics and that between 1921 and 1972, the duration of the Unionist regime, Derry was the place that the abuse of that power was at its most blatant. Ms Cosgrave may have subverted my 'authority' (in Anne Game's sense of the word) in the interview and the experience may have troubled me thereafter, but neither at the time of the interview, nor when writing up my thesis did I explore why she said what she had said; rather, I assumed or reassumed the authoritative voice of the objective researcher. As I have already indicated, I was, at the time, oblivious to the alternative writing strategies discussed by Clifford and Marcus (1986).

6. The ineluctable nature of sectarian identities is captured in a well-worn local joke. The joke takes various forms, but most often it concerns a Jewish man. The man is stopped in the street by a menacing gang who challenge him to identify himself. He says, 'I'm Jewish.' The gang members reply: 'but are you a Catholic Jew or a Protestant Jew?'

7. I would not deny that what transpired in my interviews was influenced by the fact that I was a young man and that most of my interviewees were elderly women. Nor would I deny the current conventional wisdom which insists on the inextricability of gender, class and ethnicity (for example, Aretxaga, 1997). But, for the purpose of this article, I think that the single-minded focus on ethnic identity is warranted. Harris has argued that in Northern Ireland 'religious affiliation is the most important characteristic of any individual, normally outweighing even that of sex' (1986: 148). A large claim: all I can say is that while gender loomed large in my thesis and the issue of reflexivity with respect to gender was raised by at least one social scientist who read a draft, my gender identity was never explicitly challenged in the way that Ms Cosgrave challenged my ethnic identity.

REFERENCES

Aretxaga, B. (1997) *Shattering Silence: Women, Nationalism and Political Subjectivity in Northern Ireland* (New Jersey: Princeton University Press).

Asad, T. (ed.) (1973) *Anthropology and the Colonial Encounter* (London: Ithaca Press).

Bell, D. (1990) *Acts of Union: Youth Culture and Sectarianism in Northern Ireland* (Basingstoke: Macmillan Education).

Bell, D. (1998) 'Modernising History: the realpolitik of heritage and cultural tradition in Northern Ireland', in David Miller (ed.), *Rethinking Northern Ireland* (London: Longman).

Behar, R. and Gordon, D.A. (eds) (1995) *Women Writing Culture* (Berkeley: University of California Press).

Bhaba, H. (1994) *The Location of Culture* (London: Routledge).

Bowes, A. (1996) 'Evaluating an Empowering Research Strategy: Reflections on Action-Research with South Asian Women', *Sociological Research Online*, vol. 1, no. 1, <http://www.socresonline.org.uk/socresonline/1/1/1.html>

Brewer, J.D. (1991) 'The Parallels Between Sectarianism and Racism: the Northern Ireland Experience', in Central Council for Social Work Training (ed.), *One Small Step Towards Racial Justice: The Teaching of Anti-Racism in Diploma in Social Work Programmes* (London: Central Council for Social Work Training/ The Midas Press).

Brewer, J.D. with Magee, K. (1991) *Inside the RUC: Routine Policing in a Divided Society* (London: Clarendon Press).

Brewer, J.D. (1994) 'The Ethnographic Critique of Ethnography: Sectarianism in the RUC', *Sociology*, vol. 28, no. 1, pp. 231–44.

Burton, F. (1978) *The Politics of Legitimacy: Struggles in a Belfast Community* (London: Routledge and Kegan Paul).

Clifford, J. and Marcus, G.E. (1986) *Writing Culture: The Poetics and Politics of Ethnography* (Berkeley: University of California Press).

Cochrane, F. (1997) *Unionist Politics and the Politics of Unionism Since the Anglo-Irish Agreement* (Cork: Cork University Press).

Donnan, H. and McFarlane, G. (1983) 'Informal Social Organisation', in J. Darby (ed.), *Northern Ireland – The Background to the Conflict* (Belfast: Appletree Press).

Feldman, A. (1991) *Formations of Violence: the Narrative of the Body and Political Terror in Northern Ireland* (Chicago: University of Chicago Press).

Finlay, A. (1989) 'Trade Unionism and Sectarianism Among Derry Shirt Workers 1920–1968', unpublished PhD Thesis, University of London.

Foster, J.W. (1991) *Colonial Consequences Essays in Irish Literature and Culture* (Dublin: Lilliput Press).

Friedman, J. (1997) 'Global Crises, the Struggle for Cultural Identity and Intellectual Porkbarrelling: Cosmopolitans Vs Locals, Ethnics and Nationals in an Era of De-hegemonisation', in P. Werbner and T. Modood (eds), *Debating Cultural Hybridity Multicultural Identities and the Politics of Antiracisim* (London: Zed).

Game, A. (1991) *Undoing the Social: Towards a Sociology* (Buckingham: Open University Press).

Gouldner, A.W. (1970) *The Coming Crisis of Western Sociology* (London: Heinemann).

Hall, M. (1994) *Ulster's Protestant Working Class – A Community Exploration*, Island Pamphlet 9 (Newtownabbey: Island Publications).

Hammersley, M. and Gomm, R. (1997) 'Bias in Social Research', *Sociological Research Online*, vol. 2, no. 1, <http://www.socresonline.org.uk/socresonline/2/1/2.html>

Haraway, D. (1988) 'Situated Knowledges: the Science Question in Feminism and the Privilege of Partial Perspective', *Feminist Studies*, vol. 14, no. 3, pp. 575–99.

Harris, R. (1972, 2nd edn 1986) *Prejudice and Tolerance in Ulster: A Study of Neighbours and 'Strangers' in a Border Community* (Manchester: Manchester University Press).

Heaney, S. (1990) *New Selected Poems 1966–1987* (London: Faber and Faber).

Hochschild, A.R. (1983) *The Managed Heart: the Commercialization of Human Feeling* (Berkeley: University of California Press).

Hyndman, M. (1996) *Further Afield: Journeys From a Protestant Past* (Belfast: Beyond the Pale Publications).

Jackson, J. (1983) 'Foreword', in Robert J. Cormack and Robert D. Osborne (eds), *Religion, Education and Employment Aspects of Equal Opportunity in Northern Ireland* (Belfast: Appletree).

Lee, R.M. (1995) *Dangerous Fieldwork*, Qualitative Research Methods Vol. 34 (London: Sage).

Leonard, M. (1994) *Informal Economic Activity in Belfast* (Aldershot: Avebury).

McVeigh, R. (1995a) 'Cherishing the Children of the Nation Unequally: Sectarianism in Ireland', in Patrick Clancy et al. (eds), *Irish Society, Sociological Perspectives* (Dublin: Institute of Public Administration and Sociological Association of Ireland).

McVeigh, R. (1995b) 'The Last Conquest of Ireland? British Academics in Irish Universities', *Race and Class*, vol. 37, no. 1, pp. 109–21.

Marcus, G.E. (1994) 'What Comes (Just) After "Post": the Case of Ethnography', in Norman K. Denzin, and Yvonna S. Lincoln (eds), *Handbook of Qualitative Research* (London: Sage).

Miller, D. (1998) *Rethinking Northern Ireland: Culture, Ideology and Colonialism* (London and New York: Longman).

Moerman, M. (1974, first published 1968) 'Accomplishing Ethnicity', in Roy Turner (ed.), *Ethnomethodology: Selected Readings* (Harmondsworth: Penguin).

O'Dowd, L. (1990) new 'Introduction', to Albert Memmi, *The Colonizer and the Colonized* (London: Earthscan).

Patterson, H. (1999) *Sunday Times*, 11 July.

Poster, M. (1997) *Cultural History and Postmodernity Disciplinary Readings and Challenges* (New York: Columbia Press).

Rhodes, P.J. (1994) 'Race of Interviewer Effects: A Brief Comment', *Sociology*, vol. 28, no. 2, pp. 547–58.

Rolston, B. (1998a) 'Crimes of Passion: Sociology, Research and Political Violence', *Irish Journal of Sociology*, vol. 8, pp. 93–112.

Rolston, B. (1998b) 'What's wrong with multiculturalism? Liberalism and the Irish conflict', in David Miller (ed.), *Rethinking Northern Ireland* (London: Longman).

Sartre, J.P. (1990, original introduction, 1957), to Memmi, A., *The Colonizer and the Colonized* (London: Earthscan).

Scheff, T.J. (1994) *Bloody Revenge Emotions, Nationalism and War* (Boulder and San Francisco: Westview Press).

Shirlow, P. and McGovern, M. (1997) *Who are 'The People'?: Unionism, Protestantism and Loyalism in Northern Ireland* (London: Pluto Press).

Smyth, M. and Moore, R. (1996) 'Researching Sectarianism', in Marie Smyth (ed.), *Three Conference Papers on Aspects of Segregation and Sectarian Division* (Derry Londonderry: Templegrove Action Research Limited).

Song, M. and Parker, D. (1995) 'In-Depth Interviewing: Commonality, Difference and the Dynamics of Disclosure in In-Depth Interviewing', *Sociology*, vol. 29, no. 2, pp. 241–56.

Stanley, L. (1996) 'The Mother of Invention: Necessity, Writing and Representation', *Feminism and Psychology*, vol. 6, no. 1, pp. 45–51.

Stanley, L. and Wise, S. (1983) *Breaking Out: Feminist Consciousness and Feminist Research* (London: Routledge).

Suttles, G.D. (1968) *The Social Order of the Slum* (Chicago: University of Chicago Press).

Whyte, J. (1983) 'Is Research on the Northern Ireland Problem Worthwhile?', inaugural lecture delivered before the Board of the Queen's University of Belfast (Belfast: the Queen's University of Belfast).

Woolgar, S. (ed.) (1988) *Knowledge and Reflexivity: New Frontiers in the Sociology of Scientific Knowledge* (London: Sage).

4 The Impermeable Identity Wall: The Study of Violent Conflicts by 'Insiders' and 'Outsiders'

Tamar Hermann

From the viewpoint of social scientists, conflict situations are much more interesting than harmonious ones. If for no other reason, this is because, in the socio-political arena, conflicts of various levels and intensity are far more common than harmonious states. Thus, essentially, all branches of social research focus on one form or another of conflict: economics deals with the struggle over allocation of scarce financial resources; psychology is concerned with the conflicts within a person's soul and between the individual and his or her immediate environment; sociology investigates the friction between groups within a society; political science examines the struggles between political actors for control of national pinnacles of power, while the study of international relations addresses the rivalry between states or supra-national bodies in the international sphere.

The common thread running through these diversified areas of research is the question of the rationality of conflicts, or at least their functionality. Although clearly very costly in terms of human lives and suffering, as well as of valuable material resources, conflicts were, and still are, rife. Prolonged harmony, on the other hand, which seems to be basically more compatible with rational behaviour, or *economic management*, in terms of minimising costs and allowing for prosperity and well-being, has always been a relatively uncommon state of social interaction.

The problem in the study of socio-political conflicts, as well as finding ways to resolve them, is that social scientists, who are themselves members of society and of a specific socio-political group, often either take a stand on the conflict they are researching, or are, in one way or another, involved in it. They are quite unlike their colleagues in the natural and life sciences, for example, who regard the objects of their research from an external vantage point.

Physicists does not identify with or, alternatively, feel alienated from the particles that they are investigating; nor do biologists relate with the protozoa they are studying on a personal level. Therefore such researchers can and normally do conform with the demands of the positivistic (empiricist) scientific school for academic objectivity. A categorical demand is placed by this school on all researchers – including social scientists – to remove all shadings of personal values and attitudes from their studies. However, an economist, even if personally functioning in an economic system on the other side of the globe from the one they are studying, willingly or unwillingly and consciously or unconsciously, brings a personal identity or normative stance into the analysis. In other words, they never cease to be a particular person of a given descent and with certain ideological inclinations – humble or wealthy, a denizen of the developed world or of a developing country, an advocate of capitalism or an adherent of socialism or Marxism. The psychologist, too, is male or female, married or unmarried, a parent or childless and is not a *tabula rasa* when analysing the problems of patients or when conducting any sort of psychological research. This is also, of course, the situation of the researcher in sociology, political science, or international relations.

Indeed, this well-known fact is in clear conflict with the above-mentioned requisite for the researcher's normative and attitudinal neutrality *vis-à-vis* their object of inquiry (Taylor, 1967). The awareness of this *problematique* gave rise, in recent decades, to the hermeneutic approach that currently dominates a considerable number of the domains within social research. According to this approach, there is nothing – neither the research data themselves nor their analyses – that is not subjective, particularly when looked at from the perspective of power relations (Foucault, 1982). Social research, it is thus argued, is never unaffected by the investigator's preconceived values and specific identity, and should make no pretence of having these unattainable qualities. The proponents of this approach maintain that, in many respects, social research unavoidably replicates the power relations between the investigator and the investigated. Therefore, they demand that the researchers, in their writings, present and analyse their positioning in no less detail than that devoted to the objects of their study. Only in this way, they argue, can the context of the analysis be made clear to the reader and perceived in the right perspective, and even taken with the proverbial grain of salt when necessary. These *rules of scientific conduct* are rejected by the mainstream on the basis that they interfere with the essential processes of validation or refutation. By opening the door to manifested subjectivity, it is argued, relativism is legitimated, and this, in its turn, blurs the line between scientific study and other modes of reality construction, such as political advocacy or journalistic reporting.

In most social sciences, the golden path between the two epistemological schools – the positivistic and the hermeneutic – has not, thus far, been found and researchers must choose which of the two approaches to employ.[1] Yet, with regard to the study of violent conflicts,[2] both the positivistic demand for objectivity and the hermeneutic requirement for honest reflexivity are extremely difficult to meet. This is, first and foremost, because researchers, who are after all human beings and moral personas, operate under the weight of the emotional baggage visited upon them by the pain and suffering that accompany most conflicts. Few academics, even if they are geographically, ethnically, nationally and/or religiously complete 'outsiders' to the conflict, are able to maintain even a semblance of aloofness when dealing with tragedies such as the genocide in Rwanda or the non-ending massacres in the former Yugoslavia. (For an account of such an 'involved outsider', see Gourevitch, 1998.) Simply by being members of the human race, researchers of a conflict become part of it. It is worth noticing, however, that in the study of violent conflict researchers of the pure *outsider* type – that is, those who base their views on a study of the situation from afar and on a basically unbiased scrutiny of the facts – are a rare breed. The more common type of researcher is, in fact, an *involved outsider* – one who is personally connected to the conflict by virtue of belonging to one of the national, religious or ethnic groups involved in it, or because of an identification with a general political stance such as anti-racism, anti-colonialism or non-violence that is relevant to the analysis of the specific conflict.

Such emotional baggage, which often interferes with the proper conduct of academic studies of violent conflicts, is, of course, even heavier when the researcher is an *insider* – a member of a socio-political group involved in the conflict and also a resident of the place where it is taking place. This personal involvement essentially turns the researcher into a participating observer, even when this is not the professed methodology of the investigation, and makes the study potentially prejudiced. Some would go as far as to argue that in such cases the researchers are not only participant observers but are, in a way, themselves the subject of their research. In this capacity they may be morally responsible – and, in some cases, accountable in practice – for violence committed by the group to which they belong against the opposing group. No less problematic are situations in which researchers belonging to one side of the conflict or those close to them, are potential or actual victims of violence from the opposing side. A study of a violent conflict conducted from either of these two positions – that of perpetrator of violence or that of victim – cannot possibly aspire to the objectivity demanded by the positivistic research school. But under these same conditions, the demands of the hermeneutic approach, which call for sincere reflexivity and impartial acknowledgment of the real power relations between the parties to the conflict, are no less difficult and are, perhaps, even inherently impossible.

The following brief discussion of the role of identity in studying violent conflicts is based to a considerable extent on the experience the author acquired while leading an Israeli research team which, in the years 1996–98, studied three decades of peace activities in Israel (1967–98) and their contribution to the launching of the peace process.[3] It is also based on her prolonged cooperation with Palestinian pollsters in the context of an ongoing Israeli–Palestinian survey project entitled 'Israeli–Palestinian Peace Index', which follows in *real time* the developments in Israeli and Palestinian public opinion with the unfolding peace process.[4]

As far as Israeli–Arab relationships in general, and Israeli–Palestinian relationships in particular, were concerned, the years investigated in the first project were of a mixed character. Prior to 1991 the main feature of these relationships was their zero-sum definition by both sides, a definition that, unsurprisingly, was accompanied by much physical violence – from fully-fledged wars to border skirmishes and local terror attacks. However, since the autumn of 1991 (when the Madrid Peace Conference was convened), and even more so since 1993 (when the Oslo I Accord was signed), the overall situation has changed. Although violence has not ceased, and in certain respects has even increased, the process of *rapprochement*, rather than the conflict itself, has become the focus of Israeli–Arab relations. As a result the former, zero-sum definition of the relations has apparently been replaced by a *mixed-motives* one, resulting in a situation that allows for a dialogue between the two sides, academic researchers included. This change actually provided the above-mentioned project's *raison d'être*: to

assess the influence of peace/conflict resolution grassroots organisations on the initiation of the peace negotiations and on the way
in which they were conducted.

The identity of the researcher, the issue which stands at the heart
of this chapter, was the first, and perhaps most severe problem
encountered by the teams upon the launching of this project. In the
case of South Africa, and of Northern Ireland as well, the formation
of a team representing both sides of the conflict proved an attainable
task. This appeared to be an unfeasible arrangement in the
Israeli–Palestinian context and the study of this case was therefore
conducted by two teams, each working independently: the Palestinian team studied the activities and groups on the Palestinian side,
while the Israeli team studied those on the Israeli side. Cooperative
Israeli–Palestinian peace endeavours were also studied separately by
the two teams.

As both the Israeli and the Palestinian teams discovered at the very
earliest stages of their work, a joint team was unable to get the *real*
stories of the organisation of either side. Thus, despite the obviously
negative norm implied by such a nationality-based separation, the
researchers accepted the fact that, given the overall context of this
particular conflict, a joint Israeli–Palestinian team could never
penetrate the surface and uncover the genuine perceptual motiva-
tions and practical considerations of the two sides. A particularly
difficult aspect of investigation by a joint team seemed to be the
complicated relations between the peace activists of the two sides,
for, although they sincerely sought a solution to the conflict, even
the most committed peace seekers could not repudiate their own
national collective. The difficulty of carrying out a joint research
project became even more discernible while actively studying the
joint organisations: the activists or leaders of the Israeli peace
movements often expressed sceptical views of the future relationship between the two peoples when only Israelis were present, but
maintained a façade of optimism when Palestinian activists or
researchers were also in attendance. In addition, the information on
the joint organisations gathered by the Palestinian team in the Palestinian branches was found to be quite different from that gathered
by the Israeli team in the Israeli branches. Furthermore, the development, at the analysis phase, of a joint Israeli–Palestinian
interpretation of the data gathered appeared to be very difficult or
even impossible due to the very dissimilar historical and national
narratives of the two sides, as well as to the clearly asymmetrical

power relations between them, as occupiers and occupied. These built-in characteristics were inescapable, and were reflected in the relations between the teams as well.

The joint survey project mentioned above revealed other difficulties in conducting cooperative research in the context of a protracted conflict. The most severe of these were the difficulties in agreeing on the proper terminology and operational definitions of events and processes, such as wars and their consequences, for example, liberation or occupation, or population movements, expulsion or voluntary leaving. (On the problems of carrying out joint research, see Newman, 1996.)

Based on this experience in studying a violent conflict – although apparently at a stage close to its management if not its resolution – the main argument elaborated in the following parts of this short chapter is that the researcher's identity, mainly in terms of *insider* versus *outsider*, is crucial to their ability to conduct such a study in an objective and scientific manner. Furthermore, the difference between insider and outsider, some sources of which have been already mentioned above, turns out to have distinct implications for the main three stages of the study: data gathering, analysis, and dissemination of findings. In general, it seems that while insiders have an advantage in carrying out the first stage, their specific identity constitutes an obstacle in the second and third ones. Outsiders, on the other hand, face considerable difficulties in the first, data-gathering stage, due to their second-hand familiarity with the conflict context, a stumbling-block that often interferes with their work. However, this distance is exactly what makes them better equipped to deal with the second and third stages of analysis and dissemination of findings.

THE DATA-GATHERING STAGE

It appears that researchers who belong to one of the sides of a conflict, that is, insiders, are best qualified for gathering the hard data on their own side: they are proficient in the language, familiar with the socio-cultural and political contexts, have detailed and sometimes first-hand information regarding relevant events, and have incomparable access to primary resources and informants.

When the language or languages used by the sides in a conflict are less widely known ones (such as Hebrew, Arabic, Serbo-Croatian, Basque, or Tamil, to name just a few of the languages of the sides involved in current violent conflicts), the advantage of inside over outside researchers is most apparent. Even the best and most faithful translations of the claims of the respective sides unavoidably impair the authenticity of the data, and hence the validity of their analysis. For example, in our research we found that the texts of the Israeli peace movements that were translated into English for foreign readers often transmitted a somewhat different message than did the Hebrew originals, and yet researchers from other parts of the world studying the Israeli–Palestinian conflict and its resolution base much of their analyses on these translations. For example, the translations, which in the original Hebrew often bring to mind modern or biblical words related to the conflict, or idiomatic expressions known to be in use by one or another political camp, often fail to evoke the intended historic connotations or cultural nuances. We also found that the conversion of Israeli peace movements' brochures and articles into English or French often put a stronger emphasis on moral argumentation and universal values than their Hebrew sources. This emphasis, which is not highly compelling to the greater part of the Israeli readership, is meant to appeal to a target audience known to be interested in such a discourse. The outside researcher, who is usually not linguistically equipped to compare the original text with its translation, cannot detect these differences and therefore may well get an erroneous impression regarding the internal Israeli dialogue on the conflict. Researchers from the inside – native speakers of the language – are clearly less likely to make mistakes of this sort.

During the course of our study, we faced the distorting impact of the difficulties of expressing oneself in a foreign language, a serious problem in so far as direct communication with the people of the sides involved in the conflict is concerned. We realised that in order to overcome this language barrier the Israeli interviewees found it helpful to develop a *myth* describing the evolution of the organisation they represent and the key events in its history. They presented this myth time and again to the outside researchers who, as a result of its being repeated so coherently and consistently, usually accepted it without question. First-hand familiarity with the local context, which only insiders usually have, often helps the researchers to recognise and circumvent such myths and uncover the less obvious complexities of the conflict and its internal contradictions.

Accessibility to the vital information found in official sources such as archives is of immense importance. Formally, all interested parties have equal access to such sources, but in reality insiders have much better chances of getting to the primary resources than do outsiders. For example, the fact that one must present a local identity card or university permit in order to enter certain archives and libraries in Israel (and in other countries as well) creates a situation whereby the identity of the researcher is immediately established. This frequently affects the nature of the material which the archivist or librarian will give the researcher. In Israel, permission to photocopy documents, particularly these dealing with some aspects of security, is even more dependent on the user's identity.

Access to public figures in official positions, for interviews or information, is also often much easier for insiders. This is particularly true in relatively small and intimate societies such as those of Northern Ireland or Israel where the social distances are short, especially between such groups as the political and academic elites. Even in the case of informants who do not have formal roles, such as former politicians and retired military officers, researchers who are insiders have better chances than outsiders to get to them, as the social-networking factor operates to their advantage.

None the less, in so sensitive a socio-political issue as a violent conflict, even insiders face some problems of accessibility. In our study, we found that in order to approach the subjects of our study – that is, the people in the peace movements, and particularly the radical ones among them – and to obtain information and data which were important to the study, we first had to present them with a sort of political *certificate of honesty*. This could be achieved, for example, by expressing sympathy with their highly critical view of the Israeli side and its conduct in the context of the conflict. A similar situation, though in the opposite direction, arose when interviewing active politicians or military personnel about the conflict: we practically had to make a virtual *declaration of loyalty* before they would communicate to us any information, assessment or materials. In other words, in a society functioning under the pressures of an often violent conflict, even the researcher from within is often required to have the appropriate political credentials in order to receive cooperation from the subjects of the study, a condition which is clearly not in line with the neutrality dictated by the rules of positivistic research. It is almost impossible for outsiders to enjoy such cooperation.

In at least one realm, however – getting through to the *other side* of the conflict in order to obtain materials relevant for their study – insiders are usually less capable of obtaining data than outsiders.

Even when insiders do succeed in making their way through the walls of suspicion and hostility, and sometimes through bureaucratic obstacles and military checkpoints as well, the ensuing interaction often replicates the power relations between the sides – between occupied and occupier, oppressor and oppressed, perpetrator of violence and its victim, and so on. Our study confirmed the hypothesis that even if some contact with the relevant actors on the other side of the conflict is established, the researcher's affiliation to the stronger side in the conflict significantly affects the interaction with the weaker one: in most cases, the researcher is perceived as being personally *guilty* of offences committed by the side with which he is affiliated. Thus, the Israeli researchers gathering data on the conflict on the Palestinian side found themselves in a defensive position, which clearly detracted from their impartiality in the investigation of the claims presented to them.

Occasionally, even passing through a border or a boundary for the purpose of carrying out research on the other side can actually be physically dangerous. This was so in the case of the so-called 'peace lines' in the Shankill and Falls Roads in Belfast, and the Green Line, the pre-1967 border between Israel and the West Bank in the Israeli–Palestinian case. Thus, even when an Israeli researcher succeeded in getting to the relevant offices and informants in certain areas within the West Bank or the Gaza Strip, the suspicious or even hostile atmosphere and the lack of freedom to roam freely in the area severely impaired the communications necessary for the work of data gathering to be properly carried out. Such forays were much more productive when the researchers were accompanied by their Palestinian colleagues. Palestinian researchers, on the other hand, had considerable trouble getting into Israel at all, and their access to Israeli decision makers or formal documents was negligible at best.

Such difficulties of access, physical danger, and the unpleasantness often associated with gathering information on the *other* side – obstacles directly connected with their identities – encourages the tendency which prevails among researchers affiliated with one side of a violent conflict to focus their studies on *their own* side. Furthermore, it curtails their ability and desire to investigate the other side to the same depth.

Notwithstanding these important drawbacks, the effectiveness of insiders in the first stage of data gathering is, by and large, usually better than that of the outsiders.

THE ANALYSIS STAGE

The identity of the insiders may turn out to be considerably less constructive during the, second, analysis stage of the study: their socialisation into the conflict from early childhood on may interfere with researchers' ability to carry out impartial analyses, and often may also limit or even obviate their ability to be genuinely reflexive. Moreover, unlike outsiders they are inescapably caught between psychological and social demands to take their own community's side in the conflict, on the one hand, and their professional obligation to meet academic standards of proper investigation on the other. In their effort to resolve these difficult dilemmas, insiders often tend to go to one extreme or the other, that is, to be either overly fault-finding in so far as their community's role in the conflict is concerned, or insufficiently critical of it.

A good illustration of this *problematique* can be found in Israeli historiography. Sorting through studies of the Israeli–Palestinian conflict reveals that almost all of them fit into one of two main interpretative frameworks: the first is the almost non-reflexive traditional Zionist framework, which presents Israel and Israelis as victims of ongoing, baseless Arab hostility, along with a strong emphasis on the ever-present danger of physical annihilation and, consequently, a description of the measures taken by Israel as being purely defensive. For many years, this interpretation of the roots and dynamics of the conflict was the only one given a seal of approval by the mainstream. About ten years ago, however, an increasing number of very critical studies written by Israeli researchers of a younger academic generation began to appear. The researchers who adopted this framework, often dubbed 'the new historians', focus on analysing from *within* the purported colonialist character of the Zionist movement and the mechanisms that grew out of it. According to this school of interpretation, these mechanisms were applied to the Arab residents of Israel for the purpose of removing them from their lands and also denying them their national and even human rights. If the predecessors of the new historians tended to avoid self-criticism, the researchers associated with this school of thought are strongly disposed toward excessive criticism of the Israeli side, on which they place almost total responsibility for the conflict while deprecating the responsibility of the Arab side. Not surprisingly, the researchers who use this alternative interpretative framework have been rejected and strongly denounced by both the

Israeli public and the academic mainstream, but commended for their *objectivity* and sympathy by the Palestinians and many outside researchers of the conflict.[5]

In addition to the difficulties that insiders may have in presenting a balanced account of the conflict, which is one of the results of their tendency to be either insufficiently or overly critical of their own side, they also tend to put an excessive emphasis on the unique aspects of the conflict they are part of while understating these aspects that are recognisable in other conflicts as well: they thus lose the insights offered by a comparative-analytical study. This tendency reduces their ability to utilise theoretically the data successfully collected during the first stage. Researchers from the outside, on the other hand, are more capable of recognising these features, which are common to all violent conflicts, and are more proficient in putting specific ones in wider comparative-analytical frameworks, thereby gaining a deeper insight into the specific case as well. (A fine example of the ability to see the Israeli–Palestinian conflict 'from the outside', in a comprehensive perspective, is Lustick, 1993).

This problematic tendency of overstating uniqueness was revealed already during preparations for the data-gathering stage of the above-mentioned international project, when the common operational definitions (in particular of *peace movements* and *non-violent means to resolve conflicts*) were being constructed and the methodology selected. However, the tendency towards idiosyncratic perceptions became much more problematic at the stage when general and comparative conclusions drawing on all three conflicts and the efforts at their resolution was reached. Each of the four teams participating in the study was apparently facing significant difficulties in rising above the case study it had explored and in which its members were personally involved. Thus, while capable of pointing to the similarities between the two case studies to which they were outsiders, the members of all the teams were noticeably less successful in identifying the common variables in the context of their own conflict. Thus, the Northern Irish team, conceptual captives of their own recent experiences, and without distinguishing enough between their own and the other conflicts, made some sweeping generalisations regarding the role of religion as both the source of violent conflicts and as a means of resolving them. The South Africans strongly emphasised the issues of racism and redistributive justice, although the other three teams were less convinced of the universal validity of these factors. And, finally, the Israelis and

Palestinians specified the centrality of national aspirations and territorial rights as the crucial elements, although these were not seen as highly relevant by the other two teams.

THE FINDINGS DISSEMINATION STAGE

The dissemination of the findings of a study on violent conflicts is relatively easy due to its headline-capturing and newsworthy topicality and perceived relevance: politicians, the media, and the wide public all over the world are avid followers of news about conflicts. Yet, it is also problematic, in a sense, for that very same general interest in the subject: if the findings are not trivial, their publication often evokes strong reactions by the protagonists and interested observers of the conflict. These reactions are related to the historical facts as presented in the study, but even more to their interpretation. Thus, the primary loyalties and political agendas of the researchers, and in some cases their academic professionalism as well, are often questioned.

Living and working *in loco*, researchers from the inside are very likely to be alarmed by such criticism. Although they often fail to acknowledge it, in many cases the expectation of such reactions from their immediate environment influences at least the tone, if not the factual content, of their writings about the conflict. Outsiders, on the other hand, because of their personal detachment from the context of the conflict, have to deal only with the references to the academic quality of their publication and are therefore more capable of producing a balanced analysis.

In so far as our study of Israeli peace movements is concerned, the decision on whether to delve into the roots of their low political efficacy or to make do with some general, descriptive comments on their activity, certainly affected our final report. We took into consideration the fact that the exposure of various structural and operational shortcomings of these movements would damage our relationships with the leaders and activists of these movements. As our team's members were all socially and professionally close to people involved in peace activism, the decision to go for the first option, to be more critical, was indeed costly in terms of personal relations. However, since we live and function in an overall secure and democratic context, and because all of the relevant people understood the advantages of getting a sober and non-laudatory account of this sort of activity, our dilemma was relatively easy to solve. The situation is much more difficult for inside researchers operating in violent or less tolerant contexts, where a report of this kind might even put them in fear of their well-being and safety.

When it comes to the criteria for publishing, scandals are good for business. Therefore, when a commercial publisher is making the decision as to whether to publish a book on a violent conflict, the decisive consideration is often the degree of sensation which such a publication will generate. On many occasions this approach has exploited the drawing power of provocative data about a conflict, thereby endowing them with more apparent validity than the facts themselves support. Such publishers often seek and even encourage highly critical writings. At the other extreme, there are conservative publishers who, to maintain their reputations, will not publish studies whose findings are not consonant with mainstream public opinion. The interest in having their works published by such publishing houses, which are also often the most respectable from the academic point of view, impels some researchers to present a conformist version of the conflict, even if the facts they have uncovered do not reinforce it. In this respect the choice made by insiders is basically no different from that made by outsiders. However, the professional assessment of the quality of the research products of the two sorts of researchers is often different: studies of the conflict written by outside researchers, even if considered neutral by objective referees, are frequently considered invalid by reviewers affiliated with the sides to the conflict, who claim that the outside researcher *doesn't understand* the facts because of their being an *auslander*. When it comes to inside researchers, considerations of yet another type are involved, in what are allegedly neutral quality assessments, and may be in the form of an accusation of some visual distortions caused by their affiliation with a certain group. On occasion, depending on the zeitgeist, pressure is exerted on researchers to publish studies that take a critical, reflexive approach. In most cases the writer has no possibility of defending him or herself against such stipulations since, in the case of academic journals, for example, the views of reviewers are usually expressed anonymously. Writers therefore often try to adjust their report in advance to what they anticipate will be desirable in the eyes of the reviewers. The result may be, of course, a study of low academic value.

In conclusion, it appears that it is extremely difficult to meet the basic challenge of conducting a study of a violent conflict that is free of preconceived values and, even more so, of emotion. Another alternative, of achieving genuine reflexivity when going through the different stages of exploration, elaboration and summary, is also difficult, if not impossible. The identity of the researcher, whether that of an insider or of an outsider, is of exceptional significance in this case, and also seems to have differential influence during different stages of the research process. Apparently, some of the negative influences of the researcher's identity cannot be remedied, but an awareness of them might mitigate their effects.

However, increasing awareness to the implications of the researcher's identity is, in itself, hardly a satisfactory remedy to the practical problems they create. A workable way of dealing with the identity issue is by constructing research teams composed of a combination of insiders and outsiders. The cooperation between them must be properly designed so that each type of researcher will fulfil a greater role at the stages in which their identity-related qualifications are an advantage, and a smaller one where their identity may be a drawback. If successful, this research strategy may produce a better study of the conflict than one produced by a homogeneous group. A particular case of such cooperation between insiders and outsiders, which was discussed above, would consist of teams composed of researchers affiliated with the rival sides in a violent conflict. The question of the operational extent of such a strategy is indeed a moot point, especially since the experience of our project was quite unpromising in this regard. As described above, we actually fell short of constructing a joint Israeli–Palestinian team. However, the success of the other two joint teams participating in the project in producing commendable case studies suggests that the Israeli–Palestinian case may not be a representative example of the efforts to overcome the identity problem by balancing or compensating for the identity pitfalls of one researcher or team with that of the other.

At the same time the success of the other two teams may suggest that the ability to conduct a joint study depends to a considerable extent on the stage at which the conflict stands at the time of its investigation. Apparently, the fact that in 1998 both South Africa and Northern Ireland had already progressed towards the resolution of their major conflicts, and were at a stage far ahead of the progress made at that time in the Israeli–Palestinian context, facilitated such joint ventures. In other words, it seems that one's identity and its repercussions are highly dependent on the context, for in the research of violent conflicts the negative repercussions of one's identity are similar to those found in life in general.

NOTES

1. For the difference between these two theoretical 'lenses' in the study of conflicts see Rothman, 1992: 70–74. Rothman mentions a third, still evolving 'lens' – critical theory – which, he maintains, both criticises and wishes to transform the status quo. In practical terms, this approach is meant to bridge the gap between the former contradictory approaches, but has not yet become a comparable alternative to them in terms of its acceptance in academic circles.
2. It should be emphasised that the discussion here refers to physically violent conflicts, not to situations of 'structured violence' – 'where those at "the bottom" of some hierarchically structured relational system, cannot – by reason of involuntary membership in certain ethnic, class, religion and/or other groups – obtain fair access to the social, economic, political, educational, legal, and/or other resources typically enjoyed and presided over by the mainstream' (Galtung, 1969: 171).
3. The study was conducted under the auspices of the Aspen Institute in Washington, DC, as part of an international comparative project that also included the South African and Northern Irish case studies.
4. This project is sponsored by the Norwegian Labor Union (FAFO) in the framework of its People to People programme.
5. For a short but representative style analysis of 'the new historian', see Pappe, 1995. For a critical view of the 'new historians' school, see Karsh, 1997. For a more balanced view see, Bar On, 1998.

REFERENCES

Bar On, M. (1998) 'The Historians' Debate in Israel and the Middle East Peace Process', in I. Peleg (ed.) (1997) *The Middle East Peace Process: Interdisciplinary Perspectives* (Albany: Suny Press).

Foucault, M. (1982) 'The Subject and the Power', *Critical Inquiry*, no. 8, pp. 777–93.

Galtung, J. (1969) 'Peace Violence and Peace Research', *Journal of Peace Research*, vol. 6, p. 171.

Gourevitch, P. (1998) *We Wish to Inform You That Tomorrow We Will Be Killed With Our Families* (New York: Farrar, Straus & Giroux).

Karsh, E. (1997) *Fabricating Israeli History* (London: Frank Cass).

Lustick, I. (1993) *Unsettled States, Disputed Lands* (Ithaca: Cornell University Press).

Newman, D. (1996) 'Writing Together Separately: Critical Discourse and the Problems of Cross-ethnic Co-authorship', *Area*, vol. 28, no. 1, pp. 1–12.

Pappe, I. (1995) 'The New History and Sociology of Israel: A Challenge to the Old Version', *Palestine-Israel Journal*, vol. II, no. 3, pp. 70–76.

Rothman, J. (1992) *From Confrontation to Cooperation: Resolving Ethnic and Regional Conflict* (London: Sage) pp. 70–74.

Taylor, C. (1967) 'Neutrality in Political Science', in P. Laslett and W.G. Runciman (eds), *Philosophy, Politics and Society* (Oxford: Basil Blackwell).

5   Research for Empowerment in a Divided Cambodia

Helen Jenks Clarke

INTRODUCTION

Much social knowledge in Cambodia has been the victim of thirty years of armed conflict. At the lowest point, during the period of Khmer Rouge rule, violence was explicitly directed at eradicating social knowledge and returning the country to 'year zero'. Today, probably as much social research[1] in Cambodia originates in humanitarian organisations as in the one university and several institutes of the country. The university is modest and elitist and most institutes are oriented toward producing policy advice for the government or explaining Cambodia to the world, while the humanitarian organisations attempt to develop knowledge to inform their work with the poor.

This chapter argues[2] that it is important for Cambodians to be involved in research in order to regain knowledge that has been lost and to empower them for the future. Regaining social knowledge may help people to overcome their divisions and to 'move on'. A case study of one organisation's attempts to develop knowledge to inform its work illustrates the difficulties of doing this type of research in a violent and divided society.

CAMBODIA AS A DIVIDED SOCIETY

That Cambodia is described as a divided society may seem like an anomaly: Cambodia is homogeneous in ethnicity and religion – 95 per cent of the people are Khmer and most are at least nominally Buddhist. Language does not divide them. Only five per cent of Cambodians are of other ethnicities – Chams, Vietnamese, or various small groups of highlands people. But the division in Cambodia about which we are concerned is among the Khmers themselves.

In Cambodia, ethnicity, language, religion do not divide: history does. Over the past thirty years, individuals and villages have had very different experiences and therein lies the basis for social division. Cambodia went from a colonial period characterised by indifference, manipulation and extraction to a supposedly democratic monarchy in 1953, characterised by corruption, inept government and intrigue. Norodom Sihanouk – first when he was king and then, when he became prince (so as to participate in government) – attempted unsuccessfully to prevent the downfall of his government. A series of disastrous decisions included assent to an American request for permission to pursue Viet Minh troops across the border into Cambodia.

By 1970, the Communist Party of Kampuchea had become an armed guerrilla movement, General Lon Nol had staged a coup against Prince Sihanouk, and Cambodia found itself engulfed in a civil war. In 1975, the Communists, called the 'Khmer Rouges' (Red Khmers), completed their control of Cambodia with the capture of Phnom Penh. There followed 'three years, eight months and 23 days',[3] a period of deliberate murder, starvation and overwork in which approximately 1.7 million people – out of a population of only 10 million – died. This is close to two out of every ten people living in Cambodia at that time.

In 1979 the Khmer Rouge revolution was dislodged in what was called by some a 'liberation', and by others an 'occupation' of former Khmer Rouge soldiers and Vietnamese troops, and the civil war resumed. Since the withdrawal of Vietnamese troops in 1989 and the signing of the Paris Peace Accords, even as the civil war continued until the final Khmer Rouge defections of 1998, Cambodians have attempted to come to some agreement about which model of society to use. With the civil war over at long last Cambodians can now look to the future – but models of the future depend, at least partly, on how people see their past and Khmers retain deep disagreements on the meaning of the past thirty years.

The divisions are based in personal and group experience of the civil war period of 1970–75, the horrific 'Pol Pot' revolutionary years of 1975–79, and the continuation of the civil war. Divisions during those periods were physical, geographic and social. In the 1960s, the US war in Vietnam spilled over to Laos and Cambodia. US carpet bombing, lasting from 1969 to 1973 (Kiernan, 1996), was not long confined to the Vietnamese border area – as had been agreed by Sihanouk – and eventually covered the entire eastern half of Cambodia. To escape the bombing, millions of Cambodian peasants left rural villages and moved to the cities, losing their lands and becoming displaced urban squatters. By the time the US bombing stopped, the civil war had become so entrenched and the Khmer

Rouge had gained so much ground, that the cities continued to swell with displaced people who had lost all, including their ancestral lands. The city of Phnom Penh more than doubled in population during that period.

On 15 April 1975, Khmer Rouge troops entered Phnom Penh. Within three days, all the cities of Cambodia were evacuated. Those forced at gunpoint from the cities were the 'new' people, forced to live in communal proximity with the 'old' country people to whose lands they were haphazardly and forcefully assigned. Children were separated from parents, couples divided, older or sick people were killed or died of neglect. The 'new' people tried to hide their city origins and experience, and the 'old' people learned to ferret them out. Movement was next to impossible and only a lucky few managed to escape to Thailand or Vietnam.

The years that followed the arrival of Vietnamese troops in 1979 to drive the Khmer Rouge out of Phnom Penh resulted in further divisions. The Khmer Rouge, now reduced to a rearguard and a government in exile, moved mostly to the northeast of Cambodia and the Thai border area, taking whole villages with them, either at gunpoint or by using fear of the Vietnamese to impel the movement. Camps on the Thai border filled with hundreds of thousands of Cambodians applying for refugee status overseas. The worldwide diaspora of those years marks one of the basic divisions in Cambodia, between those who stayed and those who left. In the eyes of some Cambodians, the ones who managed to leave were the ones who 'had it easy', who did not experience the deprivations of the 1980s. This is not to say that life in the camps, prior to going overseas, was easy – not at all – as the refugees continued to be terrorised by Khmer Rouge and Royalist bandits who controlled some of the camps at night. But some of those 'border people' were accepted as refugees in Europe, North America and Australia, and left for more promising lands.

In the 1979–89 period, devastated by civil war and revolution, Cambodia returned to being a pawn in the Cold War. Essentially, the world abandoned the country, despite its experience of genocide. For rebuilding, the government could call on only its own resources, those of Vietnam (itself rebuilding after thirty years of war), the Eastern Bloc, and the resources of a handful of relief agencies. Famine killed thousands during this period, partly because rice could not be distributed because the infrastructure had been destroyed. In addition, not enough food could be raised because approximately half the draft animals had died during the Pol Pot period. Landmines came to be a scourge, used on both sides of the continuing war. Medicines were not available and schools were taught in the open air by those who had received instruction only in the grade ahead of the one they were teaching.

Current divisions in the Cambodia of the 1990s, then, reflect a country's experience of loss: loss of families and friends, of personal history, of social history and of trust. Loss of trust means that anyone can be suspected of having been a Khmer Rouge or of cooperating with them, of being a 'Communist',[4] or of being 'one who left', who went overseas. The ones who went overseas and only returned recently have – beside material wealth and educational advantage – the freedom to leave at any time since they carry foreign passports, whereas most Cambodians have none and cannot seek any other haven.

Cambodians are divided also, because of loss of history and knowledge. The Khmer Rouge leaders called 1975, the year they gained control of the entire country, 'Year Zero'. One goal of the Maoist revolution was to rewrite Cambodian history and they were appallingly successful. Libraries and schools were gutted, historical and government records burned, Buddhist libraries were used to house pigs. Teachers, doctors and judges were murdered, overseas students were enticed home to 'join the revolution' only to be taken from the airport to prison and the killing fields, monks were defrocked, and with court dancers and musicians, killed. With the practitioners and records destroyed, knowledge and history were erased. It really was 'Year Zero'.

In the years since the Khmer Rouge were driven out of Phnom Penh, even as the civil war resumed and continued for almost another twenty years, a major concern has been to re-establish that which has been lost. The surviving court dancers, too old now to perform, teach in the Department of Fine Arts of the Royal University of Phnom Penh. Cambodians and foreign advisers struggle to preserve what remains of the Archives and the Library. Preservation efforts continue at the great temple complex of Angkor Wat, even while others chip away at the bas-relief and steal statues to sell in the lucrative Thai and world art market. Recently, efforts have begun to re-establish basic knowledge about Cambodian society, how it worked, and what they valued in the time before Year Zero.

RESEARCH TO RECOVER KNOWLEDGE

Research establishes knowledge and tests assumptions; it can contribute to reconstructing a record of history that appears to have been lost and it serves as a basis for action. Research can help Cambodians reclaim knowledge and decide on meaningful models for their society.

Published research about Cambodian society in pre-contact, colonial, and pre-war times was characterised by a remarkable shallowness,[5] and the Khmer Rouge destroyed much that was available in Cambodia.[6] Pre-war knowledge was limited, followed in the Khmer Rouge period by the obliteration of most of the learned people of the society and deliberate destruction of most of the written records that had accumulated. Recovery of knowledge about historical Cambodian society – both of the court and of the village – is difficult because so few of those sources remain.

More recently, political tension, continuing during the civil war and even among factions of the democratically elected government, has inhibited and distorted research. Now, with Cambodia at peace, social science investigation will help to relieve our lack of knowledge regarding current conditions. In a more open and stable period, research can begin to elicit and establish knowledge about Cambodian society in its wide variety of forms.

Some assumptions about divided societies require a long time-line and a comparison with the past that, in Cambodia, appears 'lost'. Consider the assumption that war-torn societies are different: something makes distinctive those societies that have experienced a long history of war. The assumption that the experience of war 'tears' or damages a society is easy to make but difficult to research and to prove without having a historic base to use for comparison.

As another example, the violent nature of contemporary Cambodian society is observable and widely acknowledged but it is casually attributed to a variety of causes. For instance, a common argument relates domestic violence to the historic experience: 'Domestic violence ... has reached epidemic proportions ... One reason is Cambodia's legacy of political violence. Coming after a decade of war, the era of the Khmer Rouge ... unleashed a culture of violence that still takes a toll on women.'[7] The fact of rampant domestic violence cannot be denied but its basis in war and revolution has not been established.

The horrific violence of the civil war and revolutionary periods baffles Cambodians. They do not understand how 'Khmer killed Khmer', and many are repelled by the violence observed in Cambodia today. Their accounts are anecdotal and provide no systematic explanations for the violence. The origins of violence and its relation to behaviour observed in contemporary Cambodia cannot be known without investigation.

The structure and organisation of Cambodian families and Cambodian communities, too, are assumed to have changed as a result of thirty years of war. We do not know whether research can re-establish the historic record about Cambodian communities but current methods certainly can record the varieties of contemporary social organisation. In recent years, a common assertion has been that Cambodian communities were destroyed by the war experience and that currently the basic unit is the household (Ovesen et al., 1995). Current research now is challenging such assumptions (Krishnamurthy, 1999; McAndrew, 1998).

RESEARCH TO EMPOWER

As well as recovering knowledge, research can empower; it can support people to allow them to act from knowledge. The older generation can be asked to document how things used to be and a picture, no matter how sketchy, can be built from the reclaimed knowledge. When added to investigations regarding the contemporary society, this research prepares the way for informed decision making. Research becomes a tool to design action and provides legitimisation.

In any society, people use models of society as the basis of action. Such models may be based in ideal types but more frequently they are based upon perceptions of the way society actually is and where it can go from here.

For too long, the models used in Cambodia were imposed. The Khmer Rouge model was one of agrarian socialism: self-reliant communes replaced families, barter displaced the need for money, and there was no further need to interact with one's neighbours or the world. Now, international and national organisations – humanitarian non-government organisations (NGOs) or financial bodies established for economic assistance to developing countries – also have their models of society. These revolve around whatever terminology is currently fashionable, whether it is basic needs, sustainable development, or globalisation. They have little or no cultural reference to the countries in which they work.

It is vital that people become involved in determining the model toward which their society is moving but they, too, must be aware of and able to explain the differences found in their society. 'Common-sense' models of a society need to be replaced by well-researched ones. Widely divergent models can be modified by knowledge gained from research, to serve as a basis for empowerment and for action in a newly rebuilding country (Smith, 1999).

TWO APPROACHES TO LEARNING ABOUT VIOLENCE

Given the lack of basic data about contemporary and historic Cambodia, a number of organisations have found that conducting research is a necessary forerunner to designing action interventions. The American Friends Service Committee (AFSC) is not a research organisation and we recognised the necessity to conduct research only because it became evident that we needed more information before we could design a new project, called 'Local Capacities for Nonviolence'.

Socio-Cultural Vulnerability and Coping Strategies (SCVCS)[8]

When recently we decided we should aim our work towards community-based peace activities, we also realised this was a new type of work and we needed base-line data with which to design a project. A peace project from the point of view of socio-cultural vulnerabilities suited our needs and we began a research project called 'Socio-Cultural Vulnerability and Coping Strategies' (SCVCS) in January 1998.

Our basic assumption is that in Cambodian society vulnerable groups develop coping strategies. Research establishes how a group's vulnerabilities affect behaviour, or are displayed in coping strategies. In this research, our first objective is to assess those vulnerabilities, to understand how vulnerable households, communities and other types of groups continue to be affected by their experience of the past or the present. We look to see how they cope in different situations by using trust, cooperation and caring for one another. We also assess their ability to plan and take effective action, to avoid and resolve conflict and to use resources.

A second objective is to identify, analyse, and disseminate the implications of the coping strategies for the policies and programmes of government, national and international institutions, and NGOs. The third objective is to provide training in research methods and analysis to a core research team and local field research teams working at the community level.

The project was originally designed as a participatory action research project. A dearth of any local capacity in this approach and a donor view that information on socio-cultural vulnerability and coping strategies needed to be generated quickly – within a two-year period – reshaped the project's methodological orientation.

In looking for partner agencies we were determined that the research should focus on vulnerable groups who were themselves interested in finding out about their own coping strategies. We sought partnerships with other groups who shared this approach in their work. The partner organisations who joined us included those working with street children, disabled people, internally displaced or 'border' people and their neighbours who have been in the middle of recent military clashes, and migrant communities located in an ecologically fragile environment.

We had first to develop a research team, in a country having barely any research experience. First, we hired a core research team, made up of the expatriate research coordinator, the Cambodian research-training associate, and three Cambodian research assistants, to develop the research design and provide leadership for the research, and to enhance the capacities of the field research teams. Then, we enlisted the cooperation of seconded staff from the four partner organisations to make up the field research teams. Both groups have worked together to conduct the research, gathering preliminary information, developing case study frameworks, formulating data collection instruments, data gathering, and data analysis. The core research teams have done capacity-building activities for the research and feedback/disseminating to the partner organisations and to various other audiences.

The first six months of the project essentially focused on building up the research relationships with the partner organisations, establishing the criteria for selecting the research sites, and recruiting the research associate and assistants who compose the core research team. The next eight months dwelt on discussions within the core research team on the substantive issues of socio-cultural vulnerability and coping strategies. The period also entailed the development and facilitation of formal as well as on-site training activities on information-gathering tools and techniques, as well as on community organising. It was also during this time that the research working group conducted the preliminary information gathering in the different villages and settlements of the partner organisations. Reflection on the findings from this preliminary data collection directed the team toward developing case studies on specific topics of socio-cultural vulnerability and necessarily, toward the individuals, households, and groups of people who live these varying forms of socio-cultural vulnerability. The period of data gathering now has given way to analysis and final report preparation.

The research has shown that even in a situation of extreme and prolonged violence and its aftermath, vulnerable people can and do draw on many resources that facilitate their coping on a daily basis. These coping strategies can provide a basis for positive social action in new situations in the current period.

Community Experience with Violence[9]

Daily life in Cambodia is not a matter of constant warfare. Yet, recourse to violent behaviour is frequent and not unexpected. In tense situations, the first option is to turn away but many factors – maintaining status or having nothing to lose, saving face and keeping one's honour – make the recourse to violence acceptable. Lack of trust, a history of genocide and the need to use survival strategies, the universal loss of relatives to revolution, warfare and grinding poverty – all appear to contribute to making Cambodian life quite remarkably violent.

Another AFSC research project has been an investigation into violence in Cambodian villages (Swift, 1999). The project took place over five cycles of research and reflection. The expatriate researcher worked in a number of provinces and reported back to the reflection group who directed his further work, extending over a period of five months. The objective of the research was to learn how Cambodians living in rural villages think about the concept of violence and how they structure their experiences of violence in the context of their communities.

Some of the questions the researcher asked were:

- What actions do you consider to be violent?
- What has been your actual experience of violence?
- What do you and your neighbours do about it?
- What are the reasons behind the use of violence?
- How do others regard violent behaviour?
- After violence has occurred, how do the involved people relate to each other?
- What actions do you think would help to reduce violence in your village?

The richest material came from research in the two provinces where the researcher was well known, where trust has grown over several years. In the two provinces where he was not known, the answers to questions sometimes directly contradicted the results from the first two sites. The people there minimised the issues of violence or problems in their village and, perhaps deliberately, limited the researcher's access to a variety of community members. He found that people are extremely sensitive about the experience and practice of violence.

LESSONS LEARNED

The research on the experience of violence leads to conclusions that can, to some extent, be applied also to the research on vulnerability. Investigations on violence and on vulnerable groups require a previous relationship of trust between researcher and villagers. *The picture gained of the experience of violence or vulnerability will be incomplete where trust has not been established.*

Work in the different provinces indicates marked differences in the perceptions of violence, the underlying reasons for violence, and the reaction that violence elicits in others. *The paradigm of violence in one Cambodian community cannot be considered to hold true in other communities.* Perhaps a similar conclusion can be made that the experience of vulnerability will not be the same, nor will similar coping strategies emerge, between different vulnerable groups.

Both research projects have indicated that the meaning of 'violence' is very broad (both in English and Khmer) and the different types of violence played out in the communities indicate the complexity of the term. There is micro-level violence – such as neighbourhood disputes, disputes between neighbours, domestic violence, and violence while drunk. Then there is macro-level violence, where rich or powerful people use the threat – and reality – of violence or oppression against poorer and less powerful persons. There are links between these two levels of violence but the interventions to address each level are quite different and might, if not handled carefully, have a negative effect on interventions to address the other level. *Research into violence must look at the micro- and the macro-levels, find the links between the two, and point to interventions that will effectively address both.* Research results of the coping strategies of vulnerable groups project will be used at various levels to inform interventions, from that of national government policy to community-level NGO development projects. Practitioners using the results of the research will need to be careful to determine and coordinate the links between macro- and micro-level interventions.

Participation is an effective and legitimate way to establish trust. Our original plan to use strictly participatory methodology in the SCVCS study was thwarted by constraints of time and research capacity. To the extent that we had to streamline the process, the research became less participatory and more extractive. The study of community violence was designed to be fast and not participatory. In both cases, we ran into barriers between researchers and the villagers. Those villagers not involved in conducting research to explain their own issues have less reason to cooperate. They are especially quick to sense hierarchical differences between themselves and visiting researchers. To the extent that they were not in partnership with the research team, not doing the research themselves, they could resist troublesome questions. We were brought face-to-face with the lesson that *where trust is lacking, villagers have much to lose by being too open.* Research exposes informants who are not in control of the research process. If villagers are participants in the research process, not just subjects, they can determine how the information will be used. A participatory research process allows villagers to see how answering questions about their vulnerability or about the violence in their lives can lead to finding solutions amenable to them. A participatory research process, in which trust has been established as the first step, empowers villagers to build their own models of society.

Without participation, villagers do not 'own' the research. Resistance or violence may then become an impediment. In a violent society researchers are at risk. They need to be aware and to ask, are our questions about the issues of vulnerability and the experience of violence provocative? Do they increase the likelihood of violence occurring? Do they increase the vulnerability of the group? Villagers may view the research process itself as dangerous (talking to strangers – especially about others – makes you more vulnerable) or it might result in violent reactions as old wounds are reopened.

Researchers in our projects have had to deal with the threat of violence in a number of instances. Among the research team working with street children who live in an urban squatter community, only those who had worked there for a long time were allowed to conduct interviews. The core research team could not enter the squatter community because the partner organisation could not be sure of their safety.

In the migrant villages, we discovered that the demands of competing village chiefs had split loyalties in the community and the field research team had become entangled in the conflict. The research team's point of view derived from their in-depth interviews with people who had been involved in the formal land titling efforts of one of the village chiefs. It differed from the point of view of village workers in a resource management project who relied on very different types of information from another village chief involved in establishing new land claims for his followers. Both chiefs used the presence of our staff to legitimate their claims. Threats by the two chiefs and the brandishing of guns by their loyal followers put researchers, village workers and villagers at risk.

Researchers who come from outside the village, even if they visit repeatedly, are subject to threat. Our researchers entered each village 'correctly', with no promises of gifts, so at the start they had no natural allies in the village, no one to stand up for them. The benefits that come of research may not be immediately evident to villagers who have never had a chance to join in the research process. It takes a while for villagers to understand how they can guide and employ the results to broaden their understanding of the world and their place in it. Furthermore, researchers who are newcomers will make mistakes, ask the wrong question of the wrong people, and ask provocative questions, ones that are too sensitive to be tolerated and ones that show some people in a bad light. All these sources of tension can precipitate violence.

CONCLUSION

Thirty years of warfare have resulted in a divided Cambodia. Now, while the country is at peace, Cambodians have an opportunity to begin to understand those divisions and to determine their future.

This chapter has examined two research projects, one investigating the coping strategies of vulnerable groups and the other exploring the meaning and experience of violence in Cambodian life. Conducting research in a divided and violent society has yielded some important lessons. The first is that researching vulnerability and violence requires the establishment of trust. Participatory research methodology can help to establish trust and allows villagers to 'own' research so it is accessible to them and answerable to their concerns. Failure to do so may result in an incomplete picture and endangerment of villagers and research staff.

Secondly, due to the lack of historic records or their destruction – because of Cambodia's particular history – at this time we have only a rudimentary basis for understanding Cambodian communities.

Therefore, comparisons from one community to another are risky, because we do not have a full understanding of the context in which vulnerability is observed or violence is expressed.

A third lesson is that different kinds of violence are expressed at domestic, community and national levels. It is important to understand how violence is expressed at the micro- and the macro-levels, the connections between the levels, and how to design effective interventions that address the connections. It may be that research exploring coping strategies of vulnerable groups will indicate a similar need for a multi-layered approach by groups using the research results.

Research helps to bring back, to re-establish some knowledge. Even in a violent and divided society, research can empower Cambodians to rebuild society using their own models, as opposed to those of others to which they have been subject for such a long period.

NOTES

1. Rebecca 'Pem' Catalla and Judy Saumweber provided extremely helpful background information in the preparation of this paper. Their comments on the final paper are also appreciated, as are Navi Ngin's. These three were deeply involved in the research project Socio-Cultural Vulnerability and Coping Strategies. The results of that Cambodian research, published May 2000, can be found at www.go.to/scvcs. I especially want to acknowledge the comments and support of Robert Clarke.
2. The point of view presented in this chapter is one of a development practitioner, not of a researcher. Some of the staff involved in the research discussed here have provided valuable input into the chapter but they may have a very different view of the functions of the research in which they have been involved.
3. This is a phrase repeatedly invoked to denote the agony of that period, in which every day of survival was counted.
4. The epithet 'Communist' is remarkably tenacious. It was applied to the Khmer Rouge, and also to those who displaced them. The Vietnamese-backed government of the 1980s and the State of Cambodia government of 1989–91 were avowedly 'Communist', supported by the Communist People's Party. However, after 1991 and the Paris Peace Accords, the CPP changed to be the Cambodian People's Party. Although the governments put in place by the 1993 and 1998 elections are decidedly market-oriented, Prime Minister Hun Sen and his allies continue to be labelled, incorrectly, as 'Communist'.
5. In preparation for a conference, 'The Meaning of Community', literature reviews were prepared by the Working Group on Social Organisation in Cambodia, May 1999. The reviews of the existing literature on the broad topic of Cambodian society were prepared by Esther M. Watts (English language literature), Ellie Brown (French language), and Dr Prum Tevi

(Khmer language, with translation to English by Mr Leang Seak Meng) and are unpublished.
6. May Ebihara's PhD dissertation, *Svay, A Khmer Village in Cambodia* (1968) is the only extensive English-language sociological study of pre-war Cambodian village life.
7. Internet publication: *On the Record//Women of Southeast Asia Fight Violence//*Volume 5, Part 1 – March 4, 1999. I do not intend to highlight this source as being particularly mistaken, it is just one example of many.
8. Rebecca Catalla kindly supplied information presented in this section.
9. I am indebted to Judy Saumweber for input into this and the next section.

REFERENCES

Ebihara, M. (1968) *Svay, A Khmer Village in Cambodia*, PhD dissertation, Columbia University (Ann Arbor, MI: University Microfilms).

Kiernan, B. (1996) *The Pol Pot Regime: Race, Power, and Genocide in Cambodia under the Khmer Rouge, 1975–79* (New Haven: Yale University Press).

Krishnamurthy, V. (1999) 'The Impact of Armed Conflict in Social Capital: A Study of Two Villages in Cambodia' (Phnom Penh: Social Services of Cambodia and the World Bank).

McAndrew, J.P. (1998) 'Interdependence in Household Livelihood Strategies in Two Cambodian Villages', Working Paper No. 7 (Phnom Penh: Cambodia Development Resource Institute).

Ovesen, J., Trankell, I.-B. and Ojendal, J. (1995) 'When Every Household is an Island: Social Organization and Power Structures in Rural Cambodia' (Uppsala: Department of Cultural Anthropology, Uppsala University and SIDA).

Smith, L.T. (1999) *Decolonizing Methodologies: Research and Indigenous Peoples* (London: Zed Books).

Swift, P. (1999) 'Violence in Cambodian villages', unpublished ms.

6 The Role and Process of Action Research in the Management of Violent Community Conflicts in Nigeria

Isaac Olawale Albert

Violent conflicts have been a regular feature of social life in many parts of Nigeria since the early 1990s. Existing studies, most especially Otite and Albert (1999), show that this problem results from religious fanaticism, political exclusion, overpopulation, the accident of a hostile environment in some specific cases, freer access of the civil populace to sophisticated light firearms, and a chaotic network of subaltern micro-ethnic groupings constantly jostling for access to increasingly dwindling political and economic resources. It is therefore common to read in the Nigerian daily newspapers about one group taking up arms against the other or agents of the state as we found in the Niger Delta (most especially among the highly violent 'Egbesu boys') and in Lagos (among the 'Oduduwa boys').

The response of the government to these conflicts has been quite weak. Most of the conflicts usually start with some early warning signals (appeals, threats, issuance of ultimatum, etc.) all of which gave ample room for the government to engage in preventive diplomacy if it so desired. The warning signs are, however, often ignored. Government responses usually come after the first bullet had been fired and some casualties have been recorded. What usually follows is the government's deployment of anti-riot policemen (popularly known in Nigeria as 'Kill-and-go') in the warring community, in line with its constitutional duty of maintaining law and order. Once the physical hostility is halted, the policemen are withdrawn from the warring community and the people are literally left with their problems. This situation often enabled the parties to the conflict to go back to the battlefield and the cycle of violence continues. In some cases, the government sets up a commission of enquiry to look into the root causes of the conflict and make recommendations on how a lasting peace can be restored to the community. The reports of such commissions are rarely published. This often gives room for rumour-mongers to go to town with insider knowledge of the contents of the report. The party that considers itself disadvantaged by the report would therefore regroup to launch another attack, believing that its interests cannot be met through any official intervention. Several community conflicts have relapsed into a worse state of violence as a result. People from these warring communities in Nigeria therefore have little or no confidence in the ability of the government to help them resolve their differences. They see it as their responsibility to promote peace in their communities. The paradox however is that most of these communities are entrapped in their problems; none is inclined to take the first step towards championing the peace process. People also lack the necessary skills for dealing constructively with their problems. This is probably one of the reasons most of the communities sometimes jump at the offer by outsiders to help them deal with their problems.

Since 1994, a number of non-governmental organisations (NGOs) have been actively working in some of these conflict-prone Nigerian communities. The work of most of these NGOs is, however, limited to conflict resolution training. Most of the organisations lack the courage, or expertise and financial resources for embarking on mediation activity. One of the few NGOs that have successfully started such work and that seem to have the means of de-escalating community conflicts in Nigeria, is Academic Associates PeaceWorks (AAPW). The author was the research and intervention officer of AAPW between 1997 and 1999.

AAPW, which has its headquarters in Lagos, has a vast experience in the area of managing violent community conflicts. It has contributed immensely to the de-escalation of several violent ethnic and religious conflicts in the country. These include the conflicts in Zango-Kataf, Wukari, Tafawa Balewa, Igbo-Ora and Ugep. It is currently working on the Ife–Modakeke conflict in Ile-Ife (Osun state), the Tiv–Jukun conflict in Takum (Taraba state) and the Warri conflict (Delta state). All these violent conflicts, except the ones in Ugep and Igbo-Ora, are well known to members of the international community, having received wide publicity by some international news media (most especially CNN). The violent encounters between the Ife and Modakeke, Tiv and Jukun in Wukari, Itsekiri and Ijawin

Warri, Ijaw and Ilaje at Ilaje-Ese Odo area of Ondo state all involved the use of modern weaponry – bombs, machine guns, etc. Each of the conflicts endangered the internal security of Nigeria and diverted the attention of the government away from fundamental issues in community development.

Not much is known, however – most especially outside Nigeria – about the work of AAPW. Our intervention projects are usually conducted under conditions of secrecy against the background of the belief that too much media coverage of a peace process can mess it up. The Nigerian government – at federal, state and local government levels – as well as the people of the conflict areas in which we have worked is however quite familiar with the achievements of the organisation. Some international organisations that have working relationships with AAPW are also familiar with the nature of our work. Such organisations include Responding to Conflict in Birmingham, in Britain; Nairobi Peace Initiative; Centre for Conflict Resolution, Cape Town in South Africa, the Community Board Programme in Illinois. The major funders of AAPW's projects include the British High Commission in Nigeria, the British Council, the United States Agency for International Development, ActionAid, and most recently the United States Institute of Peace (USIP).

AAPW makes and builds peace in Nigerian communities. It also engages in preventive diplomacy by monitoring early warning signs of community conflicts and taking appropriate steps to prevent their escalation into violence. The successes recorded by the organisation depend largely on the calibre and resourcefulness of its staff. AAPW is headed by an American woman with vast experience in intergroup dynamics and mediation, who is also a gifted conflict management trainer. The organisation further benefits from the experience of a retired major-general in the Nigerian army who is a professional strategist, as well as two research and intervention officers, both of whom are experts on conflict transformation. The four programme officers have brought our research experiences to bear, very powerfully, on the work of AAPW. The results have been remarkable. Programme officers' duties include evolving intervention strategies for conflict situations, carrying out action research, analysing the issues, parties and interests in a conflict situation, organising conflict resolution training and problem-solving workshops. The basic goal of AAPW is to help communities bedevilled by violent conflicts find solutions to their problems. The organisation does not pretend to have solutions to the problems of the people; what it basically does is to work with them with a view to enabling them to have a better understanding of their situation and as a result seek ways out of these problems.

The mediation work of the organisation is facilitated by members of the Nigerian Corps of Mediators (NCOM). Set up by AAPW in 1997, NCOM consists of a number of prominent Nigerians (retired ambassadors, state governors, local government chairmen, notable retired civil servants, etc.) who were trained in mediation processes with the support of Responding to Conflict from Birmingham. It must be mentioned, however, that before this training, most members of the corps have acquired vast practical experience on how to deal with violent conflicts in their respective professional callings. Three members of NCOM are retired career diplomats. One of them represented Nigeria at the United Nations. One of them is currently serving as the envoy of the UN Secretary General in a crisis-ridden part of Africa. Another member is a traditional ruler, while two others are former deputy governors in Nigeria. All members of NCOM are very influential in their localities and in the larger Nigerian society.

Before AAPW intervenes in any conflict (whether through conflict resolution training, problem-solving workshops or facilitated peace negotiation), it usually carries out *action research* into the conflict situation. These action researchers are usually different from those to be invited later to mediate in the conflict. The idea of leaving the task of conducting the research to an intake worker is not peculiar to the Nigerian situation under focus; it is a world-wide practice (Moore, 1996: 117), though some have argued that it is better for mediators to do such research. Conducting research is believed to have the potential of enabling the mediator to build rapport and credibility with the parties to the conflict. In the Nigerian situation, conducting research would overburden the professional mediators, many of whom, as I have mentioned earlier, are retirees. It is difficult for them to penetrate into the difficult terrains where young scholars might need to go to collect their data. Furthermore, the professional mediators have not been trained in the skills of conducting such fieldwork. AAPW therefore relies on the employment of young scholars in the social sciences and humanities for its action research.

This chapter will address the relevance of such action research for managing ethnic conflicts. It will also discuss how such research is done – how our research teams are constituted, the kind of data the researchers go after, their interdisciplinary and multidisciplinary methods of data collection, issues of values and ethics in the fieldwork; how the researchers analyse their data, and how the research is reported, reanalysed and used for managing conflicts. We shall also discuss the extent to which this kind of approach to conflict management has led to *positive peace* in Nigeria.

BASIC VERSUS APPLIED RESEARCH

Research can simply be defined as 'a systematic inquiry designed to further our knowledge and understanding of a subject' (Hult, 1996: 11). Stringer (1996: 51) sees it as 'systematic and rigorous inquiry or investigation that enables people to understand the nature of prob- lematic events or phenomena'. Reasons for conducting research vary from one person or situation, to the other. Research could be conducted to discover new information about people, objects or the environment; to update our knowledge of some situations and to interpret our experience most especially in the light of the experi- ences of others.

Within the framework of the foregoing, research can be broadly divided into two types: basic or pure research and applied or action research. The difference between the two is often difficult to establish because of their close relatedness. The focus of basic research is on 'understanding rather than the immediate solution to a problem' (Elmes et al., 1995: 444) while an applied research focuses on solving a practical problem (p.443). The focus in this presenta- tion is on the applied researcher who is also known variously as 'action researcher', 'analytical researcher', 'proactive researcher' in the existing literature. Most scholars refer to it interchangeably as action research. Stringer tried to shed light on the difference between basic and action research:

> A fundamental premise of community-based action research is that it commences with an interest in the problems of a group, a community, or an organization. Its purpose is to assist people in extending their understanding of their situation and thus resolve problems that confront them. Put another way, community-based action research provides a model for enacting local action-oriented approaches to inquiry, applying small-scale theorizing to specific problems in specific situations ... Traditional research projects are complete when a report has been written and presented to the contracting agency or published in an academic journal. Community-based action research can have these purely academic

outcomes, and may provide the basis for rich and profound theorizing and basic knowledge production, *but its primary purpose is as a practical tool for solving problems experienced by people in their professional, community or private lives. If an action research does not make a difference, in a very specific way, for Practitioners and/or their clients, then it has failed to achieve its objectives.* [Stringer, 1996: 9–11, original emphasis]

For Hubbard, applied research 'focuses on matters which are not merely of "academic interest"' by responding to the needs of the broader community and attempting 'to provide information which is relevant to the existing reality outside the university environment' (1993: 204). The basic researcher is interested in knowing largely as an academic exercise. Their goal is to expand the frontiers of knowledge. The action researcher on the other hand, seeks to know as a first step to generating ideas on intervention. Action researchers apply the tools of anthropology and other disciplines to the practical resolution of social problems (Goodenough, 1963; Lewin, 1946).

Basic research and applied or action research coexist in some cases. The data, theoretical inductions and concepts from basic research could become useful information for the action researcher. Without the data of the basic researcher, 'the applied researcher would soon dry up and sputter to a halt, unless applied researchers become of necessity basic researchers' (Elmes et al., 1995: 46). Writing in similar vein, Datta noted:

The distinction between 'basic' and 'applied' research is not always clear. The textbook definition of basic research stands for a kind of theoretical investigation the relevance of which may not be manifest, while applied social research is said to be policy-related and empirically-based – of a sort that has direct and immediate usefulness ... Is there, however, an inherent contradiction between the two? Can these be divided into watertight compartments? With reference to a specific point of a research scenario, can we pronounce authoritatively: Applied research stops at this point: from here basic research takes over? In addressing these questions, I would like to argue that the notion of basic research is not merely one of theory or concept. It should also comprise a contribution to the methodology including research design and that very inter- esting area which brings together consideration of methodology and of philosophical questions, viz. interpretation. In this broad sense, almost every piece of applied social research has in-built components of basic research. [Datta, 1993: 19–20]

Applied research has close semblance to what Majchrzak described as 'social policy research' which he defined as a 'process of conducting research on, or analysis of, fundamental social problem in order to provide policymakers with pragmatic, action-orientated recommendations, for alleviating the problem' (1984: 21).

This kind of research is usually carried out by researchers who work with the government or development agencies. Many academics, doing applied, action or social policy research started first as basic researchers before becoming what they are as a result of the demands of their work. The author is one of those few Nigerian scholars that has found himself integrating both the basic and applied research in the desperate attempt to generate ideas on how to deal constructively with violent community conflicts.

THE ROLE OF APPLIED RESEARCH IN CONFLICT MANAGEMENT

In developing a systemic view of peace-building and conflict resolution, the Institute of Multi-track Diplomacy (IMTD) has recommended that peace works be approached from nine different perspectives or 'tracks':

(1) government,
(2) non-governmental/professional organisations,
(3) business,
(4) private citizen,
(5) research, training and education,
(6) activism,
(7) religion,
(8) funding and
(9) communication.

Each of these nine tracks, as Diamond and McDonald noted 'represents a world unto itself, with its own philosophy and perspective, purpose, language, attitudes, activities, diversities, culture, and membership' (1996: 5). Research, training and education belong to the fifth track. Track Five is therefore aimed at promoting peace through learning. The primary goal here is:

... to generate and transfer information about issues of peace and conflict, peacemaking and conflict resolution, and to suggest policy or action implications arising from that information. The assumption is that the more we study and learn, the more capable we are of collectively and concretely doing something about the enormous problems that face the planet. Another is that alternative ways of resolving conflict are possible. Moreover, in order to change the world, we must begin by educating people ... Track Five is the brain of the system; it serves as the intellect or mind function for the whole. It analyses, synthesizes, and produces information for the rest of the system – information on which the rest of the system depends ... The positive aspect of Track Five is the wealth and richness of its contribution to the whole system. Brilliant minds are probing complex and intricate issues and finding, discovering, uncovering and creating powerful and useful insights and information that can be translated into action that is beneficial to the world community. [Diamond and McDonald, 1996: 70]

The first step in Track Five is researching into the conflict situation. Research initiatives are often fired by researchers' troubled feelings about an observation or experience. They want to know why certain things are happening around them and what could be done. They are most particularly interested in knowing more about things and processes that challenge their existing ideas or vision of life. If what researchers have observed or experienced is complimentary, they ask themselves the question 'how can the situation be sustained or further improved upon?' But if uncomplimentary, researchers channel their energy towards understanding why and how the problematic situation can be reversed.

Nigerian experience shows that action research sheds light on six important aspects of a conflict situation.

The True Identity of the Parties to the Conflict

Action research unearths the true identity of the parties to the conflict. Parties to a conflict can be divided into two main categories: the primary parties and the shadow figures or 'stakeholders'. The primary parties are those that directly participate in the physical violence. They kill and are killed. Media reports on the conflict often focus on them. Unlike the primary parties who are well known, the identity of shadow figures or stakeholders in a conflict are usually hidden. They therefore prefer to operate behind the scene directing the primary parties on how to respond to the conflict situation. The terms 'shadow figures' or 'stakeholders' here refer to the people or group behind the primary parties who have a stake in the causes, courses or outcome of the violent conflict. Researchers need to identify these stakeholders in their work because no sustainable peace agreements can be worked out without including their interests and needs in any consideration. They supply the combatants with moral, ideological and financial support. It is sometimes possible to stop the physical violence by ensuring that these stakeholders withhold their support to the combatants.

In the Ife–Modakeke conflict, the shadow figures were found to have included, on the side of the Modakeke, the *Alafin* (leader) of Oyo (Oba Lamidi Adeyemi) and on the Ife side, the *Ashipa* (leader) of Oyo (the late Chief Amuda Olurunosebi). The *Alafin* supported the Modakekes for two main reasons. First, the Modakekes are Oyo migrants in Ile-Ife. It therefore behoves the *Alafin* to protect his subjects against 'external aggression' but it was difficult for him to do this publicly. Second, the *Ooni* (leader) of Ife and the *Alafin* of Oyo are the most estranged traditional rulers in Nigeria. Since the early twentieth century, the occupants of the two offices have been contesting supremacy as the custodian of the Yoruba political and cultural traditions. It is therefore in the interest of the *Alafin* that the peace of the *Ooni*'s domain be *disturbed* by the Modakekes. The Modakekes would not take any major political decision without consulting the *Alafin*. On the other side, the Ife people were supported in their struggles against the Modakeke by the *Ashipa* of Oyo for one major reason. Though an Oyo Chief, the *Ashipa* was (until his murder in 1997) an avowed enemy of the *Alafin*. It was therefore in his interest to make the *Alafin*'s friends his own enemies and *Alafin*'s enemies his own friends. He therefore provided the *Ooni* with all moral support needed for fighting the *Alafin boys* in Ife territory (namely the Modakeke's). The implication of identifying these shadow figures or stakeholders is to build up a good knowledge of the many interests and personalities that the conflict managers might have to take into consideration in their peace process. For example, any peace agreement struck with the Modakeke people by the Ifes that do not enjoy the support of the *Alafin* might not be sustainable since the Modakekes defer to his good judgement in many things.

Apart from the specific situations that we mentioned concerning the Ife–Modakeke crisis, shadow parties/stakeholders in community conflicts in Nigeria are usually dominated by retired military officers and politicians. The army officers, whether serving or retired, are seen as achievers in their community. Their opinions therefore carry heavy weight in the community. These military men often reside outside their communities. They come home occasionally to help the communities analyse their problems and to provide the necessary support for the violent struggle. The politicians on the other hand also help members of the communities to reinterpret or analyse their conflicts. They often ally themselves with one particular side in the conflict and in the process help to further divide the people.

The History and Structure of the Conflict

The action researcher operating in the field of conflict management performs the role of helping the conflict manager to understand the history and structure of the conflict. That is, the researcher helps to put the significant events in the conflict in a proper time perspective. This is with a view to identifying the stage in the interaction between the parties at which the conflict occurred, and the stage at which the conflict escalated into violence. The structure of a conflict, as Druckman noted, is composed of 'the sources of differences between individuals and groups' (1993: 251). What are the primary and secondary issues in the conflict? This author has always assumed that there are three major causes of community conflicts: inadequate resources (which necessitate unhealthy competition), conflicting value systems (most especially when the people are intolerant) and psychological needs of individuals and groups (most especially when the environment is stressful). Druckman (1993: 25–9) put this differently. According to him, violent conflicts can be caused by conflicting interests, understanding of the conflict environment and ideological differences. An action researcher must try as much as possible to clearly articulate how these serve as a catalyst to the conflict.

The Processes of the Conflict

The third function of the action researcher is that of identifying and analysing the processes of the conflict. The researcher addresses the extent to which the parties to the conflict have been tough, soft or moderate in how they go about the conflict. In other words, the researcher needs to paint a vivid picture of the power relations of the parties. Which of the parties has power over the other, what is the source of such power (resources, information, access to decision makers, political influence, moral authority, population size, etc.); and how is such power being mobilised in the conflict situation? What arguments or languages do the parties use for articulating their positions, interests and needs? Are the parties constantly adjusting their positions as situations demand, or are they static in their demands?

The Processes that Led to the Use of Violence

The fourth function of the action researcher is that of shedding light on the conflict processes and behaviour. This refers to the strategies used by the parties in the conflict. The researcher must be able to account for the processes that led to the use of violence. Several conflicts around the world have escalated into violence just because those in position of authority failed to take the right action at the right time. When should action be taken to resolve a conflict? Is it when the conflict is still at the latent stage or when it had escalated into full-blown violence? These are questions which the researcher must address.

In one of his works, Professor William Zartman noted that internal conflicts usually unfold in four different phases, each of which had specific opportunities for de-escalating the ugly situation. The four phases are those of articulation, mobilisation, insurgency and warfare. He elaborated on these:

> The first phase is one of cultural protest led by groups of educated elites petitioning the government for political reform with political means. Such groups express many different and specific grievances and expect redress. The second phase ... involves the formation of a single movement led by charismatic organizers who seek to unite the disparate groups and force the attention of the government to the grievances by means of coercive civil action. The third or insurgent phase turns from political to violent means of pressure through a mass movement with a more ideological and action-oriented leadership that contests the ability and legitimacy of the government to meet its demands. In the fourth phase direct military confrontation is used to overthrow the government or to secede from the state, with a leadership drawn from the field. [Zartman, 1995: 13–14].

Action researchers must be able to identify which stage of the conflict has been reached at the time of their research and the path to that stage. For example, why have the parties taken up arms against each other and not resolved the conflict at the stage of articulation or mobilisation? Is it because all past attempts at resolving the conflict were not welcomed by one of the parties? Which of the parties seem to be taking a hard line? What are the interests and needs of this hardliner? Is the hardline position a consensus in the group or the handiwork of a few individuals? Is the failure in past peace efforts due to the inability of the interveners to do a good job? All these questions must be carefully answered by the action-researcher, so that those who will be using the resulting report for their interventions will know the kind of challenges and opportunities that await them.

Provide Information

The fifth role of action researchers is that of providing the information that will help their readers to understand the context of the conflict. By 'context', as Druckman noted, we are referring 'both to broad systemic influences and to more immediate interventions in conflict by third parties' (1993: 35). This author's field experiences in Nigeria have shown that what is reportedly responsible for a conflict is sometimes not the entire picture necessary to understand the violent situation. There are sometimes factors or parties apparently remote to the conflict which have to be put in the proper perspective. It is necessary to know the domestic, regional and international politics shaping the conflict. It is also necessary to know whether the conflict is a genuine entity in its own right or merely a symptom of other unresolved problems in the larger society. Some of the community conflicts in contemporary Nigerian society have been found to be due to social, economic and political stress. The researcher must shed bright light on these contexts of conflict, as a way of building up an inclusive picture of the conflict, so that the intervener can take them into consideration in their analysis of the problems.

Develop Strategies for Dealing with the Conflict

The sixth and final role expected of action researchers is for them to use their field experiences to guide possible interveners towards strategies for dealing with the conflict. As researchers, they are better educated about the conflict situation and environment than others. They must be able to state in their work whether the conflict is escalating or stabilising and why. Are the issues moving from specific to general? What chances are there for immediate intervention in the conflict? Which intervention approaches are best suited for which kind of conflict?

PROCESSES OF THE RESEARCH

Every research – whether basic or applied – has four stages: conception, deskwork, fieldwork and report writing. The emphasis in this chapter is how the fieldwork is done, that is, how the data for writing the research report is collected. Data for an action research can be collected through direct observation (participant or non-participant observation), review of secondary literature and interviews. We need to elaborate more on the interview methods. Unlike the collection of documentary evidence and the use of observation which can be generalised, interviews are usually conducted with prominent individuals in the society. Such people often exert power in that society and are selected for interview because of the amount of oral information at their disposal. To this extent, identifying the informant is usually an important task in the fieldwork.

There are three major approaches for identifying useful informants in a warring community: 'positional approach', 'reputational approach' and 'decision-making approach' (Moore, 1996: 118–120). Positional approach involves the researcher selecting for interview those who occupy key formal positions of authority in the community. These people are often assumed to be those charting the direction which the community conflict has been taking. We found this to be misleading in some Nigerian communities. Some of the traditional rulers in the communities are actually *not* in charge. The leadership of the conflict had literally been hijacked by some hardliners who hitherto had little significance in the communities. The chiefs in such a community even defer to the 'good judgement' of these hardliners as a way of not being labelled as a saboteur of the ongoing revolution in their community. A researcher using the second approach (that is, the reputational approach) for identifying their informants will normally interview people considered to have the appropriate reputation in the community. This hardline category of people could have become very prominent in the community as a result of their hardline stance in the conflict or in terms of the degree of their losses. The third approach, that is, the decision-making approach, places emphasis on the identification of people who were previously involved in decision making on how to deal with the conflict in the past. This approach assumes that if such people are contacted they might supply information that could guide the mediators to identify the ground upon which something else could be built. The research questions that researchers set for themselves will dictate which of these approaches to be used and when. Information can be collected from any of these people using focused, non-focused, structured or non-structured interviews.

It is, however, necessary for the action researcher to see the conflict environment as a lawless society where anything could happen. A person undertaking research in a violently divided society is like a peacekeeper who could get hurt in the process of bringing peace to others. Researchers therefore need to think carefully before launching themselves into the field: they need to ask themselves a number of questions. Do they have the resources (contacts, language, dressing patterns, observance of traditional ethical codes, etc.) to successfully work in the conflict area? Does the researcher really know the conflict environment? Can they do the work alone or go to the field with people familiar with the conflict environment? Do they actually understand how the parties in the conflict perceive themselves in relation to others? If so, are they well equipped to avoid doing things that could ignite the anger of his interviewees?

In summary, there are two problems involved in investigating violence in a divided society. The first is acceptability of the researcher to those being researched and the second is the personal biases of the researcher. Can the researchers achieve neutrality in their assessment of problems that have kept the society divided for that long? What hope of objectivity is there in such research? Writing on the implications of personal biases and acceptability of the researcher, Shipman noted, 'In practice, the personal involvement of the scientist in the issues he investigates increases as they become of pressing public concern. It is not just that the scientist will be exposed to personal as well as professional criticism, but that attacks on his personal motives for undertaking the work will be extended to challenge his competence as a scientist' (1981: 35). Since win–lose expectations characterise all conflict environments, each of the parties to a conflict situation will always want to see itself reported to be right and its perspective to be the most morally defensible in the conflict situation. The success of the research therefore tends to be assessed by parties to the conflict from the perspective of the extent to which their particular interests are protected.

Researchers have different ways of dealing with the question of validity and objectivity in their work. The author's research team usually includes people from the conflict area, but the team leader is usually drawn from outside the conflict area. Each of the co-researchers advises the lead researcher on their own people. This usually enables the informants to speak freely during interviews on the assumption that their own person in the research team is unlikely to engage in anything that could injure the interests of his or her own people. The role of the lead researcher is to ensure that the collection of the research data and their analysis is conducted in a scientific rather than a sentimental way.

In the author's experience of data collection, the aim is to ensure that all shades of opinions are listened to and all perspectives are represented in the research report. Where it is safe to do so, the researchers present judgements and conclusions; where it is dangerous to do so, they simply present their data and leave the reader to form their own opinion on the situation.

In order to ensure the validity of the information available to him, the researcher must be prepared to triangulate data. By triangulation I mean the procedure whereby researchers judge the validity of the data by the extent to which different and contrasting methods of data collection yield similar findings on similar research subjects (Denzin, 1989b; Bloor, 1997: 37–50). Researchers could, for example, try to confirm the validity of oral information with some archival or ethnographic sources. The main goal of triangulation is to reduce measurement biases in a research.

Researchers must also try to get to the *heart of the matter*. Consequently, they need to go beyond a mere collection of positional statements from informants; they must dig deep into unravelling the interests and needs of the parties to the conflict. By positional statement I mean what each party says they want. This is different from what they *must have*. In fieldwork in Ile-Ife, for example, people said 'The Modakekes are ingrates. They must move away from our community. We can no longer live with them.' This perspective was noted but was not taken as all that could be known. Researchers explored further in order to identify the interest of the Ife people. They sought to know why the Modakekes were being accused of ingratitude. Why are the Ifes saying they must be expelled from Ile-Ife? The answers were: 'We welcomed the Modakekes here in the early nineteenth century. No sooner had they settled down among us, when they started launching military attacks on us, trying to claim our land. We want to regain the control of our land.' What was revealed here was the interest of the informants. In order to understand the informant's needs, other questions were asked: 'But the Ifes constitute the majority in Ifeland and the Modakekes are not claiming that they own Ife. As a senior partner in this relationship, why can't the Ifes try to work out a peaceful way of resolving this conflict?' The answer from the Ifes was: 'We can tolerate the Modakekes only on the condition that they are prepared to keep paying us [the Ife people] tenant rates for their farmland and are prepared to subordinate themselves to our king, the Ooni of Ife. We cannot tolerate a situation in which they want to turn a Ward [a stranger settlement] in Ife into an independent town. If they want autonomy let them go elsewhere.' This statement clearly unveiled the needs of the Ife people and shows that they are prepared to tolerate the Modakekes on some negotiable conditions which in the conflict situation it might not be easy to articulate. In conflict situations, people often hide their needs and endlessly rearticulate their positions. Those who therefore take the positional statement (for example, 'the Modakekes must go away from Ile-Ife') of conflicting parties too seriously, might find it difficult to resolve the conflict. It is essential that the action researcher helps the intervener get as close to the needs of the parties as possible.

In the urgent efforts to get at the position, interest and needs of the informant, researchers must not lose sight of the context in which they are operating. They need to ask themselves: who actually is this informant? The informant or respondent must be identified by social characteristics that are significant to the purpose of the research. For example, the researcher needs to know the gender, age, occupation and length of the respondent's residence in the neighbourhood. The failure to take any of these variables into consideration could result in the researcher being misled in their conclusions.

Fieldwork in a violent society is best done within a multidisciplinary framework. The research data are best collected using the qualitative research methods such as acquisition of archival records, participant observation, interviews, and ethno-methodology, etc. As Cuba and Cocking noted, qualitative data often lead the researcher towards revealing patterns – typical ways in which things happen in complex behavioural settings (1997: 105). Qualitative analysis often gives the reader a sense of having a direct experience and understanding of the social setting which the researcher wishes to reveal. Qualitative research methods are therefore usually targeted at the following:

- Identifying the variation in response to a phenomenon (for example, the roles of individuals as different from those of groups in a conflict situation)
- The stages in a process (for example, stages of latent conflict, open disagreement and violent encounters in a conflict situation)
- The social organisation of specific groups or settings (for example, how stakeholders outside a conflict environment control the conflict process externally). [Cuba and Cocking, 1997: 104]

Focus group discussions are usually taken as an important element of qualitative technique of data collection. This method is difficult to employ when researching a violent society since researchers will find it extremely difficult, if not impossible, to bring the two sides from the conflicted society together for the purpose of being jointly interviewed about the conflict situation. The parties can, however, be interviewed separately. Focus group discussion also can only be employed where the data to be collected are from third parties to the conflict or whilst the process of conflict resolution training or problem solving for the parties to the conflict is ongoing.

PREPARATION AND USE OF THE RESEARCH REPORT

A research project is not complete until the research is written up. This is as arduous a task as that of conceiving the research and doing the fieldwork. Researchers must make sure that what they write reflects an accurate picture of the conflict situation. They must not be subjective in the interpretation of data. Their conclusions must be borne out of concrete evidence and sound reasoning. The question that researchers must keep asking themselves as they write is: Can I defend the positions that I have taken in this paper? Do I have concrete evidence for backing what I am saying? Even in a situation where researchers have enough evidence to back what they are saying, they could still employ euphemisms to describe what is obviously a bad situation so as not to offend and alienate the affected party. Of course, while doing this, the facts of the case must not be misrepresented. A group may have killed members of the other groups in ways that suggest that they could be said to be lacking in humanitarian feelings. Rather than using negative adjective to describe the situation, the researcher could merely provide the figure of people killed, how they were killed and the public opinion about such events. Some euphemisms or other strategies might be necessary for explaining bad situations in a violently divided society. This is necessary because, as part of the peacemaking and peace-building efforts, the parties to the conflict might read the research report. The language of the researcher could prejudice the work of those trying to mediate in the conflict.

We can illustrate the point made above with a very recent example. From 8 to 10 February 1999, AAPW was in Jos, Plateau State organising a workshop for members of the peace support network which AAPW established in some Nigerian communities. As the meeting was going on, AAPW received a letter from a prominent citizen of one of the communities being studied. He wrote to complain about how the researchers that worked on the conflict in his community used some pejorative adjectives to depict the actions of his people in the conflict. He was of the opinion that the archival documents on the conflict were interpreted in a manner that suggested that the researchers were biased. He therefore accused the researchers of partisanship and threatened legal action should the research report be published before the offensive adjectives were removed. He was a typical hardliner in the conflict; however, when the team took another look at the researchers' report, his position could be appreciated. Though minor, when the mistakes in the paper were re-examined against the background of the complaints received, it became clear that the researchers' mistakes were indeed grievous. The mistakes had to be corrected – not only for moral reasons but also because the complainant was one of the hardliners expected at the problem-solving workshop planned for his conflict-prone community. If his genuine interests were not satisfied before the workshop he could incite members of his community, expected at the workshop, to be less prepared to compromise.

So as not to be seen to be taking sides or saying things that are not true, action researchers in the field of conflict management must try as much as possible to avoid the use of ambiguous statements in research papers. The language in which the paper is written must be clear and precise. The report must be written in a manner that makes it to be accessible to both professional practitioners and lay persons. It must not be shrouded in the mists of technical languages and complex statistical procedures that often characterise traditional scientific research reports (Stringer, 1996: 151).

Every research report that is completed by AAPW is usually given to a number of internal reviewers within AAPW and some external consultants drawn from the universities in Nigeria. These assessors include both the mainstream academic researchers and conflict management practitioners. The usual practice is for each of them to carefully go through the paper and criticise it from their different perspectives. The first draft is therefore sent back to the researchers for revision. Once the revised copy of the research report is considered good enough, members of the management board of AAPW meet to take a closer look at the issues in the conflict as well as the fears and needs of the parties. This usually helps to determine the kind of people that could be invited to intervene in the conflict. The ethnic, religious and professional background of every member of the Nigerian Corps of Mediators is carefully taken into consideration as efforts are made to identify the right calibre of mediators for the conflict. Once the mediators are identified, they are immediately invited for a Case Study Analysis Meeting. At this meeting, researchers who studied the conflict are asked to present their analysis for the benefit of the mediators at the meeting. The case study is carefully analysed by the mediators. The issues in the conflict, the parties, the fears and needs of the parties and possible intervention mechanisms are carefully outlined. A time-line is also set for the intervention project. All intervention programmes of AAPW take this general pattern.

As noted earlier, there is usually a variety of intervention mechanisms that could be used in a violent society such as Nigeria: conflict resolution training, problem-solving workshops, conciliation, mediation, arbitration, etc. The intervention methods most favoured by AAPW are those that enable the parties to the conflict to have effective control over the process of conflict resolution: these are conflict resolution training, problem-solving workshops and mediation.

Conflict resolution training is aimed at combining a range of elements: a raising of awareness (that is, educating people about conflict) with the imparting of skills for dealing with it (Schultz, 1989); teaching problem solving, which is also known to some scholars as 'inter-active problem solving' (Kelman, 1986); 'third party consultations' (Fisher, 1983) or 'collaborative, analytical problem-solving' (Mitchell and Banks, 1991), which enables representatives in a conflict 'to interact in an analytical rather than coercive manner as well as giving scholarly insights into the parties' mutual predicament' (Mitchell, 1993: 78). A main plank of the approach is to eliminate negative stereotypes held by parties in conflict situations about each other and help to rehumanise their relationships. By learning together how to respond to conflict, the parties to the conflict are made to realise that they can actually solve their problems by themselves. Writing on conflict management training, generally, Rothman noted *inter alia*: 'As with education for critical thinking, conflict management training is designed to help parties clarify their own epistemologies and question their own assumptions about conflict in ways that lead to enhanced creativity and imagination in planning for its management' (1992: 75).

Against the background of the foregoing, AAPW usually starts their intervention programmes with conflict resolution training, especially for young people. The intervention in the Tiv–Jukun crisis in Wukari was started by organising conflict resolution training for the young people who had served as combatants in the conflict. It was agreed by all interviewed during the fieldwork, that they were the most important people in the conflict. The researchers were told that once the cooperation of the combatants was enlisted, tension would recede. The youth were trained in Jos, Plateau State some hundreds of kilometres from the war front. Another conflict resolution training session was organised for the community and local government leaders in Wukari. This was followed by a problem-solving workshop for selected members of the community. Much has been achieved in this community and almost all the issues in the conflict have been amicably resolved. The intervention programme in Tafawa Balewa in Bauchi State and Zango Kataf in Kaduna State took a very similar pattern. In Ife-Modakeke, the intervention programme began with conflict resolution training for women, community-based organisations and secondary school teachers. This enabled AAPW to reach the elders and traditional chieftains, including the *Ooni* of Ife and the *Ogunsua* of Modakeke, in the community. AAPW has since conducted problem-solving workshops for the youth leaders and elders in the warring communities. The peace process in Wukari is still ongoing.

At the end of the workshops in each of these communities, AAPW usually constitute the participants into a Peace Support Network which subsequently monitors the peace process in the community. In Ugep, Cross Rivers State and Igbo-Ora in Oyo State, the members of the Peace Support Network took charge of the peace process after the conflict resolution workshop was organised for them. In Ugep, the people constituted themselves into Yakurr Peace Committee, while in Igbo-Ora the people constituted themselves into the Igbo-Ora Peace Monitoring Committee. The achievements of these two organisations are noteworthy and could be usefully emulated by other conflict-prone communities. They did not wait for any external interveners. Once they acquired the skills for dealing with their problems, they started working and the communities now have what could be described as sustainable peace.

In April 1998, the British High Commission in Lagos, which has been the greatest single funder of the intervention programmes of AAPW, commissioned an external assessor to evaluate the activities of AAPW and assess their impact and effectiveness. The evaluator, Dr Robert Dodd of ActionAid in Britain, traversed a distance of over 4,000 kilometres (Dodd, 1998: 2) meeting the people of the various Nigerian communities where AAPW had worked. In his report, the evaluator Dr Dodd noted *inter alia*:

> Over the years AA [ActionAid] has built up considerable expertise in peace and conflict analysis and has augmented its skills by drawing on the experience of specialist institutions and individuals within Nigeria and through international contacts ... During 1996–97 AA carried out over 30 workshops throughout the country and provided training in conflict management to around 1,500 individuals. This was an impressive achievement by any standards. The workshops are much appreciated. Several people, some of whom described themselves as former fanatics, told the evaluator that they had been surprised that techniques for conflict resolution even existed. What they learned during the workshops was that it was possible for antagonists on both sides of a conflict to hold legitimate grievances and that these differences could, with care, be reconciled without recourse to violence. Conflict management was of overriding importance, they said, and peace was preferable to conflict. It was clear, therefore, that the combined content, form and presentation of the workshops had been highly successful and that they had an impact on the way that people thought about conflict and peace. In particular was the diffusion and dissemination of values which would lead to conflict avoidance and to peace-building. [Dodd, 1998: 51]

Commenting on the contribution of research to the work of AAPW, Dr Dodd noted:

> An important component of AA's work is the documentation and analysis of community conflicts in various parts of Nigeria. These are undertaken by people who generally have an academic background and who have an understanding of peace and conflict issues. These case studies are of a high order and their analyses offer valuable insights into the root causes of the disputes ... The documentation of community conflicts in Nigeria represents an important contribution to the understanding of disputes. It provides AA staff with an authoritative base on which to work and will be an invaluable resource for the Peace and Conflict Centre at the University of Ibadan. Continued British Council/BHC support to these initiatives will be important to the wider aims of conflict management. [Dodd, 1998: 71, 13]

The activities of AAPW take the normal pattern of defining the problems in conflict-prone communities; then the context of the conflicts in the society is explored and the analyses are carefully completed before intervening in any community conflict in Nigeria. Action research plays a key role in all these activities preceding conflict management. Finally, the staff of AAPW was particularly trained to do action research. There are very few universities around the world that provide training in what is considered to be a luxury. Until 1996, when this author formally joined AAPW, his academic works in the field of urban violence (Albert et al., 1994; 1996) were produced, not from an action research practitioner's point of view, but from a *basic* research approach. Now, both basic and action research are used. Many action researchers such as the author, whether in the field of peace and conflict studies or in the fields of development, found themselves using action research approaches out of necessity, without prior training. However, action research can and must be taught to students of peace and conflict in order to empower them to affect people's lives positively in violently divided societies. Those developing curricula in this area will hopefully find the AAPW's experience quite instructive.

REFERENCES

Albert, I.O. et al. (eds) (1994) *Urban Management and Urban Violence in Africa* (Ibadan: Institut Francais de Recherche en Afrique – IFRA).

Albert, I.O. et al. (1996) *Informal Channels for Conflict Resolution in Ibadan, Nigeria* (Ibadan: IFRA).

Albert, I.O. (1996) *Women and Urban Violence in Kano, Nigeria* (Ibadan: Spectrum Books).

Albert, I.O. (1999) *The Task of Community Peace Works in Nigeria*, Report on the Workshop for the Peace Support Network organised by Academic Associates PeaceWorks at New Jos Hotel, 8–10 February (Lagos: Academic Associates Peace Works).

Bloor, M. (1997) 'Techniques of validation in qualitative research: A critical commentary', in Gale Miller and Robert Dingwall (eds), *Context and Method in Qualitative Research* (London: Sage Publications Ltd).

Cuba, L. and Cocking, J. (1997) *How to Write about the Social Sciences* (Essex: Longman).

Datta, A. (1993) 'National integration and development: Paradigm of an interface between basic and applied social research in Namibia', in K.K. Prah (ed.), *Social Science Research Priorities for Namibia* (Dakar: CODESRIA).

Denzin, N.K. (1989a) *Interpretive Interactionism*, Newbury Park (Thousand Oaks, CA: Sage).

Denzin, N. (1989b) *The Research Act: A Theoretical Introduction to Sociological Methods*, 3rd edn, (Englewood Cliffs, NJ: Prentice Hall).

Diamond, L. and McDonald, J. (1996) *Multi-Track Diplomacy: A Systemic Approach to Peace* (West Hartford, CT: Kumarian Press).

Dodd, R. (1998) *Evaluation of the British High Commission Conflict Management Programme in Nigeria* (Lagos: ActionAid).

Druckman, D. (1993) 'An analytical research agenda for conflict and conflict resolution', in Dennis J.D. Sandole and Hugo van der Merwe (eds), *Conflict Resolution Theory and Practice. Integration and Application* (Manchester and New York: Manchester University Press).

Elmes, D.G., Kantowitz, B.H. and Roediger III, H.L. (1995) *Research Methods in Psychology*, 5th edn (St. Paul, MN: West Publishing Company).

Fisher, R.J. (1983) 'Third party consultation as a method of conflict resolution: A review of studies', *Journal of Conflict Resolution*, vol. 27, pp. 301–34.

Goodenough, W. (1963) *Cooperation in change: An anthropological approach to community development* (New York: Russell Sage Foundation).

Hamilton, D. (1998) 'Traditions, preferences, and postures in applied qualitative research', in Norinan K. Denzin and Yvonna S. Lincoln (eds), *The Landscape of Qualitative Research: Theories and Issues* (Thousand Oaks, CA: Sage).

Heron, J. (1996) *Co-operative Inquiry: Research into the Human Condition* (London: Sage).

Hubbard, D. (1993) 'Gender research approaches and structures', in K.K. Prah (ed.), *Social Science Research Priorities for Namibia* (Dakar: CODESRIA).

Hult, A.C. (1996) *Researching and Writing the Social Sciences* (Needham Heights, MA: Simon and Schuster).

Keeton, M. and Tate, P. (1978) *Learning by experience – What, why, how* (San Franscisco: Jossey Bass).

Kelman, H.C. (1986) 'Interactive problem-solving: A social-psychological approach to conflict resolution', in W. Klassen (ed.), *Dialogue toward inter-*

faith understanding (Jerusalem: Tantur Ecumenical Institute for Theological Research).

Lederach, J.P. (1995) *Building Peace: Sustainable Reconciliation in Divided Societies* (Tokyo: The United Nations University).

Lewin, K. (1946) 'Action research and minority problems', *Journal of Social Issues*, vol. 2, pp. 34–46.

Majchrzak, A. (1984) *Methods for Policy Research* (Thousand Oaks, CA: Sage).

May, T. (1997) *Social Research: Issues, Methods and Process* (Buckingham: Open University Press).

Miller, G. and Dingwall, R. (1997) *Context and Method in Qualitative Research* (London: Sage).

Mitchell, C.R. (1993) 'Problem-solving exercises and theories of conflict resolution', in Dennis J.D. Sandole and Hugo van der Merwe (eds), *Conflict Resolution Theory and Practice: Integration and Application* (Manchester and New York: Manchester University Press).

Mitchell, C.R. and Banks, M. (eds) (1991) *Handbook of Conflict Resolution – The Analytical Problem-Solving Approach* (London and New York: Pinter).

Moore, C.W. (1996) *The Mediation Process: Practical Strategies for Resolving Conflict* (San Francisco: Jossey-Bass).

Otite, O. and Albert, I.O. (eds) (1999) *Community Conflicts in Nigeria: Resolution, Management and Transformation* (Ibadan: Spectrum Books).

Rothman, J. (1992) *From confrontation to cooperation. Resolving ethnic and regional conflict* (London: Sage).

Schultz, A. (1989) 'Concept and Theory formation in the social sciences', in J. Bynner and K. Stribley (eds), *Social Research: Principles and Procedures* (Harlow: Longman).

Shipman, M. (1981) *The Limitation of Social Research* (London and New York: Longman).

Stringer, E.T. (1996) *Action Research: A Handbook for Practitioners* (Thousand Oaks, CA, London, New Delhi: Sage).

Zartman, I.W. (1995) 'Dynamics and constraints in negotiation in internal conflicts', in I. William Zartman (ed.), *Elusive Peace: Negotiating an End to Civil Wars* (Washington, DC: The Brookings Institute).

Zuber-Skerritt, O. (1992) *Action Research in Higher Education* (London: Kogan Page).

7 Researching Ethnic Conflict in Post-Soviet Central Asia

Anara Tabyshalieva

This chapter presents an overview of some peculiarities of research in Central Asia. There are different factors which in their various ways make conflict research in the region complex. The identified parameters show just the rough picture of constraints for researchers. For example, double standards not only make conflict research difficult; they can also cause conflict itself. Finally, the application of double standards across the region makes it unlikely that researchers of different nationality, ethnicity, gender, age and so on would produce similar results.

FROM 'UNDISPUTED' SOCIETY TO ... DISPUTES

For a long time, the 'camp mentality' that divided the world into insiders and outsiders helped to mobilise hundreds of nationalities of the Soviet empire into a 'new community of the Soviet people'. Nowadays, the post-Soviet establishments of Central Asia are using old tools of this Soviet legacy by emphasising ethnic supremacy.

Many of the region's current problems can be attributed to decades of Soviet rule. For instance, the creation of the Central Asian national republics has provided the underlying framework of current conflicts. One of the results of Moscow's 'benign' policies is today's territorial boundaries, which many in the region would like to change. This problem has its roots in the Soviet 'divide and rule' policy, manifested in the boundary demarcations made nearly sixty years ago. Having little knowledge of the region, the Soviets divided Central Asia among the region's five largest groups, which were previously united by tribe, territory and Muslim religion rather than ethnicity. Central Asians were encouraged to develop ethnic cultures that would replace their tribal and Muslim identity. The region was artificially divided into two major areas, the first one consisting of Kazakhstan and the second one incorporating the rest of Central Asia. Meanwhile, the officially pronounced proletarian internationalism aimed at developing a monolithic Soviet society existed mainly on paper. Now that Moscow's hand has weakened, it is not surprising that ethnic conflicts have flared up, as previously the repressive Soviet apparatus prevented their emergence.

During the Soviet period, Stalin (as well as Krushchev and Brezhnev) deported various peoples to Central Asia, which further changed the region from a relatively homogenous to a multi-ethnic and multi-religious area. Relations between natives and Slavs were complex and confused due to the rhetoric of Soviet propaganda, which created an illusion of equality of all people under the Kremlin's leadership. The rigid hierarchy of the Soviet system enforced divisions among ethnic groups throughout the USSR. Russians were often given the best positions, while the natives of the 14 non-Russian republics were usually not allowed to advance. In the local capitals of Central Asia, indigenous peoples comprised the minority of the population. This demographic imbalance was especially true in Kazakhstan and Kyrgyzstan, where Russians dominated many of the key positions in the country's intellectual and industrial life. The use of non-Russian languages was severely restricted.

Ethnic and religious coexistence of numerous groups is a current issue in the newly independent states, which so far seem to be ill-prepared to deal with the kind of diversity brought about after the sudden collapse of the empire. Under Soviet rule, the centrally controlled administrative and military apparatus enforced ethnic stability, suppressing any ethnic or religious conflict. However, with disintegration of the USSR, such forces have vanished and the Central Asian republics have been left to their own devices. Inexperience and reliance on old methods has led to strife and unrest, demonstrating an urgent need to research and develop a new model of ethnic coexistence in Central Asia. With the weakening of the repressive Soviet system, a number of deadly clashes occurred throughout the region.

BURDEN OF ETHNIC VIOLENCE

In Kazakhstan, demonstrations in Almaty in 1986 were the first open expression against the Russian colonial regime, and the brutal rule of Moscow. People dared to disagree with employment policy. It is still unknown how many people became the victims of security forces.

Cruel clashes between locals and minorities (originally from Caucasus) in Kazakhstan (Novyi Uzen) in 1989, and Meshetian Turks in Uzbekistan's part of the Fergana Valley in 1989, reflected a new era of ethnic intolerance in Central Asia. Violence against minorities (mainly Armenians) has occurred in Turkmenistan in May 1989, and Tajikistan in February 1990, revealing social and economic crises and the inability of the government to prevent and resolve conflicts.

The most devastating event in the post-Soviet history of the region was a civil war in Tajikistan (1992–97), in which 60,000 people were killed – one per cent of the national population. Nearly one million people – or one out of six Tajiks – was displaced by the war. Sixty thousand fled to northern Afghanistan because of the civil war, which erupted after Tajikistan's independence. Some also fled to other Commonwealth of Independent States (CIS) countries and Russia.

It is illustrative to take the riots in Osh that occurred between Uzbeks and Kyrgyz in South Kyrgyzstan in 1990 as an example. The riots began as a conflict over redistribution of land to local residents and continued as savage ethnic cleansing in several places. Officially, three hundred people were killed and over a thousand wounded; more than five thousand crimes were committed and hundreds of houses were destroyed. These figures are most likely underestimates. When compared to previous conflicts in Central Asia and the Soviet Union, the conflict was coloured by the cruelty of both sides involved. The murders were merciless. Sometimes the bodies of those murdered were burned, so that they would be unrecognisable. Both sides committed mass rapes of the women of the other side and humiliation took many forms.

In August 1999, an armed group led by an Uzbek commander moved to Batken in south Kyrgyzstan, and took several hostages. The rebels demanded that the president of Uzbekistan stand down, that the Islamic Movement of Uzbekistan be allowed to operate in the Fergana Valley, and that the political prisoners affiliated with the Islamic Movement be released in exchange for the hostages. Several hundred rebels took about 25 hostages, including four Japanese geologists. During the two-month crisis, 27 Kyrgyz citizens were killed and the number of internally displaced people reached about six thousand; bombing by Uzbekistan's planes caused victims among civilians. The latest case of conflict in Batken, interpreted by governments as a religious one, is on an even more dangerous scale. If in previous clashes there were internal actors; now new outside parties involved in the conflict are interested in its further escalation in Central Asia.

A flashpoint of conflict is the Fergana Valley, a highly fertile and densely populated region of Central Asia, and home to twelve million people. The region was divided between three states – Kyrgyzstan, Tajikistan and Uzbekistan – after the collapse of the Soviet Union. This division, using boundaries drawn up by Stalin, bears no resemblance to the ethnic make-up of the region. Another major problem involved in researching conflict in the Fergana Valley is the isolation of the region. For each of the three republics, the Valley is a peripheral region, far from the capital and the seat of influence. Though the problems of the Fergana Valley, because of its high population and its history of bloody conflict, are among the greatest and most potentially deadly in the region, they are studiously ignored by national mass media in the three countries. In all three capitals of states, sharing the Valley, very little is read or heard about events in the Fergana Valley. The peripheral nature of the region in the eyes of many researchers from national centres, where most higher education institutions are concentrated, means that there is a dearth of research, seminars and information sharing in those capitals.

The maxim of the eighteenth-century Italian economist Caesar Bonesana who said: 'Happy is a nation without history', can be applied to the case of ethnic violence in the Fergana Valley. Presently this sub-region contains many major sources of conflict, making it a likely venue of severe unrest in the future if preventive measures are not taken. Many experts, and well-known leaders of international organisations, such as chairman of the Organisation for Security and Cooperation in Europe (OSCE) Knut Vollebaek, and OSCE High Commissioner on National Minorities Max van der Stoel, warned in the autumn of 1999, that Central Asia (meaning first of all instability in the Fergana Valley) could experience conflicts worse than those in the Balkans. Although some have noted that the Fergana Valley is a massive time-bomb, there exists a potential for avoiding and preventing violent and deadly conflicts. Of course, no single measure will eliminate ethnic tensions, but it is possible to reduce the threat of destabilisation and ethnic cleansing, and save the lives of potential victims. However, current attempts to improve and research the situation do not match the level of instability and economic hardship. The Fergana Valley can serve as an incubator for a more peaceful future in the whole of Central Asia if proper efforts are made, or it can become a source of disaster for the entire region.

THE LEGACY OF SOVIET RHETORIC

Peculiarities of conflict research stem from the Soviet era. The legacy of Soviet rhetoric left a perception of conflict as evil, which should not be mentioned. There are numerous taboo questions, including any naming of the recent bloody conflicts, to which researchers do not receive honest answers. It is common for many people to believe that merely talking about conflict with outsiders can provoke it. Native researchers in particular face this problem, and are advised to steer away from difficult issues and to adjust their findings to put a positive gloss on them.

Government officials in all three countries are extremely unwilling to talk about the recent riots and instability, preferring to create a picture of inter-ethnic harmony. The official line is 'do not talk about the riots because they have happened and never will again.' The silencing of people reporting on conflicts in the region is from the highest level. When the governor of Osh region openly spoke about trouble on the border with Uzbekistan, he was dismissed within days. Native researchers are strongly discouraged from tackling conflict, though double standards mean that foreigners are given help to carry out their studies. There is a lot of suspicion in state circles that talking about the problems will cause old wounds to be reopened and consequently there is a desire to hide the conflict from the people. However, it seems that the reverse is true: if the problems are not addressed, they cannot be healed.

All Central Asian countries have a bitter legacy of violent conflicts, which were not investigated in-depth, and no publications on them are available in the region. The most alarming trend is that no serious action was taken to understand what happened, or to mitigate pain and mutual suspicion between all ethnic groups, even those who were not directly involved in the riots. No special programmes on civic education and economic cooperation have been established. Ideas of ethnic cleansing remain embedded in the collective consciousness of some groups, and such ideas could easily surface should the economic and social situation in the region dete-riorate further.

DOUBLE STANDARDS

Research in Central Asia is complicated by problems of double standards, which occur on many levels. First, they occur on a global level. In some cases, rich or larger countries believe they have a good understanding of the affairs of poorer or smaller countries and the right to intervene, when they are unable to solve or even understand many of their own problems. This means, for example, that some researchers for international organisations may arrive in their region of study as 'parachutists', who try to conduct research extremely quickly on the basis of previous work done elsewhere, and whose work is more widely accepted worldwide than that of local researchers. This problem is especially acute in Central Asia, which until recently was a closed society and so has very little literature for researchers to study in order to understand the region's culture and history.

As S.A. Dudoignon notes:

Most people studying contemporary Central Asian societies pay little attention to their recent history. The economical, social and political history of [the] last decades of the Soviet period, though rich and diverse, remains understudied. Therefore, many observers tend to interpret all the social phenomena which appear exotic to them and which cannot clearly [be] seen as a part of the Soviet legacy, as survivals of pre-modern times. Hence, a common impression of stillness, backwardness and conservatism prevails. Such points of view are [the] only ones currently tolerated about Central Asia in Western media, which, as we know, tend in general to systematically promote ethnic substantialism – if not racism – when speaking of non-Western societies. [Dudoignon, 1998, p. 1]

Second, at a regional level, governments in Central Asia do not take each others' national interests into account, while they are always looking to promote their own. This leads to the unwillingness of some governments to accept researchers from other Central Asian states to carry out research on their territory. For example, Uzbekistan's government has virtually sealed off its section of the Fergana Valley to researchers.

Third, within each state, double standards exist in the relationship between state and society. The state is allowed to do what society cannot because it is better organised and has power. One example of this in all states is the pressure that the state puts on its citizens to pay taxes on time and not hide profits, while the state itself does not have a transparent budget and often pays salaries late, if at all. More generally, the state maintains the right to control society without admitting that the state itself should be controlled by the society. The government's unwillingness to be transparent and the lack of a traditional interface between officials and researchers means that access to governmental statistics and information on social and economic situation is limited. It is necessary to spend time cultivating relationships with civil servants. This lack of cooperation does not only occur at the administrative level, however. The non-governmental, higher education and other sectors all seem to have very little desire to coordinate their activities, though of course there are exceptions.

In Central Asian countries, under the pressure of the West, and its desire to develop new links with influential regimes, even the leaders of the region's most autocratic states are anxious about creating a democratic image for their countries. For example, in Uzbekistan, the president publicly demands 'more courage' from parliamentarians in revealing human rights violations while, at the same time, attempting to silence the political opposition leaders. Turkmenistan's president tries to demonstrate the democratic character of his one-party regime. An officially sponsored Human Rights Center, under the protection of the president, was opened in Turkmenistan, even though, according to Freedom House, the country has the lowest level of political rights.

SPLITTING UP

Central Asia embraces a territory larger than Western Europe, having a population of about 55 million people. This region has never been a monolithic set of people or states, despite official proclamations during the Soviet era, and the diversity of the region is obvious today. Increasing political polarisation between newly independent states acquires ethnic coloration and is more acute in Central Asia than elsewhere in the former Soviet Republic. Kyrgyzstan and Kazakhstan have adopted relatively open and democratic free-market systems, while Uzbekistan, not willing to reform its political institutions, remains stuck with an authoritarian regime and a relatively closed economy. Justifying his authoritarian rule, the leader of Uzbekistan points out the need to combat the Islamic threat, facilitate market reforms, and 'prepare' the society for democracy. Turkmenistan is an extreme case of a totalitarian state, which has reverted to medieval tyranny. Turkmenistan's president uses his own personality cult as the basis of his authority, comparable to the political systems in North Korea or Iraq. After declaring 'a decade of stability and prosperity', the 'Father of All Turkmen' muzzled any opposition in Turkmenistan. Tajikistan has all but collapsed under a quite unpopular pro-Russian government that was unable to control the country's situation, providing a sad example of how a modern state can implode due to regional and clan-based clashes.

Members of the domestic opposition in these three states fled to other countries to avoid political repression.

Post-Soviet Central Asia is fragmenting due to the continuing divergence of political, economic and geopolitical interests. The largest ethnic minorities in all Central Asian republics have irredentist hopes, or desire autonomy as a way to resolve the current painful transition. A combination of historical, geographical, geopolitical, socio-economic and cultural factors make conflict research in Central Asia difficult. The Soviet Union left a region split by illogical boundaries and containing a highly ethnicised populace with numerous economic and social problems.

Geopolitical friction between all the Central Asian states makes inter-state research, information sharing and travel complicated. Uzbekistan and Turkmenistan have frozen relations with their neighbours, and introduced visa regimes. Tajikistan is the most regionally fragmented country; although the five-year war ended in 1997, political violence remains a main threat for any research or open discussion. It is becoming increasingly dangerous to cross the borders of any state having a common boundary with Uzbekistan. The new, heightened security has resulted in shootings of Tajikistan, Kyrgyzstan and Kazakhstan citizens along the Uzbekistan border.[1]

The mistrust between states in the region has led to a great deal of difficulty in looking at grassroots conflicts over the borders between Kyrgyzstan, Tajikistan and Uzbekistan, and conducting research over these borders. For a long time, the problems of water sharing and water consumption were discussed within a narrow round of politicians who did not listen to the opinions of economists, ecologists, sociologists and other scholars. Moreover, many economic problems were resolved by political methods, without taking into account the real situation in the area. Many factors destabilising the ethnic and religious situation are increasing (unemployment, crime, economic problems and others). Governmental decrees and decisions are simply declarative and there is no serious control over their implementation. Activities of state bodies in the field of inter-ethnic policy are not coordinated and are sometimes chaotic; numerous structures are separate and maintain a bureaucratic approach, without considering the long-term perspective of inter-ethnic relations. Efforts by public organisations are sporadic and isolated, and based on short-term projects. One possibility for reducing tensions in the Central Asian region would be to increase cooperation, and information sharing among the regional powers, research institutions and grassroots organisations.

The geographic interdependence of the Central Asian states necessitates cooperation to research and assist in peacefully resolving water and land disputes, internal migration, economic integration and many other concerns. According to official sources on paper, relations between Central Asian states are flourishing. However, such collaborative efforts are the purview of top officials, while the rest of the government establishment, as well as economic and cultural entities, are not involved. Consequently, regional cooperation typically attempts to look impressive on paper, but has not accomplished a great deal in practice. This lack of regional cooperation is further exacerbating ethnic tensions in the region, as in many of the republics the indigenous ethnic groups have gained control of state apparatus to the detriment of other ethnic groups living in the area.

The role of non-governmental organisations (NGOs) and research centers in grassroots cooperation is still minimal. Among NGO members, social scientists and students, there are few opportunities to network and exchange ideas across state borders. Often the only opportunity that scholars have to meet with one another is in conferences, mostly organised by Western countries.

LACK OF ACCESS TO INFORMATION

The scholarly community is shrinking substantially in all republics due to the deterioration of economic situation. As Deniz Kandiyoti noted:

> The relatively modest compendium of ethnographic and sociological research produced during [the] Soviet period is not only outdated but the drying-up of research funds since the break-up of the Union has meant that social science research – which was relatively weak in the Central Asian region in the first place – has come to [a] standstill. This vacuum is now being filled by surveys, mainly commissioned by external donors, in a context where local sociological and anthropological research has ground to a virtual halt. [Kandiyoti, 1999: 500]

Conflict research mainly relies on international funding sources. The majority of local social scientists have a very low salary. In fact, local scholars and lecturers at numerous universities and academies of science are part of the hidden unemployed (or underemployed). The most active moved to business or governmental structures, including Ministries of Foreign Affairs.

The decline of all educational institutions and libraries entails a loss of many social sciences centres almost in all states. Currently very little research on Central Asia is conducted by Central Asians. Almost all publications on the region are written in the West, and by Westerners for the West. Numerous Western publications in journals and books on Central Asia remain unknown in the region. Therefore, to learn more about Central Asia, young locals must first move to the universities and libraries of Western Europe and the US.

A serious impediment preventing free research in Central Asia stems from the lack of a unified communication space. One of many legacies of the Soviet past is that the mainstream of information about Central Asian states comes mainly from Moscow. Communications in Central Asia are extremely fragmented and have no horizontal links. For example, there is no information flow or research on events in neighbouring Afghanistan or western China. Information on the Balkan crisis or Chechen war coverage in Central Asia comes mainly from Russia's sources. A new factor in the increasing fragmentation of the region is language and alphabet. Uzbekistan and Turkmenistan have adopted Latin script, whereas Tajikistan, Kazakhstan and Kyrgyzstan intend to use the Cyrillic alphabet.

The political and economic climate is not conducive for locals to conduct any research on ethnic conflict. The situation is exacerbated by the absence of free media in Uzbekistan, Turkmenistan and Tajikistan, where the government continues to censor all press materials, and all means of communication are controlled by the state.

In Turkmenistan, while the constitution provides for freedom of the press and expression, the government controls and funds all electronic and print media, prohibits the media from reporting the views of opposition political leaders and critics, and rarely allows the mildest of criticism of the government and its policies:

> Only two newspapers, *Adolat* and *Galkynysh* are nominally independent, and they were created by presidential decree. President Niyazov has been declared the 'founder' of all newspapers in Turkmenistan. Whereas cable TV existed in the late 1980s in all cities and three commercial TV stations existed in the early 1990s, they have been closed. The state controls all TV and radio broadcasts.

In October, Turkmenistan clamped restrictions on Russian public TV, and announced that broadcasts would be shown 'selectively.' The status of independent human rights monitoring in Turk- menistan is best reflected by a phrase from the oath of loyalty to the nation emblazoned on the masthead of all the country's newspapers and magazines: 'If I criticize you may my tongue fall out!' The sole local organization allowed to address human rights issues, the official Turkmen National Institute of Democracy and Human Rights under the president of Turkmenistan, acts mainly as a buffer between the Turkmen government and international bodies. International observers fare no better than would-be local monitors: the government denied Human Rights Watch repre- sentatives visas on one occasion and refused to grant them official meetings during a subsequent trip to the region in May 1998. [Human Rights Watch, 1999a]

Access to information is limited for the majority of the population in the region. There are no regional newspapers or journals circulated in the Central Asian region, except the English-language *The Times of Central Asia*, mainly for foreigners, and the journal *Central Asia and the Caucasus*, produced in Sweden. In these conditions, the NGOs are the channels of distribution of informa- tion targeted at a specific audience in the ruinous post-Soviet information environment. As well as the passive spreading of infor- mation, they are also involved in the active distribution of experience accumulated in other parts of the world to tackle conflict situations, which had not been attempted during Soviet times.

Poor development of the mass media, and the absence of books and journals reflecting inter-ethnic relations and the cultural life of ethnic groups in Central Asia do not help understanding and tolerance. Some sections of the ethnic communities in the region play positive roles, but they are more occupied with their own personal problems than with the extension of contacts between ethnic groups, the mutual exploration of the peculiarities of their cultures and histories, and the search for possibilities for common action. Therefore, the 'rumour syndrome' plays a major part in the inter-ethnic conflict. An illustration is the findings of a survey in Kyrgyzstan after the Osh conflict in 1990: in answer to the question 'What was the cause of the fight between Kyrgyz and Uzbeks?' 43 per cent of respondents said it was the allocation of plots of land. However, 39 per cent of those interviewed, answered that they began to fight after hearing that 'our folk are being beaten and killed' (Asankanov, 1996: 123). Although the Central Asian region has suffered various violent ethnic conflicts in recent years where hundreds died, there was no serious action taken to lessen the suffering and mutual suspicion between all ethnic groups. The dearth of unbiased information reaching the people often means that rumours are so widespread in the region that they are often difficult to distinguish from facts.

INCREASING ETHNIC ISOLATION

A claim to multiple identities is apt to puzzle many an outsider who, armed only with Western sociological concepts, is trained to think in terms of 'nations', 'states', and 'ethnic groups' (Gleason, 1997: 25). The confusion of the Soviet legacy has led to an exaggeration of ethnicity, a tendency to subconsciously refuse to accept that inter-ethnic tensions exist and the lack of a non-ideological sociological research base from which to consider the present tensions. Before Soviet times, ethnicity was unimportant in the region, where most people considered their regional or clan loyalties to be stronger. The Soviet system, however, encouraged the development of ethnic identities, for a variety of cultural, ideological and political reasons. Ethnicity was the fifth item on the Soviet passport, for example. During Soviet times, ethnicity was always emphasised along with the 'brotherhood of nations', and the common Soviet citizenship. This combination led to the development of ethnic identity and nationalism being hidden by the subconscious refusal of many people to accept that ethnic conflicts exist.

Central Asia is a mosaic of about a hundred ethnic groups. It is diverse in ethnic terms while at the same time it is largely dominated by a mono-ethnic elite. The mistrust between states in the region has led to a great deal of difficulty in looking at grassroots conflicts over the borders, and in conducting research over those borders. Constant conflict between the establishment, and ethnic and religious groups, contributes to instability in almost all Central Asian countries. Discontent over the employment situation has led the minority populations to mistrust state structures. Because of this, the minorities want to see proportional representation in local power structures, especially in mixed areas. Minorities' discontent over employment policy is one of the indicators of the state of inter-ethnic relations. The existing tendency to support 'our own people' has led to an ethnic imbalance in employment, in state departments.

Current requirements, such as a good command of the state language, mean that members of minority ethnic communities are barred from holding leading positions. The absence of a good system of adult education means that it is extremely difficult for people from the minority groups to learn the state language. This precludes skilled specialists with little command of the state language from filling appropriate positions. It is no accident, therefore, that the minorities put across employment policy as one of the major factors in the conflict.

The ideological vacuum is also being filled by ethnocentrism, flared up and spread by politicians attempting to prevent regionalism and intra-ethnic cleavages. All ethnic conflicts show that many participants have an entirely positive image of their own ethnic group and a mainly negative one of neighbouring groups. Propaganda in support of the ethno-nationalism in the Central Asian region provokes ideas of separatism and irredentism, which are then further reinforced by the difficulties and failures of the ruling groups.

THE RELIGIOUS FACTOR

Conflict research in Central Asia must take into account a complex religious situation and legacy of forced atheism. Since 1991, independent Central Asian states and the market economy started to form a totally new religious situation. Over 80 per cent of the population of these states (with the exception of Kazakhstan, half of whose population is non-Muslim) are Sunni Muslims. Due to the emigration of some Russians and other non-Muslim people, as well as a high birthrate, the ratio of Muslims will gradually grow. In general, re-Islamisation in Central Asia in a whole can be illustrated by the rapid growth of the number of mosques. Changes in rural areas are especially impressive: every settlement wants to have its own mosque, and former Communist party activists are replaced by people demonstrating their religiousness, for example returning from the Khajj (pilgrimage to Mecca).

Islam is mainly strong in the Fergana Valley – there was even created a Namangan Battalion, whose declared aim was to establish an Islamic state. An open struggle against 'unofficial' Islam was begun by Uzbekistan's government after 1992. Hundreds of people have been imprisoned in the Uzbek part of the Fergana Valley. The religious party, Islamic Renaissance, flourishes in Tajikistan, whereas the Islamic movement in Uzbekistan has had to flee and therefore a risk of instability is higher in Uzbekistan. Radical Islam appears to be a reaction against material hardship and social instability:

> Beginning in December 1997, the government of Uzbekistan stepped up its almost seven-year campaign against independent Muslims. It was triggered by the brutal murder of several police officers in Namangan, one of [whom] was beheaded. In response, police arrested hundreds of people in the Fergana Valley and Tashkent, many of whom were practicing Muslims who do not follow 'official' Islam. Some men were taken directly from the street simply because they had beards, a perceived sign of piety. Police routinely fabricated evidence by allegedly planting small amounts of narcotics or ammunition on suspects, and beat and threatened arrestees, both at the time of arrest and during interrogation. So in Uzbekistan, government systematically closed independent mosques and harassed religious leaders, several of [whom] disappeared. [Human Rights Watch, 1999b: 1]

At the same time, the Muslim identity of Central Asians often is exaggerated by many, especially in the Western countries and Russia. For instance, prayers are in Arabic language, which most of the people cannot understand. As was seen from the survey of the Institute for Regional Studies in Kyrgyzstan's part of the Fergana Valley in 1998, only two-thirds of those interviewed (61 per cent of the Kyrgyz and 66 per cent of the Uzbeks) have the Koran at home.

THE GENDER CONTEXT

The gender, ethnicity and age of the researcher play an important role in Central Asia. There are common impediments to women's participation in research. Double standards are widespread in the gender context. Men are allowed by society's conventions to do what women can only dream of. This can cause problems for researchers, especially in more conservative regions such as the Fergana Valley or the south of Central Asia. Traditional gender relationships often make it difficult to interview women in some conservative areas, for example, men can forbid their wives to talk to strangers or to travel to meet them.

Another problem is the patronising attitude sometimes shown to female researchers.[2] The view of recent conflicts is deeply ingrained in patriarchal signification. Many ethnic and religious traditions limit the role of women and increase discrimination and segregation in the region. Even when talking about or researching ethnic violence in Central Asia, mentions about trauma, in particular rape, and sexual violence and increased domestic violence during and after conflict are rarely mentioned. The gender sensitivity of ethnic conflicts or instability has never been a subject for research for either local or Western scholars. For example, it is quite unclear what happened to 25,000 widows, an unknown number of sexually abused women and 55,000 orphans after the Tajik war. According to a survey of the IFRS (Institute for Regional Studies) in 1998 in Kyrgyzstan's part of the Fergana Valley women respondents showed somewhat more inclination towards a mono-ethnic environment (Tabyshalieva et al., 1999: 20).

The question of the under-representation of women in the power structures was often answered by referring to the mentality of the local people. During our survey, people mentioned a proverb: 'a man with a frog's head is better than a woman with a golden head.' Access of women to decision making in politics and economics does not necessarily affect other spheres of life. They make up minorities everywhere where the most important decisions on peace and security are taken. Where responsible decisions are made, women are poorly represented due to the dominance of males in the management sphere. All this leads to the loss of valuable creative resources that women can offer.

On the one hand, we observe the unprecedented autarkic activity of women in Central Asian society, maintaining themselves and their families in extreme socio-economic situations. Such activity is reflected mainly in the sphere of small entrepreneurship. In some cases, this has strengthened the position of women in families. On the other hand, women have been removed from the decision-making echelons of power in society and the state. The number of women among the heads of organisations and institutions has sharply decreased, especially on the local administrative levels; in district, province (regional) and republican and other administrative bodies; in the government, the parliament and on all levels of power structures.

According to L.M. Handrahan:

Democratic culture in Kyrgyzstan has been divorced from citizen responsibility. The split falls neatly along donor gender prejudices. In Kyrgyzstan, democracy is vividly gendered. Civil society, as defined by NGOs and community participation, is the domain of women. Men control the elite political realm and men make up the majority of western donor representatives. In the foreign assistance interchange this means that men interact with men while women are viewed as ancillary to the main goal of promoting democracy. [Handrahan, 2000]

Rigid traditions of age discrimination complicate understanding of some gender issues as well. In traditional Central Asian culture, the position of young women is worse than that of older ones. Irrespective of whether a woman is married or not, according to ethnic traditions, she must show docility in outward appearance and agree to everything coming from older people. Public opinion is especially opposed to the idea of a young woman as a political leader or free-thinker.

'POSITIVE FEEDBACK': THE CASE OF SOUTH KYRGYZSTAN

Positive feedback is a little-known peculiarity in researching Central Asian society. The Institute for Regional Studies carried out a socio-logical survey in Kyrgyzstan's section of the Fergana Valley in 1998 (Tabyshalieva, 1999: 32). The first question we asked was 'How do you assess the state of inter-ethnic relations in the region?' A majority of the respondents estimated them as good (about 90 per cent in total). There is no considerable difference between assessments done by the Kyrgyz and Uzbek. The question failed because the respondents, perhaps thanks to the Soviet legacy, perhaps because of traditional fears of the danger of making negative statements, overwhelmingly described the relationship as 'very good' or 'good'. However, further questions elucidated a number of major problems in the relationship. The mentality of respondents influences their appraisal of the state and perspectives of inter-ethnic relations. They believe that a negative appraisal can negatively influence events. Nevertheless, practically ten per cent of respondents either said that the inter-ethnic relations are bad or avoided giving an answer.

At the same time, despite optimistic assessment of inter-ethnic relations, the overwhelming majority of the respondents (76 per cent) think that improvement of inter-ethnic relations will be promoted by the adoption of special laws providing punishment for infringement on the ground of ethnicity. A large number of respondents (79 per cent Uzbek and 71 per cent Kyrgyz) believes that such laws are needed. Nineteen per cent of the Kyrgyz respondents and only nine per cent of the Uzbek respondents think there is no need to have such laws. It is seen that the Uzbek (the ethnic minority in Kyrgyzstan) are much more concerned than the Kyrgyz with the necessity of putting into force such law.

CONCLUSION

The present research is just a first step towards the understanding of peculiarities of the study of the Central Asian region. The reliability of work can be significantly improved only in case of widening the research, including the monitoring of the main parameters, which are subject to permanent changes. Without due research and monitoring of the development of the inter-ethnic situation, the existing tensions may accumulate and lead to destructive inter-ethnic conflict.

NOTES

1. Here are some examples of insecurity for anyone who dares to travel throughout the region. In November 1999, Uzbek border guards shot and wounded three men crossing from Tajikistan into Uzbekistan on a motorcycle. In December, guards shot and wounded a Kyrgyz man who was washing his truck in a border river, and reportedly killed a Kazakh citizen. And at the beginning of this month, they shot and severely wounded another Kazakh citizen. A witness to this last shooting, Zhanat Akhmadi, gives his account: 'Baurzhan Ishakov of Sary-Aghash village wanted to cross the border by the bridge usually used by local inhabitants for visiting their relatives last week and was shot by Uzbek border guards without any warning. He is at Sary-Aghash clinic currently, receiving treatment for his wounded leg.' Uzbek guards have not said that any of the men shot were militants. More worrying to Kyrgyzstan and Tajikistan than the shootings are the increasing reports that Uzbek border guards have been moving the border posts into Kyrgyz and Tajik territory (Pannier, 2000).
2. When I was researching in the south along with a female colleague and a man from the local government, most people assumed that he was the one in charge and that we were his assistants. They pressed us (but not him) to stay and eat or relax, thus wasting valuable research time.

REFERENCES

Asankanov, A. (1996) 'Ethnic Conflict in the Osh Region in Summer 1990: Reasons and Lessons', in K. Rupesinghe and V. Tishkov (eds), *Ethnicity and Power in the Contemporary World* (Tokyo, New York, Paris: United Nations Press).

Dudoignon, S.A. (1998) *Communal Solidarity and Social Conflicts in Late 20th Century Central Asia: the Case of the Tajik Civil War*, Islamic Area Studies Project, Working Paper Series, No. 7, Tokyo.

Gleason, G. (1997) *Central Asian States: Discovering Independence* (Boulder, CO: Westview Press).

Handrahan, L.M. (2000) *Slapped by Democracy: Deconstructing Foreign Assistance*, Field Reports, Central Asia-Caucasus Institute, 19 January.

Human Rights Watch (1999a) 'Turkmenistan Defending Human Rights' <http://www.hrw.org/hrw/worldreport99/europe.turkmenistan2.html>

Human Rights Watch (1999b) 'Uzbekistan, Report 1999' <http://www.hrw.org/hrw/worldreport99/europe.turkmenistan.html>

Kandiyoti D. (1999) 'Poverty in Transition: An Ethnographic Critique of Household Survey in Post-Soviet Central Asia', *Development and Change*, vol. 30, no. 3, July.

Pannier, Bruce (2000) 'Neighbors Complain of Zealous Border Guarding', Radio Free Europe transmission, 21 January.

Tabyshalieva, A., Alisheva, A. and Shukurov, E. (1999) *Sotsial 'nye Realii Ujnogo Kyrgyzstana* (Bishkek, Kyrgyzstan: Institute for Regional Studies).

8　The Use of Epidemiological Methods in Assessing the Impact of War and Armed Conflict

David Meddings

Epidemiology at any given time is something more than the total of its established facts. It includes their orderly arrangement into chains of inference which extend more or less beyond the bounds of direct observation. (Frost, 1936)

EPIDEMIOLOGY – A BRIEF HISTORY OF A YOUNG SCIENCE

The primary focus of epidemiology is the study of disease. The rationale for such study is based on two fundamental assumptions. The first is that disease does not occur at random, while the second is that systematic investigation of populations of interest can lead to the identification of causal and preventive factors.

The recognition that a variety of factors have an influence on health is not new. In the fifth century BC Hippocrates wrote that one had to consider lifestyle, social and geographic attributes of a community in order to study medicine properly (Hippocrates, 1938). Despite this, a poor grasp of disease processes meant that this larger understanding of health resulting from the interaction of human beings and their environment remained relatively unsophisticated for well over two millennia.

One of the first major advances in this understanding came in 1855, when John Snow published a book establishing an association between household water suppliers and death rates from cholera in London in 1853 (Snow, 1855). Snow's careful documentation of the frequency, distribution, and importantly, a determinant (water supplier) of disease had a major impact on sanitation practices across Europe. His work also provided evidence that infectious disease could be spread by particles carried in water, which differed from the commonly held theory that diseases were spread by the inhalation of vapours. This approach contributed substantially to controlling

148

many of the great epidemic diseases in large parts of the world over the following century. Indeed, the major causes of death in developed countries are no longer infectious diseases, but degenerative and man-made diseases – a shift that has been labelled 'the epidemiologic transition' (Omran, 1971).

Although this transition has led to a more comprehensive concept of the term 'epidemic', epidemiology remains concerned first and foremost with examining the association between various factors and an outcome of interest. Today many health outcomes of concern are complex processes that are influenced by a wide variety of factors. This added complexity has necessitated a substantial refinement of the epidemiologic methods first utilised by Snow.

Many of the intellectual contributions to epidemiology since the end of the Second World War have centred on questions of how one assesses the presence and strength of associations between an exposure and an outcome, and how one subsequently infers something about the causal nature of such an association. The conceptual advances that have arisen from these contributions have included insights into study design, data analysis and interpretation. What has emerged is a relatively young science that, while rooted in the health sciences, has application in a wide variety of fields of enquiry.

Epidemiology and War

War is a complex phenomenon, with a wide variety of outcomes that have either a direct or indirect effect on health. A number of these, as well as antecedent causes of armed conflict, have increasingly become the subjects of active investigation. The motivation for these efforts has at times been organisational learning, academic enquiry, or national security concerns, while at other times it has been part of a civil society initiative to raise awareness or further understanding about humanitarian concerns.

Arguably the most important contribution of epidemiology to these studies has been the careful consideration given to the fundamental building-blocks of any investigation – data collection, analysis and interpretation. This is important, since the validity of any enquiry will ultimately depend on the quality of the data used and how these have been analysed and the results interpreted. Thus, while some investigations may use study designs derived from sciences other than epidemiology, insights from epidemiology may assist in determining how these designs might best be applied, and what limitations might need to be placed on the overall interpretation of the analysis.

THE IMPACT OF WAR – AN EFFECTS-BASED APPROACH TO DESCRIBING THE INDESCRIBABLE

> Anyone crossing the vast theatre of the previous day's fighting could see at every step, in the midst of chaotic disorder, despair unspeakable and misery of every kind. (Dunant, 1986 [1862])

The above quotation refers to the aftermath of the battle of Solferino, which took place in what is now northern Italy on 24 June 1859. On that day, over 300,000 men from the French and Austrian armies fought in one of the most horrific battles ever recorded. The fighting lasted more than fifteen hours, and it took three days and three nights to bury the dead. Henry Dunant, a businessman from Geneva found himself witness to the battle and organising makeshift field hospitals to care for the wounded and dying.

Dunant's account of his experience provided a gripping description of the brutal reality of soldiers locked in battle – a vocation that at the time was regarded as one of honour. However, Dunant went further than description in proposing two things: first, that societies be organised in all nations during peacetime to provide care to those wounded on the battlefield, and second, that the individuals providing this care be accorded protection and respect through an international treaty (Dunant, 1986).

Dunant's book and vision subsequently became very influential in the law courts of Europe. The emblem of the Red Cross became the internationally accepted symbol for those providing relief on the battlefield, and in 1863 the International Committee of the Red Cross was established in Geneva. The following year, twelve states gathered in Geneva and signed a convention which became the legal forerunner to what are now the four Geneva Conventions of 1949, and their two Additional Protocols of 1977. These conventions, known as international humanitarian law, constitute the body of law governing behaviour in war and at the time of this writing have been signed by 188 states. Dunant's work attests to the potential for description to lead to policy change.

Subjective description of the effects of war will always have value. The potential of this description to contribute to policy change, however, will depend on a wide variety of factors, including its perceived credibility, the context within which, and to whom it is conveyed, and the social, political, economic and cultural circumstances particular to the situation from where the description derives.

OBJECTIVITY, AND THE QUALITATIVE VERSUS QUANTITATIVE DATA DEBATE

Objective accounts are explicit about the type of information that has been collected, how this information has been collected, and what has been measured. Objectivity tends to increase perceived credibility, and many insights from epidemiology might be viewed as factors that enhance the objectivity of an investigation.

People sometimes argue that quantitative data – those things that lend themselves to being easily counted – are the only type of data that are truly objective. They carry on to argue that qualitative data – things that are inherently less quantifiable, in a conflict setting for example, a narrative description of one's experience – are always subjective. The argument usually goes on to suggest that quantitative data are somehow superior to qualitative data.

This rather polemic view is not very constructive. An obvious limitation is that there are many parameters of interest in a complex context such as armed conflict that simply cannot be counted. Furthermore, quantitative data can be, and frequently is, collected, analysed and presented in a manner that is far from objective. Conversely, a number of sound and established methodologies greatly enhance the objectivity of qualitative data.

It is probably more useful to view all types of data as coming from some point along a continuum. At one end of this continuum are data that are purely quantitative – number of people within a defined population killed or injured by weapons in a given setting over a given period of time, for example. At the other end are data that are purely qualitative – such as narrative descriptions of people's coping mechanisms for living in increasingly insecure environments. In between are data with both quantitative and qualitative elements – for example, perceptions of the relative importance of various factors that can be rank ordered.

For a given enquiry, data from anywhere along this continuum might be appropriate, and indeed one could argue that examining even a seemingly isolated aspect of something as complex as armed conflict would require looking at both quantitative and qualitative data. While a full discussion of quantitative and qualitative research methodologies is beyond the scope of this chapter, what follows is a discussion of some data collection issues, epidemiologic principles and methodologies that either have been, or could usefully be applied to examining the impacts associated with armed conflict.

The range of impacts associated with armed conflict is vast, and the range of possible enquiries into various aspects of armed conflict is correspondingly vast. For example, one might examine impacts in terms of physical or mental health, the economy, migration, political life, arms proliferation, etc. Discussion of the use of epidemiologic methods that made reference to a wide variety of these aspects run the risk of losing coherence. In the interests of simplicity and clarity then, a single research concern is developed here and, in our discussion of this concern, emphasis placed on the underlying methodological issues rather than the results themselves, in order to explore the use of epidemiological methods in exploration of the effects of war. Discussion of these methods and issues are made both in connection with the concern we have developed, but also in a general sense for application to a variety of enquiries related to researching violent societies.

ARMS AVAILABILITY – THE CONCERN

An assumption that is virtually implicit in international humanitarian law is that military arms will be found in military hands. There has been growing recognition and concern that in many parts of the world weaponry originally designed for use by trained militaries is now in the hands of untrained, and often undisciplined users (Williams et al., 1997). This high level of availability, principally of what are called small arms and light weapons – assault rifles, grenades, mortars and the like – is argued to be a factor facilitating regional instability, delayed development in post-conflict situations, and violations of international humanitarian law.

Viewed through the lens of epidemiology, the concern asserts that an association exists between high levels of weapon availability, and a number of negative outcomes. It is worth remarking that both sides of the traditional epidemiologic equation, the *exposure*, in this case high levels of weapon availability, and the *outcome* are not very explicitly defined. How does one determine that regional instability is present, or that post-conflict development is *delayed*? What, after all, does one mean by *development*? What is a *high* level of weapon availability?

Indeed, the last of these is confounded with the original concern. Part of the reason small arms and light weapons are argued to be widely available is that transfers of these weapons are relatively unregulated. Furthermore, many of the transfers involved are thought to take place illicitly, outside of formal channels, and completely without documentation (Naylor, 1995). Thus, arriving at an estimate of weapon availability in a given setting is frequently relegated to educated guesswork.

The challenge in clarifying this issue, or any of the others, does not mean that enquiry is impossible. Many knowledgeable observers would agree on certain settings as being ones where there is a high level of weapon availability, a rational definition can be constructed for the term 'post-conflict', and there are even indexes of development one can draw on to support how a study examining development has been framed (Sudhir and Amartyak, 1994). In many cases a researcher is constrained to make what most observers would feel to be a reasonable conceptual model of such issues, and to make this model explicit. In virtually any enquiry this will require a review of relevant information sources.

RATIONALES FOR REVIEW – ANALOGY AND BACKGROUND

There are a number of reasons why examining sources of information relevant to a given enquiry are important. One is to identify efforts that have addressed different, but conceptually similar research questions. Another is to establish the relevant literature and existing data sources that pertain directly to the question at hand. Both of these are discussed under separate headings below.

Public Health and Criminal Justice Parallels – Violence in Societies Without Armed Conflict

The concern that high levels of military weaponry are associated with a range of negative outcomes in countries that are at conflict or politically unstable has an analogous concern in settings where outright armed conflict is not present. In industrialised settings, a parallel concern has been expressed that high levels of firearm availability are associated with a number of negative outcomes. As it turns out, this issue has received considerable study.

Some of the study designs used in these efforts have been ecologic studies. Ecologic studies are sometimes called aggregate studies, and involve the comparison of groups rather than individuals (Morgenstern, 1998). These designs have been used in the social sciences for over a century, and have received extensive use by epidemiologists, who originally tended to view ecologic studies as simple designs that were useful in the generation of hypotheses. More recently, epidemiologists have devoted considerable attention to the complex and sometimes subtle inferential implications that arise from using group-level data (Morgenstern, 1998).

Figure 8.1 presents data from such a study design, which contrasts a measure of firearm availability with a measure of a specific negative outcome: intentional firearm deaths. The level of analysis here is the data source for which the two measures are available, and in this case is the level of a country. The implication of this is that the 15 countries for which data are provided need to have data collection systems that allow the investigator to collect comparable data for both variables.

This basic requirement is not as straightforward as it might sound. Measures of firearm availability within societies will come from different data sources in each country, as will measures of firearm deaths. Both types of sources may be expected to have varying levels of accuracy across countries. One initiative that may go some way towards harmonising international data collection on firearm injuries is the work currently underway on the International Classification of External Causes of Injury (ICECI). Once established, the ICECI system will hopefully result in more comparable data on outcomes such as firearm injuries across countries.

Some might question the appropriateness of including both homicides and suicides under the rubric of intentional firearm injury

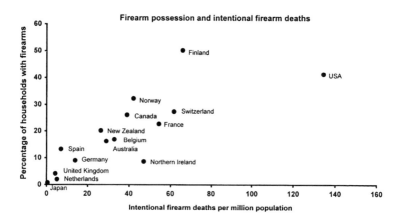

Figure 8.1   Firearm possession and intentional firearm deaths in 15 countries

in the above graph. Undoubtedly the acts of homicide and suicide are fundamentally different. Nevertheless, such aggregation is probably justifiable if one views both as a negative social outcome and our interest in these data as determining whether such outcomes have a relation with access to weaponry. Furthermore, other studies provide evidence that suicides are often acts of impulse and that a negative correlation does not exist between firearm ownership and suicides committed by other means, suggesting other methods of suicide are not substituted in settings with lower rates of firearm ownership (Maurice et al., 1989; Peterson et al., 1985; Kost-Grant, 1983; Killias, 1993).

The foregoing is largely a public health parallel, and draws on studies that have made use of data coming from health systems. Our review would not be complete without including a number of studies carried out in the criminal justice sphere. Most of these are also ecologic studies where comparisons have been made across countries on varying dimensions of the exposure (nearly always a measure of firearm availability), and criminal justice outcomes that tend to be measures of violent crime. The collective findings of these studies have tended to show a correlation between measures of firearm availability and measures of violent crime such as threats or assaults with guns (Miller and Cohen, 1997; Cukier, 1998).

After reviewing the results from enquiries studying analogous questions, the researcher is ultimately required to decide upon the degree to which these are applicable to the question at hand. An issue here would be whether anything observed in a setting at peace has relevance for a setting where an open military conflict is underway, or where there is violent political instability. While one might take the view that such fundamental differences would negate the applicability of such data, it also seems conceivable that one could argue that these relationships would tend to be exacerbated in conflict settings, where people are living under more precarious economic conditions and have experienced a general degradation of cultural norms against violence (International Committee of the Red Cross, 1999). As with the issue around making explicit one's conceptual model for issues fundamental to the enquiry, the investigator here may be constrained to presenting an argument that has face validity – that is, would appear to be reasonable to a knowledgeable observer – and supported by whatever ancillary evidence may be available.

THE IMPACT OF ARMS AVAILABILITY IN SETTINGS OF ARMED CONFLICT

What are the existing elements that contribute to an understanding about the effects of high levels of arms availability in settings of armed conflict? What have these efforts focused upon, what have they not, and what are some of the methodological issues involved?

What is Known about Levels of Arms Availability?

Perhaps a logical starting point is with the methodological issues around measuring the scope of the perceived problem. As mentioned earlier, estimating the degree of weapon availability in a setting where armed conflict is occurring is difficult. Although some databases exist that are concerned with quantifying arms transfers – the database of the Stockholm International Peace Research Institute, for example – these tend to be focused on the transfer of major conventional weapons. States rarely publish data regarding their transfers of small arms or light weapons. Moreover, many of the transfers are thought to take place illicitly or to involve arms brokers working outside the direct control of the state (Krause, 1996).

With the emergence of the concern about high levels of arms availability have come some new initiatives to tighten existing regulatory measures governing the transfer of these weapons. It may be that in the future measures to increase the transparency of these transfers will greatly assist the researcher in documenting the quantity of weapons in a given setting.

In the meantime, researchers have adopted a variety of methodologies to estimate the level of weapons availability. Frequently, these have involved approaches combining data from a variety of sources, such as security force interception of arms flows, or discoveries of arms caches, interviews with key informants, and market prices for a particularly ubiquitous weapon such as an AK-47. There are some methodological issues that arise with all of these. Security force data sources include authorities within the setting concerned, INTERPOL, or police forces from a neighbouring country intercepting cross-border arms movements.

Using such sources to subsequently make inferences about the degree of weapons availability will always bring up the issue of ascertainment. In fact, this is an issue of fundamental importance that will apply not just to reliance on official data to estimating the size of a weapon pool, but to the use of official statistics to quantify the size of virtually any phenomenon. The problem is that knowledge is never complete, and the degree of under-ascertainment present for something like weaponry is likely to be substantial. Estimating the size of what remains unascertained is often impossible, or at the very least technically difficult to do so with any accuracy.

In a similar manner, interviews with key informants are an important source of data for many enquiries, and not just those related to arms availability. Nevertheless, the validity of interview information depends very much on the competence of the interviewer and the particular context. For some issues, obtaining truthful, complete information from a respondent is very difficult (Hartge and Cahill, 1998). Integrating such data into the larger enquiry is best done after the interviewer assesses the likelihood of the information obtained being a factual account of what the respondent truly believes. Other considerations, apart from the assessment of whether the respondent's trust and cooperation were gained, are whether the investigator was capable of identifying what attributes make a particular individual important to identify, and whether those individuals identified and interviewed represent a comprehensive enough selection of potential respondents to yield a truly informative picture.

The final methodology referred to above, the market price of a particular weapon, is an indirect approach to inferring something about weapon availability. The underlying logic is that price decreases as available supply increases. While perhaps valid in principle as a means of establishing changes in availability over time in a single setting, it is difficult to imagine this as being anything other than a crude indicator of availability. For example, sometimes arms are given to insurgent groups – an exchange that would undoubtedly have an effect on traditional supply-and-demand forces. Moreover, many arms transfers that might be of interest could take place on the so-called black markets, where the applicability of supply-and-demand forces is itself a subject of enquiry.

Our discussion in this section has highlighted some of the methodological issues relating to the delineation of our exposure of interest – that is, high levels of arms availability. We have seen that data pertaining directly to the issue are rarely available, discussed some of the considerations of methodologies used to make up for this, and have seen that these methods have application to enquiries involving other aspects of armed conflict as well.

What, then, of the effects thought to be related to this high level of availability? One could choose to conceptualise the range of effects in a variety of ways. For the purposes of our discussion, we will consider two topics that might be viewed as falling under a heading of direct effects of high levels of weapon availability, and two falling under a heading of indirect effects.

Civilian Casualties

Recently, one of the most frequently cited beliefs about armed conflict is that a high proportion of individuals killed or injured by weapons are civilian. Indeed, concern about this issue is one of the primary factors driving the larger concern about high levels of availability of light weapons and small arms (International Committee of the Red Cross 1999; Aboutanos and Baker, 1997).

Many sources cite figures that either 80 or 90 per cent of all killed or injured by weapons in today's conflict are civilians. But what is the evidence upon which these assertions are based? Documents making the assertion rarely provide an explicit description of how such a figure was arrived at, so it is impossible to determine what has been *counted* as a casualty, or who is a *civilian*.

Indeed, these two points highlight the two essential methodological challenges inherent in supporting such a claim. First, one needs to have a reasonably accurate and defensible estimate of either the total number of killed or wounded, or the total number of killed or wounded who survive to reach care. This information needs to be present either for a given conflict or better yet, in a variety of conflicts. Here again we come up against the issue of ascertainment, and the inability to ascertain all such events. Armed conflict frequently results in the destruction of health system infrastructure that maintains the surveillance systems that would allow such a determination. Accordingly, ascertainment of these events frequently becomes the surveillance capacities of humanitarian organisations working in the area, if any.

The second challenge is the issue of combatant status, and making the determination that a given individual is a civilian. In the few studies that have examined this issue and been explicit about their methodologies, this has been done either by inferential deduction, for example by using employment records (Kuzman et al., 1993) or criteria such as age and sex of people who survive to reach care and have been wounded (Coupland, 1996), or by explicit ascertainment of fulfilment of prospectively established criteria (Meddings and O'Connor, 1999).

These methods highlight the potential for misclassification – another methodological issue of fundamental importance, and with relevance to any field of enquiry. Misclassification is a form of measurement error that affects discrete variables – variables with only a countable number of possible values, including binary variables for indicators like combatant status. All of the three studies above employed some method for making this distinction; misclassification would mean that some individuals were incorrectly classified.

Misclassification has different effects on a study depending on whether it is differential or non-differential. Differential misclassification means that the classification error depends on the values of other variables in the analysis, whereas non-differential misclassification means that it does not (Rothman and Greenland, 2000). For example, imagine an analysis of the rate of emphysema in smokers versus non-smokers. Classification of someone as having emphysema requires contact with the medical system. Since smokers will tend to have more contact with the medical system, they will tend to have emphysema diagnosed more often. This is an example of differential misclassification, since under-diagnosis, a classification error, will happen more often in non-smokers than smokers. On the other hand, a study examining the rate of mine injury between combatants and non-combatants must employ some classification strategy to distinguish mine injuries from other weapon injuries. Since any classification system is less than perfect, some people with other types of injuries (for example, mortar injuries) will be incorrectly classified as having sustained a mine injury. If this misclassification occurs independently of whether a given individual is a combatant or a non-combatant, this would be an example of non-differential misclassification. The importance of this difference is that differential misclassification will exaggerate or underestimate a given effect, whereas non-differential misclassification usually (but not always) tends to underestimate an effect. The results provided by studies that have objectively examined the occurrence of civilian casualties in recent conflicts do not support this proportion being as high as 80 or 90 per cent. While their combined results suggest a proportion more in the range of 35 to 65 per cent, what should be borne in mind with this is that this is still a high proportion given the protection to which civilian populations are entitled under international humanitarian law (Meddings, 1998).

Patterns of Weapon Use

One of the concerns at the heart of the issue of high levels of arms availability is that the manner in which these weapons are used has little to do with a traditional notion of disciplined militaries engaging in a military struggle. Another direct effect then, that is postulated to occur in association with high levels of weapon availability and broader than the infliction of civilian casualties, is undisciplined use of military weaponry, or use that somehow steps out of what would be considered *normal*.

There are a number of sources of information that provide insight into patterns of weapon use in settings that most observers would agree have high levels of weapons availability. News media reports of the 'taxi wars' in South Africa (Taylor, 1993), or of ethnic fighting in the streets of Karachi are examples of descriptive accounts that provide some evidence of this (Moore, 1995).

More formalised studies making use of hospital-based data have also been carried out. Some of these have relied on examination of the rate of weapon injury over time periods encompassing major politico-military transition to contrast the rate of weapon injury during conflict and post-conflict periods (Meddings, 1997). Others have explicitly established circumstances of individual injuries to classify injuries into schemes that indicate whether the injury was sustained in interfactional combat or not (Meddings and O'Connor, 1999; Michael et al., 1999).

An important issue that arises with these studies that has not been touched on in our previous discussion is the concept of a rate. The rate is a fundamental concept in epidemiology, and refers to the occurrence of an outcome of interest in a defined population over a defined period of time. Although rates are one of the earliest insights from epidemiology, the concept of a rate has application for a broad range of enquiry. Calculation of most rates is relatively straightforward, although determination of the population at risk can be challenging. Certainly in situations of armed conflict it can be difficult to establish an estimate of the population at risk, since there is usually considerable in-migration and out-migration. Here, however, use of external data sources such as pre-existing population estimates from censuses before the conflict, and possibly data on refugee movements available from organisations such as the United Nations High Commission for Refugees can assist in making such an estimate (Meddings, 1997; Meddings and O'Connor, 1999; Michael et al., 1999).

Another methodological issue that can arise with discrete events, like the occurrence of a weapon injury, is the need to adjust for time periods. This may be the time lag between the event and another event of particular importance, or, as in the case of a study involving patterns of weapons use, an adjustment for seasonality (Meddings and O'Connor, 1999). Weapons use in armed conflicts tends to vary seasonally with dry seasons being periods of higher military activity. If one is contrasting rates of weapons injury across different time periods and not accounting for an effect like seasonality the results can be misleading.

Results from studies examining patterns of weapons use support the contention that settings with high levels of weapons availability tend to be afflicted by a substantial use of military weaponry in contexts outside of interfactional combat. Moreover, these studies have also provided insights into different mechanisms by which civilian injuries are inflicted during interfactional fighting versus those inflicted outside of this context. For example, a study in Cambodia revealed that civilians injured during interfactional fighting tended to be injured by fragmenting munitions, whereas civilians injured in contexts outside of interfactional fighting most often sustained their injuries following the intentional use of a firearm (Meddings and O'Connor, 1999).

Indirect Effects of High Levels of Weapons Availability

So far our discussion has touched on two aspects that could both be conceptualised as direct effects of arms availability. However, it seems logical to expect that there would be other effects that might be associated with a high level of weapons availability aside from injury or death resulting from weapons use.

Indeed, one could imagine that impeded access to protective measures such as vaccination programmes and basic sanitation might well result in more morbidity and mortality in heavily militarised parts of the world than that due to weapons directly. This line of enquiry is in fact the focus of a recently established Reference Group on Small Arms, which is in the process of attempting to identify what routinely collected data exist with a variety of NGOs and international organisations that might shed light on this.

Methodologically, such an approach introduces the issue of making use of administrative data sources. On the one hand, such sources have the advantage of being readily available and therefore studies making use of such data tend to be relatively inexpensive. The major limitation of these studies, however, is the fact that routinely collected administrative data often does not address issues that are of particular interest. Furthermore, changes in data collection systems over time can lead to changes in things like level of ascertainment that are artefactual in nature and not genuine. Despite these potential limitations, such an effort could yield important insights and suggest directions for further research – an outcome that is relatively common when working with administrative datasets.

Arms Availability and the Concept of Human Security

An effect of high levels of arms availability that might be conceptualised as being an indirect effect is the degradation of human security. Despite the fact that the term 'human security' has begun to creep into diplomatic parlance and foreign policy agendas, there seems to have been little attempt to define the concept or assess its relation with measures of arms availability.

In the absence of any other definition, let us propose that human security can usefully be defined as a state of existence where one has access to all essential needs and the means to sustain this access, and basic rights are respected. That an environment where weapons were highly prevalent would threaten human security seems only logical. Moreover, this has direct implications for health, which is viewed by the World Health Organization (WHO) as 'a state of complete mental, physical, and social well-being, and not just the absence of disease or infirmity'. It is the social dimension of this definition, one's living environment, that would seem to be so obviously threatened by existing in an environment where weapons were prevalent and the patterns of weapons use unpredictable.

The notion of human security, and the international community's responsibilities or lack of responsibility in assuring this commodity in a world of sovereign states is probably one of the fundamentally important issues facing international diplomacy today. Its inclusion here is not so much because relevant information exists that can be reviewed and synthesised, but because it is an issue which would seem to benefit from further examination, perhaps most notably from focus group techniques and other qualitative research methodologies.

CONCLUSION

Our development of the arms availability concern has served to highlight a number of methodological issues, many of which also have more general application to other enquiries in researching violence and violent societies. As with all research, truth never exists in a single study. Complex understandings of complex phenomena ultimately come from many such efforts. The issues expanded on here can hopefully serve to enhance the quality of these undertakings.

REFERENCES

Aboutanos, M.B. and Baker, S.P. (1997) 'Wartime civilian injuries: epidemiology and intervention strategies', *Journal of Trauma*, 4 (October), pp. 719–26.

Boutwell, J.M., Klare, T. and Reed, L. (eds) (1995) *Lethal commerce: The global trade in small arms and light weapons* (Cambridge, MA: Committee on International Security Studies American Academy of Arts and Sciences).

Coupland, R.M. (1996) 'The effects of weapons: Defining superfluous injury and unnecessary suffering', *Medicine and Global Survival*, vol. A1, pp. 1–6.

Cukier, W. (1998) 'Firearms Regulation: Canada in the International Context', *Chronic Diseases in Canada*, vol. 1 (April), pp. 25–34.

Dunant, H. (1986) *A memory of Solferino* (Geneva: International Committee of the Red Cross).

Frost, W.H. (1936) *Snow on cholera* (New York: The Commonwealth Fund).

Hartge, P. and Cahill, J. (1998) 'Field methods in epidemiology', in K. Rothman and S. Greenland (eds), *Modern epidemiology*, 2nd edn (Philadelphia: Lippincott-Raven).

Hippocrates (1938) 'On airs, waters, and places', *Medical Classics*, 19.

International Committee of the Red Cross (1999) *Arms availability and the situation of civilians in armed conflict* (Geneva: International Committee of the Red Cross).

Killias, M. (1993) 'International correlations between gun ownership and rates of homicide and suicide', *Canadian Medical Association Journal*, 10 (5 January), pp. 1721–5.

Kost-Grant, B.L. (1983) 'Self-inflicted gunshot wounds among Alaska Natives', *Public Health Reports*, vol. 1 (January), pp. 72–8.

Krause, K. (1996) 'Constraining conventional arms proliferation: A model for Canada', in A. Latham (ed.), *Multilateral approaches to non-proliferation* (Toronto: York University).

Kuzman, M., Tomic, B., Stevanovic, R., Ljubicic, M., Katalinic, D. and Rodin, U. (1993) 'Fatalities in the war in Croatia, 1991 and 1992. Underlying and external causes of death', *Journal of the American Medical Association*, vol. 5 (4 August), pp. 626–8.

Maurice, S., Pommereau, X., Pueyo, S., Toulouse, C., Tilly, B., Dabis, F., Garros, B. and Salamon, R. (1989) 'Epidemiological surveillance of suicides and attempted suicides in Aquitaine, south-west France, using an original computer network of sentinel general practitioners', *Journal of Epidemiology & Community Health*, vol. 3 (September), pp. 290–92.

Meddings, D.R. (1997) 'Weapons injuries during and after periods of conflict: retrospective analysis', *British Medical Journal*, vol. 7120, pp. 1417–20.

Meddings, D.R. (1998) 'Are most casualties non-combatants?', *British Medical Journal*, vol. 7167, pp. 1249–50.

Meddings, D.R. and O'Connor, S. (1999) 'Circumstances around weapon injury in Cambodia after departure of a peacekeeping force: prospective cohort study', *British Medical Journal*, vol. 7207, pp. 412–15.

Michael, M., Meddings, D.R., Ramez, S. and Gutiérrez-Fisac, J.L. (1999) 'Incidence of weapon injuries not related to interfactional combat in Afghanistan in 1996: prospective cohort study', *British Medical Journal*, vol. 7207 (14 August), pp. 415–17.

Miller, T. and Cohen, M. (1997) 'Costs of gunshot and cut/stab wounds in the United States, with some Canadian comparisons', *Accident Analysis and Prevention*, vol. 3, pp. 329–41.

Moore, M. (1995) 'Violent death runs rampant in Karachi', *Washington Post*, 8 February, p. A24.

Morgenstern, H. (1998) 'Ecologic studies', in K. Rothman and S. Greenman (eds), *Modern epidemiology*, 2nd edn (Philadelphia: Lippincott-Raven).

Naylor, R.T. (1995) 'The structure and operation of the modern arms black market', in J. Boutwell, M.T. Klare and L.W. Reed (eds), *Lethal commerce: The global trade in small arms and light weapons* (Cambridge, MA: Committee on International Security Studies American Academy of Arts and Sciences).

Omran, A.R. (1971) 'The epidemiologic transition. A theory of the epidemiology of population change', *Milbank Memorial Fund Quarterly*, vol. 4 (October), pp. 509–38.

Peterson, L.G., Peterson, M., O'Shanick, G.J. and Swann, A. (1985) 'Self-inflicted gunshot wounds: lethality of method versus intent', *American Journal of Psychiatry*, vol. 2 (February), pp. 228–31.

Rothman, K. and Greenland, S. (2000) 'Precision and validity in epidemiologic studies', in K. Rothman and S. Greenland (eds), *Modern Epidemiology*, 2nd edn (Philadelphia: Lippincott-Raven).

Snow, J. (1855) *On the Mode of Communication of Cholera*, 2nd edn (London: Churchill).

Sudhir, A. and Amartyak, S. (1994) *Human development index: Methodology and Measurement*, Occasional Papers, no. 12, (New York: United Nations Development Programme).

Taylor, P. (1993) 'South Africa's taxi "miracle" explodes into violence', *Washington Post*, 9 February, p. A14.

Williams, P., Naylor, R.T., Mathiak, L., Batchelor, P. and Potgieter, J. (ed. Gamba, V.) (1997) *Society Under Siege: Crime, Violence and Illegal Weapons* (Pretoria: Halfway House/The Institute for Security Studies).

9 A Field Trip to Bosnia: The Dilemmas of the First-Time Researcher

Ioannis Armakolas

INTRODUCTION[1]

In this chapter I attempt to demonstrate a few of the problems and dilemmas that a researcher encounters in the field. The general tone of the chapter is one of filtering my own reflections before, during and after my fieldtrip in Bosnia, in the spring of 1999,[2] through a researcher reflexivity. Since most of the issues I address here are dealt with in more detail by other, more experienced researchers in this volume, this chapter should be read as the reflections of a first-time researcher.

All the considerations addressed here will be based on an understanding of research as a social activity involving actors interacting in a multiplicity of ways and continuously negotiating their self–other positions. The objective is to show that researching conflicts cannot be seen as an activity isolated from the general study of social phenomena. Analysis of conflicts does not take place in ideal experimental conditions. Analysis involves human beings, be they researchers or the researched. The concerns of the chapter are outlined in four parts, namely

- practical problems,
- the dilemmas and problems of studying identities,
- researcher reflexivity,
- the implications for research of the multiplicity of *sites* that constitute a conflict, including the external *observers* and actors.

My fieldtrip was carried out in a town called Pale, in what is now the Republika Srpska (Serbian Republic) of Bosnia. Pale is only twenty minutes' drive east of Sarajevo and only ten minutes from the Dayton Line that divides the two entities of the Bosnian state. The population of the town has increased as a result of the war. Most of its inhabitants are now Serb refugees from Sarajevo. The town has been a popular temporary and permanent destination of Sarajevo refugees because of its proximity to and close connection with Sarajevo. Pale has acquired disproportionate political significance during the war and also become notorious in the Western media. When the mostly Sarajevan Bosnian-Serb leadership left Sarajevo and the common Bosnian institutions, they chose Pale as the capital and location for their Assembly of the newly proclaimed independent Serbian Republic of Bosnia-Herzegovina; this new state was never internationally recognised during the war, but was subsequently incorporated in the new Bosnia created by later peace treaties. When later the Bosnian-Serb leader Karadzic, who was indicted for war crimes, was obliged to step down from office, his successor, Biljana Plavsic, broke with the Pale leadership, transferring the capital and the political institutions to the city of Banja Luka and started coop-erating with the West. Pale's significance was again drastically reduced, reflecting once again its actual size. It is still, as is Eastern Bosnia in general, particularly radical and a stronghold of the most extremist factions in Bosnian-Serb politics.

The use of some sort of ethnographic fieldtrip to approach conflict analysis research questions is quite rare in conflict literature. The comprehensive critique to traditional conflict analysis offered by Vivienne Jabri (1996) was influential in the adoption of this approach. This involves the researchers in distancing themselves from analyses of conflicts that consider group boundaries as given. Following Jabri, the process by which bounded communities are formed and maintained is considered crucial for any meaningful understanding of conflicts. This approach shares much with recent trends in social and political theory, considering identities as contingent, fluid and changeable, and focusing on the process that constructs identities rather than on any *fixed* content involved (Hall, 1992). In this line, the project and the fieldtrip were concerned with the processes involved in rendering ethnic identity predominant over other identifications and their relation to conflict.

PRACTICAL CONSIDERATIONS

A series of practical problems limit the range of possibilities available to the researcher in the field.[3] Yet all these practical con-siderations are important elements of the research and must be negotiated alongside more general questions of ethics. This section presents personal reflections on some of the practical considerations in the field.

Selection of the Area

The main consideration influencing the selection of the area for the fieldtrip is practicality. I have been lucky to have visited Bosnia before and to have monitored the local elections in Pale for the Organisation for Security and Cooperation in Europe (OSCE) in the autumn of 1998. This provided me with an initial minimal but crucial network of personal contacts that would facilitate contact with a wider group of people. This network would also function as gate-keepers and help me address specific practical problems.

My involvement in research on the Yugoslav crisis for the past nine years provided my personal motivation. During this time I moved between two academic contexts, and two discourses on the Yugoslav conflict; one in my home country, Greece, and the other in Britain. In this situation I felt like a minority in what seemed to me to be one-sided discourses. The depiction of Serbs in these two contexts as either the absolute victims or the absolute perpetrators has always made me feel uncomfortable. My fieldtrip did not solve this and did not place me firmly in one of the two camps. I had no aspirations to trace the absolute truth. Rather, the desire was to acquire some understanding of those portrayed as 'perhaps the most hated group of people in the Western world'.[4] Researching in Republika Srpska, let alone Pale, in a place whose image was constructed in a specific way by Western media was not without problems. Some of these will be discussed later in this chapter.

Access

Given a number of factors – the fact that Republika Srpska is the most isolated part of Bosnia, my very limited knowledge of the local language which made me dependent on others, and my inexperience – I think I gained access quite easily. There are three reasons for this. The first was the above-mentioned network of people. The second is the openness of the people themselves: they were very friendly and talkative and usually happy to explain their opinion about painful issues. The third reason was my nationality. The fact that I am Greek meant that they felt that 'I understood better', and therefore they were ready to speak more. For example, I often felt that some degrading comments about other nationalities were more openly made in front of me, because Greeks are on the 'correct side' in their 'geography of friends and enemies' (Ringmar, 1996), and they attributed to me more or less the same idea about these nationalities. Moreover, had I not been Greek, it would have been much more difficult to conduct interviews with the more radical young people.

Field Relations

A number of important issues arise in relations developed in the field. One such issue is trust and the reaction to my research. My nationality was crucial for establishing a significant level of trust with the people in the field. I did not have any problem telling people that I was doing research. I was always very explicit about my topics: the conflict, inter-ethnic relations and so on. They were not suspicious and they usually did not ask further questions about the details of my research. They would often joke about my interest in such morose subjects but generally they were very happy to talk to me. Many of those I met also saw my research as an opportunity to explain their point of view, which they consider under-represented abroad.

A second issue was impression management, that is, the impression the researcher gives to the people in the field. First, as mentioned above, I was open about being a researcher, my Greek nationality and my research base in Britain. Apart from that I had to have a low profile in two other aspects. These were my opinions about the conflict and dress code. I did not express any opinions about the conflict which opposed those of my interlocutors. I didn't lie but I didn't give my opinion either, since I knew that by expressing no opinion led them to believe that I agreed with them simply because I am Greek. I was more open with a small selected number of my young acquaintances, the ones that I got to know better, as will be shown below. Regarding the dress code, I adopted a low profile in that I avoided being perceived as showing off whilst attempting to look like any young southern European urbanite.

Researcher Position

An important consideration before my field research was the selection of the role of the researcher in the field. In ethnographic work, five different roles have been identified: complete participant, complete observer, participant as observer, observer as participant, and marginal native. During the Bosnia fieldtrip I opted for two different roles which varied according to the setting.

During formal interviews the role of *participant as observer* was adopted. That means that I was in an overt research role and it was clear that my relationship with the locals was a field relationship. Nevertheless, in this role I maintained an emphasis on participation and social interaction and attempted to build relationships of trust. I conducted interviews with people of all ages, both female and male, with both refugees from Sarajevo and with locals. The interviews have illuminated the play of identities before and during the early stages of the conflict. They also revealed differences according to age. In some cases my inexperience and the linguistic barriers led to failure in exploiting the full potential of the interviews and the opportunities presented by the fieldtrip. One example of this was my failed attempt to gain access to members of paramilitary groups.

Apart from the interviews, insights into my research questions have been gained through participating in the daily life of the town, especially in the environment of the young people of Pale. In these cases, the role adopted was that of a *marginal native*. In this role, I was not hiding the fact that I was doing research in Pale, and thus could not be considered a complete participant. At the same time, I was not behaving like a researcher but rather as a visitor or as a friend of my acquaintances. Most of the young people I met are refugees from Sarajevo, they study in universities in Belgrade or Pale, and they speak English. During that period I had numerous discussions with them on a wide range of topics, including my specific research questions. However, other everyday topics can be useful for the research. I also had the chance to meet the parents of some of these young people; I formally interviewed some of them and with others had short or longer informal talks. It was also valuable for my research to visit Sarajevo with some of the young people of Pale. I spent time with them there discussing everyday life in Bosnia. It was 'enemy territory' and at the same time it was a place about which they held beautiful memories of their teenage years, and the visits facilitated some fascinating discussions with them.

Research Products

The final practical issue related to research products. The first consideration involved protecting the identity of my research subjects. This was solved by the use of pseudonyms when quoting interviewees and others. A second and more puzzling issue arose. Tamar Hermann in this volume discusses the problem of the researcher who is expected to present specific research outcomes that are supportive of certain views. It seemed likely that my research conclusions would not be the ones expected by my research subjects.

Distrust about my conclusions had in fact been expressed by my informants during the course of my fieldtrip. Although people felt that I could understand them better as a Greek, some nevertheless did not hesitate to tell me that they anticipated that I would follow the example of others and blame Serbs for the conflict. *What to write* also became an issue affecting future research. I anticipated the risk to future access in this specific setting or other Serbian areas. Surely, I thought, publishing in academic outlets is remote enough and provides the safety of distance.

DILEMMAS AND PROBLEMS OF STUDYING IDENTITIES

Ethnographic literature suggests that the role of *marginal native* creates strain since the researcher is simultaneously living in two worlds: that of participation and that of research. That my trip did not last long and that my research could not therefore be considered truly ethnographic allowed me to avoid some of this strain. However, further strains were created by other features of the research. The focus on the study of identities perplexed the situation further. Below I elaborate on the identity interactions between the researcher and the researched and other general problems of researching identities, using the experience of my fieldtrip.

Encountering *Fixed* Identities

The ethnographic method provided a source of strain during my research in Bosnia. In my case the two different worlds were, on the one hand my own research, identities and political views, and on the other the projected expectations of locals because of my nationality.[5] In Pale, I was not simply a researcher – I was a *Greek* researcher. My nationality not only facilitated my research; it engendered specific expectations in the local people. Those caught up in conflict situations often have a very stable and fixed conception of their identities. This fixed conception of unified and stable identities can be extended to include the researcher. During my fieldtrip, the people that I met assigned a specific fixed conception of identity to me. The central element that determined this process was my nationality and the remaining attributes were assigned to me automatically. Religion, political views, ideas about the self and other were determined by a very fixed notion of Greek identity. For them, I was a researcher sympathetic to their cause or their people. I was someone that they could tell their story to, someone that could understand them.[6] I had to be ready to explain the reasons why the West was so hostile towards the Serbs, and of course explain it *correctly*. Applying their own conceptual framework to me confirmed that they were not completely isolated, that others could sympathise with their troubles and suffering. In effect, their own fixed identities were confirmed through their perception of my identities as fixed. This was a small contribution towards realising their imagined geography of friends and enemies and giving meaning to their suffering.

Dilemmas in Self-presentation

It was not always easy for me to avoid expressing opinions and views. It was easier for me to do so with some of my interviewees whom I would see only once or twice. It was more difficult to avoid revealing my views to people that I spent more time with and had more open-ended discussions with. After some time the solution of 'don't lie but don't tell the truth either' was not enough. I felt that not revealing my true opinions was no less of a lie. I felt that with people that I spent a lot of time with I had to, at least, imply that my views were different from the ones they thought I held. At the same time I felt I needed to indicate that there can be other alternatives from the very fixed notion of identity and community they hold; I saw this as a potential contribution to the process of opening-up of identities. After all, I had the 'correct' nationality and I could not easily be accused of having anti-Serb bias! On the other hand, this could be construed as a *research exercise* that would help me problematise the role of other identifications.

How this exposure to different possibilities is done involves ethical considerations. I was, for example, continuously trying to keep in mind the dangers of exposing the interviewees and acquaintances to the possibility of different realities only to leave them in an environment that allows little room for ambiguity and requires *taking sides* clearly, an environment that does not have a *safety net* for fluid identities so to say (this issue is addressed in Pam Bell's chapter in this volume). My plan was to demonstrate alternatives via revealing my own ambiguous position in any *fixed* identiational axis: I am Greek but at the same time a Catholic; I have Serbian friends but at the same time I have travelled in most of the former Yugoslav countries, I have good Slovene, Croat and Kosovo Albanian friends; I tend to consider other kinds of identification much more important than ethnic or religious ones, and so on.[7]

This slow process of revelation was not without problems. It was almost impossible to feel comfortable enough to reveal my religion without risking both my research and my relationship with my contacts in Pale; therefore I did not. I did however reveal some other aspects of my identity. In cases where the issues were non-contentious and therefore did not cause trouble, for example, in the case of my sympathy for the former multi-ethnic Yugoslavia, my view was to some extent congruent with the dominant Serb views on the issue. Formally, Serbs are also in favour of Yugoslavia, although increasingly after the late 1980s, in their own very exclusionist manner. In discussions on this issue, when our different conceptions of multi-ethnicity would confront each other, there would be an exchange of views and such an exchange might well have had a positive effect on some of my interlocutors.

In other cases, this process of revelation created real conflict that threatened to destroy my research. From the beginning I didn't hide that I also had friends and contacts in other former Yugoslav republics. This did not seem to matter very much. However, when I revealed that I also had Kosovo Albanian friends, this seemed to be beyond the limits of their tolerance. It seemed incomprehensible to them that I could have Albanian friends. There was a continuous attempt to prove me wrong with various arguments and examples. I had experienced before attempts to project their 'geography of friends and enemies' on to me, but it seemed that enmity with Albanians was a *sine qua non* in their particular geography. Assertions such as, 'if you have Albanian friends you cannot have Serb ones', or 'I now think that you cannot understand us', seemed to suggest to me that not only the continuity of my research, but also my relationships with these people were at stake. Their attempt was to project their geography in a way that included not only the warring parties but also the outsiders like me. In a symbolic geography of conflict, everybody, be they warring parties or outsiders, has a specific role and position, based on some *fixed* criteria positively or negatively valued by the groups in conflict. But also in that sense the success of the geography is predicated on bracketing the elements that disqualify it. Ambiguous positions (like a Greek that has Albanian friends) destabilise the foundations of this geography. Although in the end things did not go wrong, I am undecided about whether this issue had any positive effect on their conception of identities or whether it merely curtailed their trust in me.

Considering Other Identifications

The purpose of the trip was not only to trace the significance of other identifications, but to relate them to the dominant position of ethnicity in the identity repertoires of the population. Moreover, the question was not only how these relationships could be conceived in a specific time in the past but also how they were continuously renegotiated including the microprocesses triggered by my interaction with my research subjects. These were puzzling and demanding questions to explore. The most intriguing point proved to be the negotiation of cross-cutting identifications in relation to ethnic identity. The urban–rural division, for example, seemed to have central importance. Discourses on the backwardness of the local population were deployed by the people originating from Sarajevo. There was, for example, an expressed dissatisfaction by Sarajevan youngsters living in Pale about the *mentality* of the local youth. Similar ideas were expressed in other locations. Interestingly, the youngsters from Sarajevo now in Pale talked to me in derogatory terms about the inhabitants of another town proximate to Pale. They portrayed them as characteristically backward countryside people. When I visited the town in question I was again confronted with similar discourses, this time deployed against yet another town in the area.

How was gender negotiated during my fieldtrip? I am certain that my maleness did not assist me in elaborating issues of how a woman experiences a violent conflict in a male-dominated society. In my interviews, for example, I could sense that being both male and Greek deprived me of insights on female solidarity across the divide and the experiences from a conflict in which women were often put at the centre of exclusionist discourses.[8] On the other hand, my nationality made it easier for me to continue my research, meeting and interviewing women of all ages. The fact that I was a quite welcome foreigner (one generally considered to share their religion and political views) made people much more tolerant to my discussions, questions and visits to homes.[9] In a society with many patriarchal features I imagine that it would have been more difficult for me to pursue my project otherwise. I was informed by some of my acquaintances that some young men had been asking questions about my identity and what I was doing in the town. I was told that I would probably have encountered obstacles had I not been Greek. Moreover, my presence as a researcher seemed to place me amid a range of local negotiations about identities. The right of young women to be able to meet and discuss with a foreigner without having to ask permission of their young male friends was a realm of negotiation that evoked division between urban and rural populations.

This urban–rural divide was a recurrent feature of my fieldtrip. The salience of urban identity though did not entail tolerance towards the ethnic *other*. It was interesting to observe the ease with which some of my acquaintances would shift back and forth from a discourse against the ethnic *other* and the impossibility of coexistence to a discourse against the *backwardness* of rural people and their resistance to a modernised urban mentality of the Sarajevans. My fieldtrip thus convinced me that questions of identity are more complex than my original conception and that different identifications exist which interact in a multiplicity of ways. There is no evidence that cross-cutting identifications, for example, necessarily undermine the exclusionist ethnicity discourses. Assigning political significance to the various identifications encountered is never an easy or straightforward task. Ethnicity, gender, religion, ideology, age, place of origin all play their role in the constitution of the self and the collective. It means that this tends to be an open-ended process in which all kinds of different alliances and interactions are negotiated, depending on the larger social and political context.

RESEARCHER REFLEXIVITY

> I think that re-reading now pieces about Bosnia 'hurts' more... Perhaps because I am in the same places where the crimes that I read about were committed. Perhaps because I may have met people that participated in them. Perhaps because my friends here do not understand or have not been informed about what happened. Perhaps even because I am afraid that even if they find out they will not mind ...
>
> (excerpt from author's fieldwork journal, 12 May 1999)

Beyond the chimera of *objective* and *value-free* research, each researcher carries personal ideas, feelings and stereotypes into the field. The timing of my trip and its effects, the choice of research subjects and the effects of my field research on my personal feelings, ideas and expectations all illustrate this.

The Timing of the Trip

My research was carried out during the Kosovo crisis of May 1999. This affected the feelings, views and disposition of the people that I met on my trip. It would be naïve to believe that these circumstances hadn't also had an effect on me. My attitudes and emotions had gone through two phases before going to Bosnia. These two phases related not to different incidents but to the same incidents presented by different media. Before my departure from Northern Ireland, early in April 1999, I was much influenced by the bombing of Serbia-Montenegro and the way it was covered by the British media. I was disturbed by what I saw as a double-standard policy in relation to Kosovo, and upset by the failure of the media to represent the reversal in the Western policy over Kosovo, which once again targeted the Serbs. My emotions changed after I left Northern Ireland and went to Greece for almost a month before going to Bosnia. There, the public debates, media discourses and societal reactions were the reverse of those in Britain. The issue in Greece was the *criminal policy* of bombing, the killing of hundreds of civilians and the destruction of a country. Refugees appeared daily on television without viewers being informed of how they became refugees in the first place. This situation made me furious. Again, as earlier in Britain, I had the feeling that the media were simply offering a black-and-white, and for that reason distorting, view of the situation. The fact that the British media were privileging the one side of the story and the Greek media the other did not help much. In my view any one-sided coverage, any distorted view was disappointing, for media coverage of conflicts has crucial implications for issues ranging from the foreign response to the conflict, to the domestic policy adopted towards it and the dynamics of ethnic identity in the field.

I left for Bosnia only a few days after attending a public debate about the war in Athens. The debate was between a group of intellectuals, academics, former diplomats and retired politicians. Predominantly a left-wing gathering, they had always been advocates of human rights and ethical foreign policy and had confronted nationalism and racism in Greece. Yet this group was completely divided in the case of Kosovo: on whether the priority was to confront 'a systematic policy of ethnic cleansing that is a disgrace for humanity', or not to let a 'neo-imperialist bombing campaign to kill thousands of civilians and send a sovereign state back to the Middle Ages' (phrases used in the debate). I left for Bosnia with this contest in my mind. During the first few days of my trip when I re-read some articles about ethnic cleansing during the Bosnian war, I tended to prioritise the first option, that is, opposing ethnic cleansing. Later, after getting to know more people and hearing their stories about crimes, I came to the realisation that the answer is not so straightforward.

Research as *Giving Voice*

The conceptualisation of social research as other than objective, *scientific* analysis has multiplied the calls for using research as a tool for challenging the wrongdoings of the social world. Since all research is normative and *for someone and for some purpose*, it is imperative to make it useful for those in need of it, the less powerful, the ones whose voices are not heard. In this view, research is *giving voice*, empowering the underdog, representing the non-dominant alternative views and experiences of the social world. This is particularly relevant for the study of conflicts and divided societies. One of the effects of conflict situations is the marginalisation of the voices that do not serve the dominant exclusionist discourses. In this respect, giving voice in the margins of divided societies should be considered a legitimate task. The question is *who is the underdog?* But is this a straightforward identity? And is it an absolute dynamic; is it satisfactory to identify the underdog once? These questions should always puzzle researchers. The task of defining the underdog should not simply be the application of the *who is not* question, but rather the *who else is* question.

If research has such normative underpinnings, then selecting research subjects and topics becomes an important personal consideration. In the context of the Yugoslav conflict for example, research as *empowerment* was attempted by scholars and journalists to represent the cause of the vanishing multicultural Bosnia and the Bosnian Muslims. Their struggle for survival in the face of expansionist projects of Serbia and Croatia was examined. The effect was to turn an indifferent West into an active advocate of both multiculturalism in Bosnia and the protection of the Bosnian Muslims. However, it remains to be seen whether Bosnian Muslims are the only underdogs in this terrible conflict. I had to consider whether I should have disregarded Serbs and continued the practice of other researchers. Paradoxically, the ordinary Serbs that I met and studied were in a deplorable position and were therefore a legitimate normative choice. They have been demonised by the whole world and have been identified with the perpetrators of heinous war crimes. They have been isolated, victimised first by their own leadership, then by the *ethnic other* as a consequence of the war, and finally by the outside world. Contrary to expectation, these ordinary people, in whose name crimes were committed, are the group whose voice is not heard. When it is heard, it tends to be disregarded as mere propaganda, legitimisation of crime or hate-speech.

Impact of the Research on Personal Feelings and Ideas

But how did my research influence me? How was I transformed by the experience of the fieldtrip? One obvious result was that I confirmed in my own mind that Serbs are no less human than any other people. Reading my fieldwork journal again, I also realised my growing expectation that those who were subject to my partial revelation about the fluidity of my identity should be changed as a result of these self-disclosures on my part. The more I got to know people in the field and realised that they were as human as anybody else, the more I tended to expect that their *real* self was not the one resulting from the war. I was looking for other characteristics that would be revealed once I scratched the surface. A growing desire and expectation of empathy on the part of my field-acquaintances for the fate of my Kosovo friends, with whom I lost contact as a result of their fleeing the Serbian ethnic cleansing, became evident. These revealed that quite often a researcher cannot avoid some sort of personal feelings which become involved in the course of research. The limitations of research were exemplified. My frustration about the failure of my informants to be *rational* on these issues reveals the naïveté of a first-time researcher. It is one thing to get in the field and realise that conflicts are produced by normal human beings with flexible and changeable identities. It is quite another to expect that the mentalities constructed as a result of exposure to material violence and within powerful discourses and interpretations of reality and experience can easily be shifted.

THE NEBULOUS MEANING OF THE CONFLICT

From the early stages of the conflict in Bosnia, the definition of physical space and its legitimisation by the peace treaties put severe constraints on the possibilities of experiencing the *other*. Although formally, freedom of movement is maintained, practical considerations of safety inhibit it. This is quite obvious and straightforward; but I would extend this observation to include not only locals but everybody involved in one way or another in this conflict. It has been stressed by a variety of analysts that observers rather than merely *observing* a conflict effectively co-constitute it (for example, Jabri, 1996). For example, how the international community, foreign media and scholars by deploying a discourse of ethnic hatred in the

Bosnian conflict, have legitimated the exclusionist projects of the nationalist elites has been noted (Campbell, 1996: 163–80; Sorabji, 1993). *Outsiders* by constructing and reproducing a certain understanding of the conflict and its parties, lend specific meaning and judgements to a conflict situation.

The Bosnian conflict was the first civil war to generate such an enormous foreign interest, mobilised by what Martin Shaw calls 'global responsibility' (1992). As a result of this global involvement, thousands of peacekeepers, and non-governmental and inter-governmental organisations' staff poured into Bosnia. These brought with them not only their own views and prejudices, but effectively became segregated in their own little area and group and acquired minimal experience of other parts of the country, or experience of the ethnic *other*. A United Nations peacekeeper, for example, informed me that he felt better when entering the areas of the one group because they were clearly different and more civilised (the complete intermingling of populations throughout prewar Bosnia notwithstanding)! It is less obvious in the case of researchers and aid workers. Avoiding contact with the *other* may be a necessary compromise for those who need to establish trust with their research subjects; this trust would probably be jeopardised if attempts were made by them to know the ethnic *other* better.[10] All too often, however, this lack of experience of the *other* has nothing to do with research needs. It is simply a seemingly *natural* choice once someone is identified with the one of the sides involved in this conflict. In such cases, proximity is not a sufficient condition for getting to know the *other*. Pale is very close to Sarajevo, yet in the minds of many of the foreigners working or researching in Sarajevo it may as well be thousands of miles away. During my fieldtrip I met a young couple, a Sarajevo Serb from Pale and an English non-governmental worker in Sarajevo. They met in the Jahorina ski centre, the site of the 1984 Winter Olympics. They described their meeting and the original distrust of the English girl. It took her some time to understand that the boy from Pale was a young man like any other. Even when they overcame that obstacle, the young couple had to struggle with the attitudes of the girl's family back in England, for whom it was inconceivable that their daughter could become engaged to a Serb.

Research and Demonisation

If any such *observer* has a specific idea about the conflict is then any research setting unproblematically given? Do we choose our setting and pursue our research simply corresponding to the needs of our project? Is the setting in that sense void of meaning? If an observer comes to a geographical area of conflict with specific ideas about the conflict, formed before arrival in the area, then can the observer truly *observe* the setting or do they only see through the lens of preconception? Or should research on such areas of conflicts be simply a matter of identifying the geographical area and allowing the researcher to become *saturated* by the setting? Are there meanings that can only be elicited in particular settings, or can identity, for example, be usefully researched in any number of settings? Do the preconceptions about a particular place or people derived from the demonisation of those people or that place in the media or elsewhere, compromise the validity and reliability of the research itself? This set of questions raises numerous issues that concern research, especially that in violent societies. It would be impossible to address all these in this chapter. I focus only on a small part of these issues and again present my personal experience of doing research in Pale.

Research in the 'Location of Evil'

I tend to believe that there is no neutral setting, in the sense that any chosen area has a specific meaning assigned to it by the researcher before their arrival. The researcher brings with these a particular image of the setting that will be perhaps transformed as a result of research, but is nevertheless pre-existing. In that sense Pale maintains the reputation as the 'location of evil'. It is so familiar to any party interested in any way in the Yugoslav conflict, yet at the same time remains so unknown.

What were my perceptions of Pale before my first visit in 1998? I shared the image of Pale constructed abroad as the location of evil. The images that came to my mind when hearing this place-name were those of the Bosnian-Serb leadership in assembly, the war-hawks making inflammatory speeches and rejecting one solution after another aimed at mitigating the terrible conflict. I would recall the Greek war-reporter with the dramatic voice, speaking about the notorious Bosnian-Serb leaders Karadzic and Mladic and their actions. Pale was an imaginary place, where the key to the resolution of the conflict was kept but also from where the appalling war-machine was coordinated. It did not occur to me then that Pale was inhabited by people suffering in the conflict, albeit not to the same extent as those who remained in Sarajevo. I remember my surprise at meeting so many young refugees from Sarajevo in cafés. Journalists who came and went to Pale during the war were going straight to the offices of Karadzic overlooking the town. They wrote and spoke about the multicultural character of Sarajevo which was under threat, yet they avoided talking to the very people that composed this multicultural character and who were sitting under their noses in Pale.

I recall the first time I visited Pale in 1998. We had travelled with other election supervisors by coach for hours inside Bosnia, on our way to Pale. For many of us it was our first time visiting Bosnia. We were all influenced by the way this war was represented in the Western media. For hours we could see the incredibly beautiful landscapes of Central Bosnia but at the same time dozens of war-torn towns and villages, countless destroyed houses. We reached Sarajevo by afternoon. The coach took the transit road that overlooks the city and leads to the Serbian areas. It was an unforgettable moment. After hours of viewing landscapes of war we were finally there, in the very heart of the matter. No one could speak; we were all standing up and looking out of the windows at the city. They were familiar images: buildings and neighbourhoods that have become famous worldwide as sites of resistance to the worst of nationalisms and to hatred-driven violence. After a few minutes, we passed Sarajevo, and we were all astonished. In a few more minutes we entered the Serbian Republic. After asking *why?* for so long, my unreflective response was to identify the *because* with this place. In the imagination of someone coming from abroad, the two places Sarajevo/Bosnia and Pale/Serbian Republic were so close geographically but so distant in terms of values. I remember even being disturbed by the large welcoming sign written in Cyrillic. Being roughly identified with the one party in this conflict, I found myself being upset by everything that could symbolise the other/*other*.

CONCLUSIONS

Searching my archive of material from my first visit to Pale in 1998 for the purposes of this piece, I found a panoramic photo of the town taken during my stay. Looking closer I realised that this photo was taken from the Panorama, the former offices of the Bosnian-Serb leader Karadzic. Much of our image of this town has been through the lenses of this man and his activity. The town looks different from afar. Any conflict looks different from afar. There's a wide gulf between studying a conflict in a library, reading about it in newspapers, watching its images on television, being informed about it by others, and actually *being there*. Once there, personal ideas and stereotypes, likes and dislikes, normative dilemmas, the very identities of the researcher are involved in a dynamic interplay with the research subjects. Once in the field, everything is much more complicated but also more fascinating.

NOTES

1. I wish to thank INCORE and the Ireland American Funds for giving me the opportunity to work on my project by awarding me the 1998–99 Tip O'Neill Fellowship in Peace Studies. I particularly want to thank Mari Fitzduff and Gillian Robinson for their help and support throughout the period of my fellowship. I also would like to thank Delia Secker Walker and the editors of this volume for invaluable comments on earlier drafts of this paper. Naturally I remain solely responsible for the outcome.
2. Much of my analysis is inspired by Fortier (1998).
3. This section is influenced by Walsh (1998).
4. This comes from the opening statement of a 1992 BBC documentary entitled *Serbian Epics*, quoted in Zivkovic (1995).
5. One could argue here that I was in fact encountering not two but three worlds: that of participation in the local community, that of my research, and that of the expectations that local people hold for my research. However, the fact that, in the eyes of my research subjects, the reality of my participation was effectively merged with that of their expectations from my research compels me to simplify the situation and speak only of two different realities.
6. For some of the issues raised by the Serbian claims that they cannot be comprehended by foreigners and especially Westerners, see the discussion of the anthropologist Mattijs van de Port (1999). The title of his article is characteristically provocative: 'It Takes a Serb to Know a Serb'.
7. Or isn't that so? Two little words ('moral crusade') in the comments of the editors were enough to shake any unstable foundations of the researcher's (mine!) pretensions that the trip could be of any help for the field-acquaintances in that respect. If I gave the impression that my research trip was any moral 'mission', that should be due to my inexperience. The general tone of my piece and especially the following two sections should make clear that any fieldtrip does not search for any objective truth, does not 'enlighten' in any way, and it is as much for identities of the researcher as it is for those of the researched. To be sure, my personal political and academic views couldn't be more at odds with 'orientalising' (Bakic-Hayden, 1995; Todorova, 1997) approaches that advocate bringing the 'merits' of civilisation and reason to 'backward locals'. I wish to thank the editors for helping me, through their comments, clarify this point.

8. See, for example, Salecl (1994) and Sofos (1996) for the way in which women have become both the epicentre of the various nationalist discourses in the area but also the target of rape warfare.
9. Two recent anthropological studies by Cornelia Sorabji (1989) and Tone Bringa (1995) offer extremely interesting insights on the issues of the distinctions between private and public realms in the Bosnian locality. Although, neither study directly examines the Bosnian-Serb population (Sorabji examines a Muslim quarter in late 1980s Sarajevo and Bringa and Muslim-Croat village during the same period), they both provide useful analyses of the issue in the Bosnian context.
10. I thank Pam Bell for drawing my attention to this element.

REFERENCES

Bakic-Hayden, M. (1995) 'Nesting Orientalisms: The Case of Former Yugoslavia', *Slavic Review*, vol. 54, no. 4, pp. 917–31.

Bringa, T. (1995) *Being Muslim the Bosnian way: Identity and Community in a Central Bosnian village* (Princeton: Princeton University Press).

Campbell, D. (1996) 'Violent Performances: Identity, Sovereignty, Responsibility', in Y. Lapid and F. Kratochwil (eds), *The Return of Culture and Identity in IR Theory* (Boulder and London: Lynne Rienner Publishers).

Fortier, A.M. (1998) 'Gender, Ethnicity and Fieldwork: A Case Study', in Clive Seale (ed.), *Researching Society and Culture* (New Delhi: Sage).

Hall, S. (1992) 'The Question of Cultural Identity', in S. Hall, D. Held and T. McGrew (eds), *Modernity and Its Futures* (Cambridge: Polity Press – in association with the Open University).

Jabri, V. (1996) *Discourses on Violence: Conflict Analysis Reconsidered* (Manchester: Manchester University Press).

Port, M. van de (1999) '"It Takes a Serb to Know a Serb": Uncovering the Roots of Obstinate Otherness in Serbia', *Critique of Anthropology*, vol. 19, no. 1 pp. 7–30.

Ringmar, E. (1996) *Identity, Interest and Action: A Cultural Explanation of Sweden's Intervention in the Thirty Years' War* (Cambridge: Cambridge University Press).

Salecl, Renata (1994) 'The Crisis of Identity and the Struggle for New Hegemony in the Former Yugoslavia', in Ernesto Laclau (ed.), *The Making of Political Identities* (London and New York: Verso).

Shaw, M. (1992) 'Global Society and Global Responsibility: The Theoretical, Historical and Political Limits of "International Society"', *Millennium: Journal of International Studies*.

Sofos, S. (1996) 'Inter-Ethnic Violence and Gendered Constructions of Ethnicity in Former Yugoslavia', *Social Identities*, vol. 2, no. 1, pp. 73–91.

Sorabji, C. (1989) 'Muslim Identity and Islamic Faith in Sarajevo', unpublished PhD thesis, University of Cambridge.

Sorabji, C. (1993) 'Ethnic War in Bosnia?', *Radical Philosophy*, vol. 63, pp. 33–5.

Todorova, M. (1997) *Imagining the Balkans* (New York: Oxford University Press).

Walsh, D. (1998) 'Doing Ethnography', in Clive Seale (ed.), *Researching Society and Culture* (New Delhi: Sage).

Zivkovic, M. (1995) 'Ballads and Bullets in Bosnia: How Dangerous Are the Epics of Mountain Serbs?', paper presented at the American Anthropological Association Annual Meeting, Washington, DC, 15–19 November.

10 The Ethics of Conducting Psychiatric Research in War-Torn Contexts

Pam Bell

This chapter addresses some of the ethical questions encountered when doing clinical research involving a psychologically trauma-tised population, in an unstable society, under disorganised or chaotic conditions. The work experiences referred to below occurred in towns and refugee settlements in Bosnia, during and in the aftermath of the recent conflict.

The war in Bosnia claimed hundreds of thousands of lives – mostly civilians. The battlefields were homes, markets, schools and hospitals. This and an effectively thorough policy of ethnic cleansing precipitated the worst refugee crisis in Europe since the Second World War. However, it wasn't only the war carnage that shocked the world. Overwhelming evidence emerged of a carefully imple-mented strategy of the mass rape of tens of thousands of Muslim women. The Security Council of the United Nations dispatched a European Commission of Enquiry delegation to investigate the appalling reports. Their initial estimate was that over 20,000 women were affected, but subsequent assessments have suggested that up to 50,000, if not more, were victims of this policy (Guha-Sapir and Forcella, 1996). Bosnia became the focus of journalists, politicians and humanitarian aid workers. This response however was met by mixed feelings in the Bosnian population. The exposure in the media was tinted with sensation, and the journalists' hunt for raped women both distressing and distasteful (Dahl, 1993). International aid projects mushroomed, with each country or organisation bringing its own brand of support.

It soon became clear: the nature and extent of the traumatic experience largely defied the capacity of foreign programmes to deal with it. Numerous projects failed, and to date there is a dearth of assessment data available on any of the work carried out with trau-matised people in Bosnia. This is due in part to the failure of projects to meet their goals, but also because in times of extreme crisis, local health care professionals have a clinical workload which precludes research or systematic data collection. Bosnians – particularly women who have been exposed to the horrors of ethnic cleansing – are an overexposed and sensationalised population. Many attempts to help have been futile, and their current situation is desolate and insecure. The ethical questions surrounding research in this environment were, and are, daunting.

Foremost are the ethical issues raised when one considers the effects of research on such a vulnerable population. Assessing psychological trauma inevitably involves the recounting of traumatic events. Many researchers and clinicians believe that with skilful and sensitive interviewing, persons actually benefit from talking openly about their experiences. This is perhaps an attempt at self-justification, but in any event such assumptions are hard to qualify. Although victims may manifest relief at being able to talk openly about their trauma, this secure and sympathetic surrounding in which the interview occurs is unfortunately temporary. Once having *opened* the trauma, they must return to an often demanding and unsympathetic environment, without a support system to help deal with the flood of strong emotions that accompany or follow such discussion. During the interview process, it is common for many Bosnian women to choose to remain in the company of others. This makes the interviewing procedure considerably longer and rather circuitous. However the sorrow, anger and frustration are shared and contained by the group.

Given that the deeply traumatised victims undergo an emotionally challenging experience when interviewed, they, as well as the authorities responsible for their well-being, have an expectation that they will in some way benefit from the process. Setting up support/therapeutical help for interviewees after an interview is a possibility only if one works in particular contexts. Unfortunately research under these circumstances is little different from mainstream research. Justification for it does not come from the direct good one brings current victims, but from the need for the knowledge, which would help future victims. In this respect conflict regions can certainly claim an acute need. This is highlighted by the extensive review of epidemiological studies on post-traumatic stress disorder (PTSD) carried out by De Girolamo and McFarlane (1996). Only 6 per cent of studies from this review were conducted in non-Western or developing countries. Furthermore, the vast proportion of stress-related events, such as wars and natural disasters, where entire communities or populations are traumatised, occur in countries outside Western Europe and North America. This implies that many traumatised populations are either scientifically ignored, or that their situation is being addressed by Western European and North American researchers, outside the geographical, social and psychological context of their trauma. Undoubtedly, there are negative implications, examples of which are discussed below, arising from this situation, regarding both the traumatised populations concerned, and the emerging research that forms current understanding of PTSD and other trauma-related disorders.

In the area addressing war trauma involving women, the situation is bleaker still. This predicament will be addressed in more detail below. Despite the fact that war victims are psychologically, socially and politically vulnerable, there is none the less a desperate need to understand and deal with the repercussions of war-induced trauma. It is the responsibility of those conducting research to be acutely aware of the particular needs of a sensitive population, and to accommodate and adapt when necessary.

In a country devastated by war, there is little support, or even tolerance for research. Many citizens are homeless, unemployed and destitute. The basic infrastructure of economy, education, and health institutions has been destroyed. Once the basic human needs of food, shelter and medical care have been met, reconstruction becomes the priority for local authorities and international donors. Often overlooked in these emergency responses are the actual people who are being assisted. Their non-material needs are more difficult to quantify. The after-effects of rape or witnessing torture are more difficult to address than the after-effects of an empty stomach (Martin, 1994, pp. 69–80). Hospital staffs are stretched by an enormous clinical workload, and there is no place for clinical research. One could argue that allocating substantial human and financial resources to research in times of crisis is indefensible. However, enormous financial and human resources can be wasted on unsuccessful aid projects because they either target the wrong group, or offer programmes that do not meet the needs of the population. Materials and resources are offered that are of little or no value in a particular cultural setting. In order to try and avoid this, research in conflict situations should be viewed as a long-term approach towards a more effective implementation of aid programmes. Scrupulous care is called for in selecting which areas really require attention, and consultation and cooperation with local people is essential.

This leads to another ethical issue. Local professionals performing research invariably must rely on external partnerships for funding. These outside partners will inevitably have the greater influence regarding the selection and implementation of projects. Too often projects are based on the need for good publicity and a desire to please the donors. In this respect, short-term solutions and emergency relief are more popular responses. These, at times piecemeal, solutions can be at the expense of longer-term concerns – particularly involving mental health issues (Jablensky et al., 1994).

Occasionally – as was the case with victims of the mass rape policy during the war in Bosnia – their plight has been highlighted to serve the best interests of a particular group rather than to benefit the victims. The logical consequence of these factors is the premature termination of aid when public interest wanes and compassion fatigue sets in. This results not only in a huge waste of financial and other resources, but creates considerable disillusion amongst the aided population, ultimately doing more harm than good. Unfortunately, this is a situation which is unlikely to improve.

Another aspect of outside influence that deserves attention is the implementation of culturally biased programmes. International aid agencies have persistently been frustrated by the failure of their therapeutic models when used outside the cultural setting for which they were designed. The lack of research in countries experiencing conflict has led to a reliance on largely North American and Western European models, as explained earlier. International agencies bring in their own experts and methodology. While in many instances advanced Western technology would be appropriate and welcome, in the area of mental health Western models do not export well. The potential for ethno-cultural variations in patterns of PTSD is great (Friedman and Jaranson, 1992; Marsella et al., 1992, 1993). Many non-Western refugees report problems in terms of folk models of disorder and metaphors that do not fit existing classification perspectives and assumptions (Jablensky et al., 1994). Mollica (1991), for example, has observed very low levels of survivor guilt among Khmer refugees living in the Site Two refugee camps along the Thai–Cambodian border. He attributes this comparative lack of guilt in the Khmer to the Buddhist orientation of the refugees, whereas Christians in similar circumstances report high levels of guilt.

Ethno-cultural traditions have a significant influence on the subjective experience and psychological appraisal of stressful events. An improved understanding of the interplay of trauma and culture is essential to help untangle the web of causal and protective factors that result in traumas being endured, succumbed to, or recovered from (de Vries, 1996). In calling for a more culturally sensitive Diagnostic and Statistical Manual of Mental Disorders (DSM), Eisenbruch (1992) suggests that psychiatric care offered in mental health systems for traumatised refugees must emphasise a partnership between traditional healing methods and Western approaches towards diagnosis and treatment.

In this respect, Hiegel (1994) provides a refreshing perspective on the use of both Western and traditional folk medicine in his work with refugees in the Thai border camps. He instituted collaboration between traditional healers and Western health care workers, concluding that in many instances they agreed upon the same psychodynamics at work. Traditional healers however, are able to approach the victim within a *magic* or folkloric frame, thus avoiding misunderstanding and suspicion often generated from both sides in a Western doctor/non-Western patient relationship. The incompatibility of Western and non-Western notions of emotional distress is often embodied in conflicts in the administration of health programmes, ineffective interventions and failure to detect emotional problems (Farius, 1994).

Foreign programmes directed at helping rape and torture victims in Bosnia illustrate this predicament. For example, the underlying assumption of these psychotherapeutic models is that the victim will benefit from the experience of sharing her traumatic experience, and that healing can begin only with the recognition and expression of feelings of pain, humiliation, rage and guilt. Even if this premise were to be true, two factors in particular act to thwart the process. First, the idea of seeking counselling as a form of support appears to be foreign to these largely rural populations. All forms of support – including moral – are traditionally sought within the framework of a large extended family and small close-knit communities. Seeking help from an institution – be it even a community-based counselling centre – is not the accepted response that it is in some parts of Western Europe or North America. Not only is such discussion unlikely, but with regard to sexual abuse, it is close to being taboo. These women will talk about regularly hearing other women being attacked, and being forced to witness rape and sexual abuse. Almost without exception however, they deny having been raped themselves.

As a psychologist working in violent conflict situations, I believe that it is not only these critical cultural differences which can confound foreign therapy models, but the nature of the trauma itself and notably the surrounding environment. The trauma is extreme and prolonged, and occurs in the total absence of any normal support, be it familial, social, legal, financial or medical. The victims continue to be confronted by overwhelming practical burdens that are not taken into account in most Western therapy models.

Claims that it is unethical to be conducting research on a population so clearly in need of crisis intervention fail to take into account the fact that aid workers themselves – both local and international – are often the first to admit that their programmes are ill-equipped to deal with psychological trauma. They lack reliable data and results of structured research which can assist in identifying shortcomings and ideally form the foundations for an improved understanding of trauma and its effects. When assistance programmes are inadequate, mental health problems may develop or deteriorate, and in the absence of programmes addressing mental health care, otherwise effective assistance strategies may be undermined (Martin, 1994).

When conducting research under chaotic circumstances, one must come to terms with the fact that the choice of materials and approach is not always ideal. This is not only due to practical problems resulting from destroyed infrastructures, but also as a result of ensuring the best possible environment for those involved in the research. The interviewing process is a good example. In spite of the amount of material one would like to gather, the difficult and, at times, dangerous nature of fieldwork under such circumstances means that it may be necessary to settle for short, simple interviews. Because of the number of highly traumatised women who prefer to remain in the company of friends or relatives, one also needs to deal with the predicament of interviewing in groups. The choice of interviews (if structured interviews are required) should be based on clinical instruments used regularly by local mental health professionals, in order to facilitate further research, even if mainstream researchers or clinicians do not always favour these.

Given the pitfalls and problems arising from conducting research under such arduous conditions, the question arises: if research cannot be performed according to mainstream standards, should it be performed at all? I believe that it should: if we can illustrate both need and benefit, then we should engage in the research. Methodological shortcomings should be recognised openly and a clear analysis of how they were dealt with should be provided.

Neutrality is an issue that is often referred to, and the general consensus is that research cannot be neutral. This was emphasised at the INCORE Researching Violent Societies seminar in Derry Londonderry and Belfast, Northern Ireland in March 1999. The following two extracts refer to work conducted with traumatised populations in Kurdistan and Palestine:

> I do not wish to pretend that my comments here are cold scientific accounts, unfettered by emotion and personal bias. In refugee matters one is often dealing with politics and politics are not objective... In time there will be scientific and clinical studies, but for now there is only observation and opinion surrounded by emotion. [Karadaghi, 1994: 116]

> We have tried to write an objective account of the history of the current situation; however, it may be impossible for any one to do so considering the destructive climate of past and ever present times. [El-Sarraj et al., 1994: 141]

In fact most researchers in conflict settings acknowledge they are subjective and indeed that subjectivity affects their work. However, subjectivity does not only affect these individuals. All research has an agenda, be it implicit, explicit, conscious, or unconscious. Researchers have bills to pay, grants to win, positions to maintain and status to earn. Perhaps the difference between conflict research, with all its ethical dilemmas, and other social research is that the obstacles confronting researchers in violent societies are more apparent, and they are therefore obliged to tackle them.

In the final analysis one cannot answer all the ethical questions with which one is faced. However, there are two criteria that are imperative to this research. First, not to undertake research unless convinced that the end result will be of real practical value. Second, to sustain a deep respect and concern for all participants overriding any dictates of research procedure. If these principles can be maintained, then the research will be justified, despite ethical dilemmas.

REFERENCES

Brody, E. (1990) *Psychoanalytic Knowledge* (Madison, CT: International Universities Press).

Brody, E. (1994) 'The Mental Health and Well-Being of Refugees: Issues and Directions', in A. Marsella et al., (eds), *Amidst Peril and Pain. The Mental*

Health and Well-being of the World's Refugees (Washington, DC: American Psychological Association).

Dahl, S. (1993) 'The Trauma of Rape, its Effect on Mental Health and Consequences for Victim Care', in L.H.M. van Willigin (ed.), *Care and rehabilitation of rape, torture and other severe traumas of war in the republics of ex-Yugoslavia* (Utrecht: Pharos Foundation).

De Girolamo, G. (1993). 'International Perspectives in the Treatment and Prevention of Post-traumatic Stress Disorders', in J. Wilson and B. Raphael (eds), *International Handbook of Traumatic Stress Syndrome* (New York: Plenum).

De Giralmo, G. and Mcfarlane, A. (1996) 'The Epidemiology of PTSD: A Comprehensive Review of the International Literature', in A. Marsella et al., (eds), *Ethnocultural Aspects of Posttraumatic Stress Disorder* (Washington, DC: American Psychological Association).

De Vries, M. (1996). 'Trauma in Cultural Perspective', in B. van der Kolk, A. McFarlane and L. Weisaeth (eds), *Traumatic Stress: The Effects of Overwhelming Experience on Mind, Body, and Society* (New York: The Guilford Press).

Eisenbruch, M. (1992) 'Towards a Culturally Sensitive DSM: Cultural Bereavement in Cambodian Refugees', *Journal of Nervous and Mental Disease*, vol. 180, pp. 8–10.

El-Sarraj, Tawahina, A., and Heine, F. (1994) 'The Palestinians: An Uprooted People', in A. Marsella et al., (eds), *Amidst Peril and Pain. The Mental Health and Well-being of the World's Refugees* (Washington, DC: American Psychological Association).

Farius, P. (1994) 'Central and South American Refugees: Some Mental Health Challenges', in A. Marsella et al., (eds), *Amidst Peril and Pain. The Mental Health and Well-being of the World's Refugees* (Washington, DC: American Psychological Association).

Friedman, M. and Jaranson, J. (1992) 'The Applicability of the PTSD Concept to Refugees', in A. Marsella et al., (eds), *Amidst Peril and Pain. The Mental Health and Well-being of the World's Refugees* (Washington, DC: American Psychological Association).

Guha-Sapir, D. and Forcella, E. (1996) 'Armed Civil Conflicts and Women: Issues for Policy and Programme Development', paper prepared for keynote lecture at the UN Conference on Habitat II, Istanbul, June. United Nations International Research and Training Institute for the Advancement of Women.

Hiegel, J.P. (1994) 'Use of Indigenous Concepts and Healers in the Care of Refugees: Some Experiences from the Thai Border Camps', in A. Marsella et al., (eds), *Amidst Peril and Pain. The Mental Health and Well-being of the World's Refugees* (Washington, DC: American Psychological Association).

Jablensky, A., Marsella, A., Ekblad, S., Jansson, B., Levi, I., and Bornemann, T. (1994) 'Refugee Mental Health and Well-Being: Conclusions and Recommendations', in A. Marsella et al., (eds), *Amidst Peril and Pain. The Mental Health and Well-being of the World's Refugees* (Washington, DC: American Psychological Association).

Karadaghi, P. (1994). 'The Kurds: Refugees in Their Own Land', in A. Marsella et al., (eds), *Amidst Peril and Pain. The Mental Health and Well-being of the World's Refugees* (Washington, DC: American Psychological Association).

Marsella, A., Friedman, M. and Spain, E. (1992) 'A selective review of the Literature on Ethnocultural Aspects of PTSD', *PTSD Research Quarterly*, vol. 2, pp. 1–7.

Marsella, A., Friedman, M. and Spain, E. (1993) 'Ethnocultural Aspects of Post Traumatic Stress Disorder', in J.M. Oldham, M.B. Riba and A. Tasman (eds) *Review of Psychiatry* (Washington, DC: American Psychological Press).

Martin, S.F. (1994). 'A Policy Perspective on the Mental Health and Psychosocial Needs of Refugees', in A. Marsella et al., (eds), *Amidst Peril and Pain. The Mental Health and Well-being of the World's Refugees* (Washington, DC: American Psychological Association).

Mollica, R. (1991) 'The Ford Foundation Community Study in Thailand: Trauma and Disability in the Khmer Displaced Persons Camp known as Site Two', paper presented at the 14th Annual meeting of the American Psychiatric Association. May, New Orleans, LA.

United Nations High Commissioner for Refugees (UNHCR) (1993) *The State of the World's Refugees 1992–1993* (New York: Penguin Books).

11 One Size Fits All? Focused Comparison and Policy-Relevant Research on Violently Divided Societies

Albrecht Schnabel

THE RESEARCHER IN A DIVIDED SOCIETY

Research is conducted in, and on, divided societies for a number of reasons: for knowledge's sake, to write a report or a thesis, to get published, to get tenure, to inform policy makers, to develop policies for local and/or international non-governmental organisations (NGOs), or to develop policies for national decision makers at regional and international organisations. For the most part, such research will only rarely result in an improvement of the situation for those being studied. It is easy to be cynical about the impact of social science research on the improvement of the human condition. However, although the chance is very small that research results will directly or indirectly inform more effective and just policies on the part of those who can make a difference in the building and rebuilding of torn societies, this objective is still extremely important and, if approached effectively, can be successful. At a minimum, researchers need to strive for positive results of their work and they have the responsibility to make sure that their work does not worsen the situation for those whom they study.

Most researchers are driven at least partly by the desire to make a difference in the lives of those who more or less willingly answer questions, who share some of their innermost feelings and experiences to satisfy the curiosity of a stranger. People answer researchers' questions perhaps because they embrace the opportunity to talk about their great disappointment with their state, their former friends who have turned into ethnic foes, or about external actors that do or do not get involved. Or, they are disappointed with themselves and the violent and often intractable situation they find themselves in. Underneath the frustration and despair, there is often a genuine desire to understand and find solutions to the quagmire of social conflict.

Often, outsider researchers enter the subject's life with certain pre-conceptions about the nature and dynamic of the divided and violent society under scrutiny. All of us, either as researchers from outside or inside the society studied, have numerous stories to tell of moments where we are driven by doubt: on the one hand, we experience the extreme complexity of the political, historic and cultural circumstances which turned people into enemies. On the other hand, we see the human side of all this – an often misinformed and naïve account of how the world (and complex inter-group relations) work and should work, repeated over and over again by fervent protagonists eager to strengthen their power base through ethnic and nationalist propaganda and persuasion. Outsider researchers wonder how they would have acted as a member of that society. Would they have stood up and confronted the warmongers, risking their lives and the lives of friends and family? Would they have asked the difficult questions that should be asked to unveil the hidden aspects of many leaders' propaganda?

The outsider researcher becomes emotionally affected by their research – for a few days or weeks or months. Then the outsider researcher often retreats into *normal* life, most often in a secure and comfortable environment far away from their subject's unchanged situation. The subjects of the outsider researchers' inquiry are left wondering if any of what they shared will ever make a difference. Researchers from inside society are often in a different situation. Their life is more closely bound up in their field research; their work is often an attempt from within to understand the peculiarities of one's society and the reasons that have driven their society apart in violence. Their research can take them outside their own group, provide them with unique perspectives that are essential to local approaches and a more nuanced understanding of the underlying reasons and possible solutions to a society's divisions.

In order to be effective, research should be policy-oriented. Research for knowledge's sake is of course good and necessary, but knowledge should eventually feed into action. Improved knowledge about violent societies can potentially result in improved responses to the division and violence that cause societies to drift apart and go to war against each other in violent, internal conflict. Mediation and other forms of coordinated intervention in a violent society's struggle must be informed by a general knowledge of divided societies and by specific knowledge about each situation's particular characteristics. Those characteristics include a combination of social, political, historic, economic and cultural forces that constitute and shape the fabric of society. Mediation is the key to creating or rebuilding a functioning, mutually supportive social fabric that supports the end of protracted violence. This in turn facilitates the rebuilding of peaceful relations based on trust and mutual respect. Researchers require both kinds of knowledge – that of a more general nature, derived from the comparative study of the dynamics and histories of violent societies, and knowledge of a more specific nature, related to the specific nature of each conflict under scrutiny.

This combination of a general and particular knowledge allows the researcher to produce data that might eventually, if effectively communicated to the appropriate audience, lead to an improved response to the local and external management of internal conflicts. Only such a two-tiered approach to researching violent societies – along the lines of a dual-focus approach – will support effective responses to violently divided societies. Such an approach will inform analysis and lead to recommendations for policy and action. It will also hopefully benefit those who have shared their knowledge with researchers about why, how, when and in whose name some societies turn against each other, when other societies manage to integrate and cooperate to form larger, not smaller, and stable communities.

This chapter argues for the need to research violent societies through a dual-focused comparative approach. This is crucial if research is to go beyond academic discussions and inform policies at non-state, state and interstate levels. These policies can be directed at the stabilisation of, and eventual peace-building processes in, violently divided societies. International organisations and NGOs involved in long- and short-term development, humanitarian and peace operations are particularly important consumers of research and subsequent actors in peace-building activities. While international organisations tend to adopt more universal approaches to their work in violently divided societies, NGOs tend to focus on local prescriptions for local problems and environments. Nevertheless, both must harmonise universal approaches to conflict prevention, conflict management and post-conflict peace-building with local needs and circumstances. In cooperation, NGOs and international organisations can address both the challenges common to all divided societies, together with the specifics which are conditioned by each society's particular political, economic and socio-cultural fabric.

Thus, as the analyst of a specific society and perhaps also the adviser of internal and external security providers, the researcher must focus their work on both the specifics and generalities of violent and divided societies.

However, it is important to question the validity of generalisations about violently divided societies. Is it possible that one set of explanations can explain all violent societies? Does 'one size fit all'? Furthermore, is there one single type of response that is the perfect intervention in all violent and divided societies? The answer is yes and no. General, comparative research into violent societies provides us with a basic general understanding that can inform general responses. In addition, specific research into local conditions of a particular societal division and ensuing violence allows the stretching of the basic knowledge to produce an understanding and responses that fit each individual case. This combination of general and specific information, which can be provided by the researcher, can indeed be useful. Such information can result in a coordinated and cooperative response by international and local actors. Arguably then, one size will fit all.

THE UTILITY OF FOCUSED COMPARISON: THE RESEARCHER'S DUAL AGENDA

The dual-focused comparative approach, discussed by George and Smoke (1974) in *Deterrence in American Foreign Policy*,

> ... examines multiple cases and establishes its results, in the main, by making comparisons among them ... like the correlational approach, it proceeds by asking a limited number of questions or testing a limited number of hypotheses, all of which are usually closely related to each other ... [It] also resembles the intensive case study approach ... as it examines each case in some depth ... All cases are approached by asking identical questions. This standardized set of questions or hypotheses insures the comparability of results ... additional questions ... may be asked of any given case if it seems desirable to bring out unique features it may possess, so that the method has some built-in flexibility. [pp. 95–6]*

* All page references in this chapter are from George A.L. and Smoke, R. (1974) *Deterrence in American Foreign Policy: Theory and Practice* (New York: Columbia University Press).

Thus, while general lessons can be and should be derived from comparative study, specific information needs to be distilled in order to secure a comprehensive view within each individual case study.

There are advantages and disadvantages to this approach. Since this method does not look at complete sets or representative samples of cases, it is less scientific and 'cannot determine the relative frequency with which any given conjunction of independent and dependent variables occurs' (p. 96).

Moreover, because of a limited number of cases, 'findings will enjoy a lower degree of formal verification than do statistical generalizations grounded in quantitative analysis of a large number of cases' (p. 96). For that purpose, one would have to study all cases and then draw lessons. That is usually not possible or feasible. The advantages of this approach are the systematic, analytical comparison of a small number of cases, offering greater opportunity for in-depth analysis.

A key element and advantage of this approach is its usefulness in policy-relevant research. According to George and Smoke:

> ... what the focused comparison method can offer in place of a high degree of formal verification may be something more valuable – potentially a significantly greater degree of relevance to real policy problems than is usually enjoyed by statistically validated generalizations (or, for that matter, the conclusion of a single case study) ... the standardized set of questions can employ variables which policy-makers themselves find useful and tend to employ in dealing with fresh problems ... [uncovering] ... results of potential policy relevance by focusing in detail on the more useful decision-making or utility-calculus considerations. [pp. 96–7]

George and Smoke further argue that

> ... since variation among cases is addressed explicitly and analytically by the focused comparison method, conclusions can be drawn with this method that can assist directly in the diagnosis of a fresh case, historical or contemporary ... Such patterns are of obvious diagnostic assistance to the policy-maker in coping with a current ... [policy] problem, and can offer him a kind of 'contingent prediction' about the way his current situation would

be likely to develop, given the presence or absence of various conditions or factors. [p. 97]

Inter-group conflict lends itself to focused comparative study. It allows for flexible comparisons of divided societies, by giving researchers the freedom to remain sensitive to local and case-specific root problems, while pursuing a general agenda that goes beyond single-case studies which have limited value in terms of the extrapolation of general lessons. At the same time the researcher can provide a perspective for their subjects which indicates that the societal divisions and the resulting violence they are examining are not endemic or unique to their particular society. The universal aspect of their problem can then be conceptualised as requiring to be addressed globally as well as locally. The researcher does not usually come to a particular society because it represents the only case or even the worst case, but perhaps because they are a good example of a particular scenario. Only the comparative study of several divided societies in parallel is likely to yield results that can be used by local and external actors alike.

This points not only to the universal character of the problems that underlie inter-group violence, but also to the universal nature of responsibility to prevent and resolve such violence. As a global community, we are responsible to do our best to ensure basic human security in all parts of the world, not only in our own home or backyard. It is this assertion of global responsibility that is used to justify external involvement in violent societies, which are perceived not as an intrusion in that society's internal affairs, but a universal human responsibility.

SPLIT TASK/SPLIT ACTOR

This two-tiered approach – the search for general and specific lessons – sets the researcher a split task. The researcher must address the larger, general questions, about when, how, and why a society might try to solve its problems through violent means. This question, and the collection of data on it, might lead the researcher to factors such as ethnic fear, crisis of identity and belonging, oppression, weak structures of governance and law, peculiarities of the political system, poor economic conditions, poverty, environmental and natural catastrophes – amongst other reasons that have been known to be instrumental in causing the breakdown of non-violent relations. Conclusions drawn in one case might inform the research agenda of the next case. Similarities of factors across several cases might indicate that certain general trends, certain factors, foster or inhibit the deterioration of societal links and the outbreak of violence.

The researcher thus identifies the particular factors that are unique to each case. Historic experiences, irredenta, diaspora communities, the willingness and motivation of external parties to become involved, and other factors determine the unique nature of each particular conflict, whilst enriching and qualifying the general conclusions drawn from comparative study.

As Darby and Smyth note in Chapter 2, in general, researchers tend to overestimate the impact of their work, while the public underestimates it. Both perceptions lead to gross misperceptions of the possibilities and limits of research for changing and improving daily life. These misperceptions are more pronounced when it comes to the assessment of the usefulness of general/comparative versus specific/local research. Whilst many researchers believe that inquiry into universally applicable laws of conflict can have the largest impact, they often attach much less value to specific and locally targeted research. The public appetite, on the other hand, is often for research that is useful to their particular situation and context.

SPLIT AUDIENCE/SPLIT AGENDA

What is the purpose and utility of research in violently divided societies? We can identify at least three objectives it might serve:

- to contribute to the academic debate,
- to trigger more effective political action, and
- to satisfy the researcher's quest for improvement of the human condition.

In order to satisfy these objectives the researcher thus has to fulfil their role, beyond that involved in the information gathering, analysing and dissemination process. Additionally, the researcher is a feeder of information in an ongoing academic and scholarly research milieu; the researcher is an informant of policy-making and decision-making circles, and the researcher connects the academic community of violently divided societies (often peripheral communities in the developing world) with the outside academic community. Thus, the researcher may contribute to what one could call the *globalisation of knowledge* – knowledge about specific conflicts, their roots and potential remedies. This should ideally result in greater awareness and more effective and meaningful external interventions in conflicts.

Each target audience requires a different research agenda. On the one hand, the researcher needs to develop knowledge of general internal and external dynamics of conflict and external intervention in violently divided societies. This general knowledge is particularly useful in considering early prevention strategies, since with such knowledge actors can identify early warnings using indicators that point to the root causes of the conflict. On the other hand, particular knowledge, specific to each conflict and situation, will be useful to local and external actors who can use local knowledge to tailor policies and approaches to specific situations. The basic goal will be the same: to understand why violence has erupted, and how and in what circumstances it can and should be stopped and/or prevented.

How does the researcher pursue these dual agendas? As with any good research, researchers need to know what they want to find out, from whom, and why. Once those basic parameters have been established, research can pursue both agendas. The quest for answers to a number of general questions (perhaps informed through research done in other cases) will either support or challenge existing knowledge about violently divided societies. Answers to very case-specific questions address the particular socio-economic, cultural, political, historic and ethnic circumstances of a particular context.

The researcher needs to recognise that all conflicts are not alike, that not all roots of conflict in violently divided societies are the same, or that only a simplified and limited number of factors are to be blamed. In short, researchers should convey the impression that they are there to learn and understand, not to prove an argument. The comparative approach – across various cases and in search for general and case-specific knowledge – can make the research process and results more credible in the eyes of both those being studied and of the wider audience.

SPLIT DISSEMINATION AND ACADEMIC DILEMMAS

The researcher of violent societies may need to disseminate findings in various languages, that is, to speak as:

- a local, using local language, dialect, culture of expression and channels of communication;

- as an academic, applying comparative and value-neutral methodologies, and inform and consult academic and policy-making circles;
- as a generalist, who applies general findings and draws general conclusions;
- as a specialist, who explains local reasons for violence and opportunities for solutions, and
- as a journalist, who shares findings through print and broadcast media (but who needs to beware of oversimplification, sensationalism and partiality).

Few people have the skill to express themselves effectively, fairly and in a balanced way at all those levels. This may mean that each individual researcher needs to focus on what they do best, and avoid the temptation to address audiences that they are not able to address, unless they work collaboratively with, for example, journalists or others who are proficient in a different arena. The best research findings are rendered useless, perhaps even counterproductive and dangerous, if misrepresented in, for example, a sensationalist newspaper report.

Effective dissemination requires special skills in addressing specific audiences. An important aspect of research in violently divided societies can be the ability to influence policy at local, national and international levels. Researchers often need to be able to translate their findings into effectively targeted, short and succinct policy briefs that will be read by decision makers or those immediately advising them. Those in decision-making positions rarely have the time to read voluminous academic reports, or scholarly articles. Researchers who only disseminate their work in these outlets risk missing their target policy audience – the very audience that might be most effective in translating their findings into policy and action on the ground. Whilst it is necessary to produce scholarly books and volumes, results must be packaged differently for a wider audience. A policy-oriented report can afford to be brief. Properly distributed, the impact of such reports can be sizeable. Today's researcher must discover how to ensure the impact of their work – language, packaging and distribution are core elements of successful impact and output-oriented research.

Finally, the issue of academic recognition of work in this field must be considered. Research results that address broad questions and attract a large academic audience can result in widespread academic recognition for the researcher, while specifically targeted projects with local focus and input are less likely to result in academic recognition. To make matters worse, policy-oriented research will generally generate less academic credit, while more abstract, theoretical and scholarly projects will generate comparatively more academic credit. However, without academic credit, the researcher will not advance in their profession and will perhaps receive fewer opportunities to conduct research. Research institutes, universities and funding agencies must address this issue. Researchers should be rewarded for work that deals, for example, with the micro-level, and which may not result in contributions to larger academic debates, but will have immediate policy relevance. In any case, this demonstrates the necessity of the researcher pursuing both specific policy-relevant research and larger and more scholarly comparative studies – if only in the interests of career advancement.

COMPARATIVE RESEARCH IN SUPPORT OF COMPREHENSIVE SECURITY PROVISION

Just as general and specific knowledge can support and strengthen each other, so may the actions of outside and internal actors who coordinate their efforts to provide security by preventing, containing and stopping violence, and rebuilding trust and confidence among and between groups to prevent the recurrence of violence in societies.

Generic solutions that are effective in ending violence in all violently divided societies do not exist. Generic approaches that are more or less effective in specific cases do exist. Specific approaches to specific cases, addressing root causes and then dynamics of violence may compensate for gaps in more generic responses and allow them to reach an optimum of effectiveness. For instance, generic intervention approaches in a violently divided society might be composed of support for civil society organisations, electoral assistance, economic assistance and support for educational institutions and public service facilities – in order to counter social and economic conditions that foster violence. However, if, for instance, religious intolerance is fanned, perhaps by nationalist diaspora communities or the state's control over the media, then these are issues that must be addressed as well. They are most effectively addressed by a combination of external responses (by and at the expatriate community) and internal responses (for example, by the creation of alternative sources of information for citizens).

The researcher may be the informant of potential mediators and security providers in violently divided societies. The researcher may be able to perceive which actor is better equipped to handle a particular challenge. Thus, the researcher can inform the development and implementation of policy, which is a tremendous responsibility and cannot be taken lightly. Those studied by the researcher often expect that their willingness to share information, impressions and experiences will somehow translate into an improvement of their own situation. Often respondents interpret such 'improvement' in different ways, as either a sympathetic account of their cause, or as a direct contribution towards internal and external policies and actions that reduce violence.

THE RESEARCHER AS A POLITICAL TOOL?

Can the researcher afford to become involved in promoting one side over the other in an inter-group conflict? While the researcher may often be obliged to appear neutral, often perhaps even sympathetic to one group, the researcher must simultaneously remain aware of the situational impact of field research. The following example illustrates this point. A colleague lived on one side of two conflicting groups for an extended period of time. His daily e-mail reports clearly expressed his growing discontent and, eventually, utter hatred towards the other group. He would probably have developed similarly strong feeling against his hosts, had he spent the same amount of time among the people of the other side.

'Going native' can mean losing touch with a broader reality. An external, even comparative, perspective to the study of a divided society lends an added dimension to purely local experiences and perspectives, an advantage that needs to be preserved. Furthermore, the researcher must remain above local attachments, an often difficult task. Comparative research helps to keep the researcher in touch with a broader reality, and avoids too close an attachment with one particular environment. Should such attachments develop anyway, the researcher is faced with the necessity of drastic action: moving on to another case study or ending the research role and becoming an activist.

THE USE OF *PURE* RESEARCH

Whilst research that is clearly not designed to be policy relevant may not draw the same enthusiasm of support from external or internal actors, it may have the advantage of eliciting more interesting and frank responses from respondents in violently divided societies, since the research is not perceived as relating to policy making. Comparative research may have a similar advantage. Respondents may assess that it is not only their situation that is under scrutiny, and that their responses will be used to reach general conclusions rather than anything that will have a direct effect on the conflict in their own society. This may create the impression of the researcher's neutrality, detachment and interest in scholarly, rather than policy-relevant, outcomes. In some cases it may thus be useful for the researcher to maintain an identity as an independent researcher with no particular agenda (and no hidden agenda!) for the application of the research results.

RESEARCHING VIOLENTLY DIVIDED SOCIETIES, EARLY WARNING AND PREVENTION

The prevention of conflict is at the heart of motivating the evolution of approaches to conflict management. Gradually intergovernmental organisations (such as the UN and regional organisations) and their member states have begun to realise that the prevention of conflict makes more sense than attempting the management and resolution of violence that has already broken out. However, conflict prevention is hard to sell. The measurement of success in conflict prevention remains a major difficulty; how can it be proved that a conflict would have broken out had particular preventive measures not been taken? Nevertheless, enough examples exist today to show that, for instance, certain features of a society render it prone to conflict, for example, ethnic diversity, together with the absence of legal mechanisms guaranteeing the protection of minorities, or authoritarian government. Early indicators of deteriorating inter-group relations may therefore include work and legal codes that discriminate against one group, income and education inequalities, or violent attacks on minority groups.

Lessons from the observation of violently divided societies can be applied to inter-group violence at its earliest stages. These lessons inform early intervention that may prevent further escalation. Researching violently divided societies thus may provide us with the tools to monitor escalating inter-group tensions. In permissive political conditions, intervention inhibits or arrests the deterioration of inter-group relations, and contains the problem within the capacity of non-violent conflict resolution strategies.

AN AGENDA FOR EFFECTIVE POLICY-ORIENTED RESEARCH

Does one size fit all? Of course, it does not. The specific characteristics of each society and the nature of each society's interactions, peaceful as well as violent, are unique. This uniqueness must inform those internal and external agents who aim to defuse societal violence. General prescriptions and universal cures for violent conflicts are rarely feasible or effective. Organisations with global mandates, including the United Nations, cannot therefore apply general approaches unilaterally. It is necessary to share the responsibility of conflict prevention and management with regional and local actors. This entails an effective division and coordination of labour. Both regional and international organisations have much reason to be interested in developing effective approaches to assess, detect and respond to violence in divided societies.

Actors interested in addressing and alleviating such violence should ideally act in areas where they enjoy an advantage or possess special skill and experience compared to all other actors. Moreover, they should coordinate their actions and cooperate whenever possible, to avoid unnecessary overlap and allow for a maximum of integration and, thus, effectiveness of their action. Local actors may best deal primarily with local problems and friction, while external actors may be best positioned to deal with the broader factors contributing to social violence, such as poverty, misgovernment and external roots of destabilisation.

Finally, the consumers of research, those who commission or use research – international organisations such as the United Nations, governments and NGOs – frequently expect researchers to deliver research results that will produce policy recommendations. They require impact-oriented research to inform and supplement international decision making and local activism.

The sensitive task of conducting research in violently divided societies requires responsibility, sophistication and a good grasp of research methodology, analysis and dissemination. In spite of academic background and strong commitment, many activists, journalists and staff of various international and non-governmental organisations are not well equipped to undertake this work. Collaboration with those who have the necessary experience and credentials may provide the answer to this problem. Research skills must be acquired and demonstrated by a researcher in reports and publications. Researching violently divided societies is a great responsibility, is a highly complex undertaking, and requires the utmost in scholarly and human integrity. The ability to separate the general from the specific in violently divided societies, together with the ability to contribute to both conceptual and policy discussions on conflict requires professional ability that few possess. Those few must be given the means and incentives to pursue such work and make the results available to those who can improve the situation for those affected by the violence of divided societies.

There is a great need for deeper understanding of the roots of societal violence and the remedies to alleviate them. Researchers can do much to contribute to this need – if they are aware of the special requirements and complexities of conducting research in violently divided societies. Research can provide solid analysis and trigger a positive response by those actors and institutions, local and external, in a position to reduce violence and foster peaceful relations.

Conclusions

Marie Smyth and Gillian Robinson

Northern Ireland has become one of the most researched areas in the world since 1969 and the outbreak of the violence that began the period referred to as the 'Troubles'. Since then, local and international researchers have studied the Troubles, the associated violence and the subsequent peace process. Similarly high levels of research have been reported in other areas of low-intensity conflict, such as South Africa or Israel/Palestine. Whilst the positive or negative effects of such inquiry remains to be established – a point raised here by Osaghae, Darby and Smyth, and Albert – a wider issue is addressed by the range of contributions herein. Despite the relatively high level of research activity in war zones across the world, there has been little attention paid to the actual processes of conducting research in a violently divided society. A comprehensive literature search reveals that, despite the existence of an extensive inquiry methods literature, very little has been written that directly addresses the ethical and methodological challenges of studying societies undergoing ethnic conflict and other violent upheavals.

Researchers working in violently divided societies have struggled to connect with the mainstream research community. Concepts such as neutrality (addressed in this work by several of the contributors, such as Hermann and Schnabel), that seem possible if debatable in relatively peaceful contexts do not easily export to violently divided contexts. The carrying-out of the process of inquiry may have to be redesigned to take account of the devastation in the social fabric described by Clarke in her work in Cambodia. Issues of research dissemination may be determined by other local conditions commonly found in violently divided societies, such as media censorship, as described by Tabyshalieva. The mechanics of carrying out studies also vary according to the level of division within the society, and according to the level of access to literacy of the researched population, points which underpin in a number of contributions, such as Osaghae's and Albert's work. Many of these problems have not been articulated on mainstream agendas, nor have researchers from outside these contexts always been sensitive to the special demands made on researchers, research design and analysis working in such circumstances. In societies such as Northern Ireland, some research expertise has been developed in conducting investigations in violent and unstable contexts, yet the literature about mainstream research paradigms is virtually devoid of such insights. The value of bringing together an international group of researchers with practical experience of solving the problems associated with conducting research in violent and politically unstable contexts is the pooling of expertise and resources that can occur. The aim of this volume has been to consolidate and compare experiences of investigations between similarly violent societal contexts, with a view to documenting the approaches, insights and dilemmas shared by researchers internationally. We hope that this initial documentation will be valuable in supporting existing researchers in their work, and in providing relevant and useful training materials for a new generation of researchers.

From the work presented here and the preceding discussions, it seems clear that a number of aspirations are shared by many researchers in the field. First, researchers aspire to improve their accountability, not only to donors, but to the populations they work with, in ways that do not compromise the standard of their research. Research that is transparent, open and more accessible to respondents and to the wider public is a common goal.

Second, many of the researchers in this volume recognise the need to acknowledge that there is little or no neutral space in a divided society. The researcher is also a citizen, with an identity. In terms of research strategy, the development of close working collaborations with researchers or those with required expertise from the *other* side can improve the quality of the research without recourse to dubious claims to objectivity, which in violently divided societies can be tantamount to claims of super-humanity.

Third, there is a view shared by many of us that researchers and funders have ethical responsibilities to anticipate the impact of the study on those studied, and to ensure that, at very least the benefits of investigations outweigh any possible negative effects that they might have. Research can do harm, and researchers must recognise this and avoid or minimise that harm. Furthermore, researchers have the responsibility to take steps to secure resources to deal with any negative impact of their research on those researched, so that they are not left to deal with the impact of the research without support and resources.

Similarly, methods of anticipating and counteracting the negative impact of conducting such studies on researchers should be included in the project design and described in final reports. Debriefing of researchers and interviewers can be built in to study design, and the qualitative data yielded by this process can contribute to the overall analysis. Such practices can be valuable in improving research expertise in the dynamics of working in divided societies.

In summary, *quality* research in the context of a violently divided society:

- focuses on an issue or a problem which is socially relevant and valuable to understand;
- takes into account the complexity of the issue or problem and its various facets;
- is designed to collect data on the issue in a way which will inform us about those various facets;
- is carried out in a reliable, valid, ethical and professional way;
- takes responsibility for the impact of the study on those studied, the researchers and on those reading the results;
- is designed to take account of conditions in the field of study, including issues of safety;
- addresses the issues of inter-subjectivity and incorporation of polarised perspectives in the data collection and analysis;
- makes itself accountable to the constituency addressed by the research as well as to funders;
- makes explicit the loyalties and alignments of the researchers and describes measures employed to incorporate other per-spectives into the analysis, and
- approaches divided societies in an interdisciplinary manner – for example, in research which is primarily psychological in focus, that the impact of economic or political societal factors is addressed; conversely, in political or economic research, the impact of psychological or emotive aspects is addressed.

Research in violently divided societies may have some specialist features, yet in many ways, it resembles quality investigations in other contexts. Whilst perhaps these principles apply to studies conducted in all societies, yet the challenges unique to violently divided contexts described in this volume stretch the researcher to find creative and innovative solutions, and to work in ways that contribute not only to bodies of knowledge but to knowledge about conducting such inquiries.

Notes on Contributors

Isaac Olawale Albert holds a PhD in African studies (history) from the University of Ibadan where he is currently a Research Fellow. His areas of teaching and research interest include African social history, development studies (security studies and conflict resolution), gender studies, and African oral traditions and folklore. In addition to his work as a lecturer at the Institute of African Studies, he serves as the Research and Intervention Officer to Academic Associate PeaceWorks in Lagos, Nigeria. This non-governmental organisation has vast experience in the area of managing violent ethnic and religious conflicts in Nigeria. The organisation has contributed immensely to the de-escalation of the violent conflicts in Zango-Kataf, Wukari, Tafawa Balewa, Igbo-Ora, Ugep and is currently working on the Ife-Modakeke crisis in Ile-Ife. His publications include: *Community Conflicts and Conflict Resolution in Nigeria* (Ibadan: Spectrum Books, 2001) with O. Odite, *Urban Managment and Urban Violence in Africa* (Ibadan: IFRA, 1994) and *Women and Urban Violence in Kano, Nigeria* (Ibadan: Spectrum Books, 1996)

Ioannis Armakolas is a native of Greece. He graduated from Panteion University of Social and Political Sciences, Athens with a degree in international studies in 1994 and holds a Master's degree in international relations from the University of Kent at Canterbury where he also received the John Burton Prize in 1998. He is a former Alexander S. Onassis Fellow. His prior work has included research at the Institute of International Relations and the Institute of International Economic Relations, both in Athens, the Greek Ministry of Defence and field work with the OSCE. His research interests include conflict analysis, theoretical aspects of identity and conflict, critical and post-structural security studies, International Relations theory, and Central and Eastern European affairs. Ioannis was Tip O'Neill Fellow at INCORE during 1998/1999 where he worked on an inter-disciplinary examination of the transformation of identities before the conflict in former Yugoslavia. As part of this project, he conducted field research in Bosnia.

Pam Bell left her native South Africa in 1984 after graduating with Bachelor's degrees in music and psychology. She elected for psychology, and continued postgraduate studies in Australia and England, specialising in women and trauma. She spent several years counselling and lecturing psychology in Antwerp. While coordinating a student-based humanitarian project in Sarajevo during the Bosnian war, she began clinical research with local mental health professionals and was later invited to join a multidisciplinary team dealing with war-related trauma at the Sarajevo University Hospital. She is currently coordinating a collaborative project between the psychiatric departments of the Université Libre de Bruxelles and the University of Sarajevo assisting traumatised women, and writing her doctoral thesis on women and war trauma.

John Darby is Visiting Professor at the University of Notre Dame. He was formerly Director and Senior Research Fellow at INCORE (the Initiative on Conflict Resolution and Ethnicity), a joint project of the United Nations University and the University of Ulster. He has written nine books, including *The Management of Peace Processes* with Roger MacGinty (Macmillan, London, 2000), *Scorpions in a Bottle*, published by the Minority Rights Group (London, 1997) and more than 80 articles, mainly on Northern Ireland and comparative ethnic conflict. He has coordinated a five-country study of peace processes with Roger MacGinty, and is also President of the Ethnic Studies Network, an international group of more than 700 scholars, mostly working within settings of ethnic conflict.

Andrew Finlay grew up in Belfast, trained as a social anthropologist in London and now lectures in sociology at Trinity College, Dublin. After completing a PhD on sectarianism and trade unionism among Derry shirt factory workers, he conducted research on a variety of health and social problems such as teenage pregnancy, and HIV risk behaviour amongst male prostitutes and injecting drug users. Living in Dublin has rekindled his interest in debates about ethnic conflict and identity in Ireland.

Tamar Hermann is a political scientist. She is the director of the Tami Steinmetz Center for Peace Research at Tel Aviv University and a senior lecturer at the Open University of Israel. Her main academic fields are: extra-parliamentary activity and political protest movements (particularly peace movements) and public opinion as a factor in national foreign policy making and Israeli politics. Dr Hermann has recently completed an extensive study of the Israeli peace movement in the years 1967–98, which was part of an international research project conducted under the auspices of the Aspen Institute, Washington, DC. Her latest book, *Israeli Elections*, was published by the Open University of Israel, Tel Aviv, in 1999.

Helen Jenks Clarke, with Robert Clarke, is Co-Field Director of the American Friends Service Committee, Cambodia Program, and Quaker International Affairs Representative, Southeast East Asia Region. She is Chair of the Board of Governors of the Cambodian School for Prosthetics and Orthotics, serves on the Executive Committee of the Cooperation Committee for Cambodia, the Board of Directors of the Partnership for Development in Kampuchea, the Board of Directors of VBNK-A Training Institute for NGO Managers, and the Executive Committee for the Working Group for Weapons Reduction in Cambodia. She helps to supervise the joint AFSC-UNICEF Socio-Cultural Vulnerabilities and Coping Strategies (SCVCS) research project and the research on which the Local Capacities for Nonviolence project will be based. A Canadian, Helen holds degrees in anthropology and international affairs from Northeastern University and the Norman Paterson School for International Affairs, Carleton University. She has conducted social scientific research in Thailand, Vietnam, Indonesia and Malaysia and in North America.

David Meddings was born in Canada where he obtained his degree in medicine and subsequent specialisation in epidemiology. His clinical practice in Canada focused predominantly on aboriginal peoples, and included periods of practice in the Canadian Arctic and Canada's western coast. His clinical work in humanitarian contexts began in Africa in 1989 and subsequently entailed missions in Asia and the former Soviet Union. He is engaged as an epidemiologist by the International Committee of the Red Cross where he has been involved in a variety of studies examining the intersections between human health, state strength, social violence, and light weapons proliferation. He has contributed to the development of institutional doctrine for the International Committee of the Red Cross on a number of arms-related issues, including co-authoring the ICRC's *Arms Availability Study*. His other research interests include the application of epidemiologic methods in humanitarian assistance operations, programme evaluation, and the integration of applied research with policy development.

Eghosa Emmanuel Osaghae has a doctorate in political science from the University of Ibadan. He is a professor in the Department of Political Science at the University of Ibadan where he directs the Ford Foundation Programme on Ethnic and Federal Studies (PEFS). PEFS has the overall goal of building and strengthening research capacity in the study of ethnicity and its management through federalism and other means in Nigeria in particular and Africa in general. His career has taken him to appointments in the University of Transkei, University of Cape Town, South Africa, to Uppsala, and to the University of Liberia. He has also been a visiting fellow at the Carter Center, in the United States. His main research interests are ethnicity and its management, federalism, problems of the African state in comparative perspective and the consequences of political and economic reforms on these subjects. He is the author of many books most importantly *Crippled Giant: Nigeria Since Independence* (London: C. Hurst, and Bloomington: Indiana University Press, 1998).

Gillian Robinson is a Senior Lecturer at the University of Ulster and Director of ARK (The Northern Ireland Social and Political Archive). After completing her primary degree in social policy and sociology at University College Dublin, she commenced a research career that has afforded her the opportunity to research many aspects of life in Ireland and Northern Ireland including women and employment, nursing and mixed marriage. After working as a contract researcher for many years and completing her MSc at the University of Ulster she joined the lecturing staff there in 1993. Her position as Research Director at INCORE (1997 to December 2000) involved the commissioning, supervising and directing of and fund raising for research into post-conflict transitions including the Economic and Social Research Council-funded Developing and Implementing Public Policy in Northern Ireland and South Africa project. She has also been involved in the monitoring of social attitudes in Northern Ireland since 1989 and co-directs the Northern Ireland Life and Times survey series. Her interests in methodology include issues around researching violent societies and comparative methods.

Albrecht Schnabel is Academic Programme Officer of the Peace and Governance Programme at the United Nations University. He was educated at the University of Munich, the University of Nevada, and Queen's University, Canada, where he received his PhD in political studies in 1995. Before joining UNU, Dr Schnabel has taught at Queen's University (1994), the American University in Bulgaria (1995–96), and the Central European University (1996–98). In 1997 he was a research fellow at the Institute for Peace Research and Security Policy at the University of Hamburg and served on OSCE election monitoring missions in Bosnia-Herzegovina. Recent publications include the *Southeast European Challenge: Ethnic Conflict and the International Response* (Baden-Baden: Nomos, 1999), co-edited with Hans-Georg Ehrhart, and *Kosovo and the Challenge of Humanitarian Intervention: Selective Indignation, Collective Action, and International Citizenship* (Tokyo: UNU Press, 2000), co-edited with Ramesh Thakur. He currently serves as president of the International Association of Peacekeeping Training Centres and as a trainer in Early Warning and Preventive Measures for the UN Staff College in Turin, Italy.

Marie Smyth is on the academic staff of the University of Ulster and conducts full-time participative action research on various aspects of the impact of armed conflict, including the impact on civilian populations, and indigenous methods of peace-building. She has published several books and articles, and made several films. Her work has been mainly in Northern Ireland, but she also works internationally, in South Africa and Ghana, and previously in Berlin and Massachusetts. Dr Smyth is also a Director of the Northern Ireland Mediation Network.

Anara Tabyshalieva is a director of the Institute for Regional Studies in Kyrgyzstan. She was a senior fellow at the United States Institute of Peace (1996–97), and a visiting scholar (on a short-term basis) for research of Peace and Governance Programme at the United Nations University Headquarters, Tokyo (2000). She conducted the research on regional cooperation in Central Asia, supported by grant from the John D. and Catherine T. MacArthur Foundation. Anara has published several works including *The Challenge of Regional Cooperation in Central Asia. Preventing Ethnic Conflict in the Fergana Valley* (Washington, DC: United States Institute of Peace, 1999). She holds a PhD equivalent in history from Kyrgyz National State University.

Index

Compiled by Auriol Griffith-Jones

Note: Page numbers in bold refer to Figures. Notes are shown as 130*n*.